# Rescue Your
# LOVE
# LIFE

### Changing the 8 Dumb Attitudes & Behaviors
### That Will **Sink** Your Marriage

## DR. HENRY CLOUD
## DR. JOHN TOWNSEND

**THOMAS NELSON**
*Since 1798*

NASHVILLE   DALLAS   MEXICO CITY   RIO DE JANEIRO   BEIJING

RESCUE YOUR LOVE LIFE

Published in Nashville, Tennessee, by Thomas Nelson. Thomas Nelson is a registered trademark of Thomas Nelson, Inc.

Published in association with Yates & Yates, LLP, Attorneys and Literary Agents, Orange, California.

Thomas Nelson, Inc., titles may be purchased in bulk for educational, business, fund-raising, or sales promotional use. For information, e-mail: SpecialMarkets@ThomasNelson.com

Some of the names used in illustrations in this book are not actual names; identifying details have been changed to protect anonymity. Any resemblance to persons alive or dead is purely coincidental.

Unless otherwise marked, Scripture quotations are taken from The Holy Bible, New International Version®. © 1973, 1978, 1984 by International Bible Society. Used by permission of Zondervan. All rights reserved. Other Scripture quotations are from the following sources: The Living Bible (TLB). © 1971 by Tyndale House Publishers, Inc. Used by permission. All rights reserved. The Holy Bible, New Living Translation® (NLT®). © 1996. Used by permission of Tyndale House Publishers, Inc., Wheaton, Illinois 60189. All rights reserved.

Cover Design: Chris Tobias, www.tobiasdesign.com
Interior Design: Sharon Collins/Artichoke Design, Nashville, TN

**Library of Congress Cataloging-in-Publication Data**

Cloud, Henry.
  Rescue your love life / by Henry Cloud and John Townsend.
    p. cm.
  Summary: "Beginning with self-examination and setting realistic expectations, the authors explore how couples can nurture and master healthy communication, build trust, and enhance the romance in their marriage"--Provided by publisher.
  ISBN 978-1-5914-5513-4 (hardcover)
  ISBN 978-0-7852-8915-9 (trade paper)
  1. Communication in marriage. 2. Couples. 3. Married people. 4. Marriage. 5. Love. 6. Man-woman relationships. I. Townsend, John Sims, 1952- II. Title.
  HQ734.C59624 2005
  646.7'8--dc22

                                    2005017347

*Printed in the United States of America*
08 09 10 11 12 13 RRD 9 8 7 6 5 4 3 2 1

To all those couples who seek to rescue their love lives
and find the closeness and passion they desire

# Contents

# Acknowledgments

To our literary agent, Sealy Yates, and his associate, Jeana Ledbetter, for their guidance and encouragement throughout the entire writing process.

To the folks at Integrity Publishing—Byron Williamson, president; Joey Paul, publisher; Tom Williams, editor; Rob Birkhead, vice president of marketing; and Angela DePriest, managing editor—for the vision, excitement, creativity, and excellence that have helped make this book a reality.

To our assistant, Janet Williams, for her care and steadfastness in always getting those things done that needed to get done.

To our parents, Henry and Louise Cloud, and Jack and Becky Townsend, for modeling marriage for us for a combined total of well over one hundred years.

To our wives, Tori and Barbi, for their grace, their love, and the many sacrifices they have made to keep our own love lives rescued.

To the staff of Cloud-Townsend Resources, for their dedication, support, and partnership over the years.

To Steve Arterburn and the New Life Ministries gang, for all the diligence and help they bring to us.

To Bill Dallas and Church Communication Network, for their partnership and vision in giving people access to programming that promotes spiritual growth and leadership.

Special thanks from John to couples whose relationships have meant a great deal to me: Tom and Martha McCall, Ted and Jennifer Trubenbach, and Eric and Debbie Heard. You have spoken well into my own life and marriage.

And special thanks from Henry to couples whose relationships have meant a great deal to me: Bill and Julie Jemison, Guy and Christi Owen. You have spoken well into my own life and marriage.

# Read This First

If you have picked up this book, there's a good chance that it says two things about you: one, you would like your marriage to be loving, close, and passionate. And two, those things aren't happening in your marriage as they should be.

If that is so, don't give up hope. We are glad you're here, and we want you to know that there is a lot that can be done to rescue your love life! Your marriage is worth rescuing, and this book will show you how that works.

Think back for a moment to the first weeks—maybe months—of your connection with your spouse. What a magnet you guys were for each other! Most likely, you were somewhat obsessed with the other person. You felt strong desires, attractions, tenderness, and depth. You experienced emotions, laughter, and tears. When you were together, it was awesome. Apart, you missed the other.

And then . . . for whatever reason, and there are lots of them, the fire started going out. You saw a part of your mate that you didn't relate to. Maybe someone became withdrawn, self-absorbed, controlling, manipulative, irresponsible—even hurtful. Your communication and connection weren't what they had been during the good times. You began having dumb ideas about the other person, and you two started doing dumb things!

Little problems led to larger ones, and before you knew it, the desires, intimacy, and passions began to wane. In their place came distance, alienation, loss of trust, conflict, a growing numbness, and the fear that this might not ever get better. Now what do I do? Am I stuck here forever?

If this is anything like your journey, don't be discouraged. You're not alone. Many couples have the experience of what happened to that great connection we used to have, and can we ever get it back?

Take the story of Ron and Deb, for example. When they first met and fell in love, they couldn't get enough of each other. It was romantic, passionate, and full of energy and dreams for the future. Their friends envied their happiness.

But, as it happens to so many couples, they started a slow slide into alienation, hurt feelings, and fighting. Problems turned into serious issues. There were less and less good times between them. The honeymoon was definitely over, and the reality wasn't good.

The couple tried all the usual tactics: being more positive, having more date nights, and getting busy with work and parenting. But that just made everything seem worse. Though things looked better on the outside, the two felt fake, empty, and even more distant from each other.

Soon Ron began working longer hours, and spending more time with his buddies. Deb got super-involved with the kids. And the chasm of disconnection became wider and wider, until they saw no way to bridge it. In fact, the slow slide picked up speed, and before they knew it, they were contemplating divorce.

Finally, they were exposed to the principles in this book. They began working the steps. They saw the root causes of the problems they had not been aware of. They learned how they affected each other, and the relationship. They practiced tips and guidelines to resolve issues, heal hurts, and move on toward love and passion. They began opening up again to each other, and, best of all, they recaptured the passion and intimacy they had given up on!

Today, Ron and Deb are again in love with each other and are moving on in their marriage. They have experienced the rescue.

This couple's success story has been experienced by many others who have worked through these principles. The rescue concepts really work and have done so for a long time. It isn't a magic pill, but it is something much better: a proven system of looking at your love life and at yourselves, and learning how to take the steps to make things better. You'll learn how to "unlearn" those dumb ideas that started a lot of this mess in the first place!

Now, suppose the marriage is out of balance, and one of you is more interested in rescuing your love life than the other. Don't give up. There are lots of things you can do, and we will show them to you. You can maximize your own efforts to help bring connection and intimacy to your marriage. As you'll see here, one person can make a huge difference in the relationship.

So get started on your own rescue. We hope and pray the best for your love life!

# "My Lover Should Make Some Changes"

You might be wondering, as you open a book on marriage, why it would begin by telling you that it's dumb to expect your lover to change. Isn't that why you bought this book—so you could get your lover to make some changes? But as we will see, the key to improving your marriage is changing yourself first.

That may seem a little unnatural, given that you are interested in improving your relationship, not yourself. But there is a key here: *growing marriages are made up of growing people.* A relationship is only as good as the two individuals who make it up. And nothing helps the relationship more than when you shine a spotlight on yourself and see your own issues, baggage, hurts, weaknesses, and faults. As you understand what makes you tick and begin to resolve your personal issues, your capacity to love, to give grace, to improve communication, to be honest, and to solve problems is greatly enhanced. So starting with yourself is the best way for you to get what you want.

What if your mate doesn't want to deal with himself? That can and does happen. Even so, you will be surprised as you read this section to discover how much your own example and way of relating can profoundly affect the relationship—and your mate—for good and for love. And it is surprising how that can free your mate to begin to rescue himself also.

In this section, we will give you several proven principles that will help you to look at yourself and your contributions to the relationship. And we will give you guidelines to assist you in applying change and growth to yourself and to your love life.

## Change Yourself, Not Your Lover

"OK, guys," I (John) said to Dennis and Kathleen. "You have to tell us the whole story." My wife, Barbi, and I were having dinner with them for the first time. During our conversation, they had dropped a couple of hints about their marriage going through some trouble, though it was apparent that it was now in really good shape.

Dennis responded, "We probably wouldn't be where we are now if Kathleen hadn't stepped up to the plate." He turned to his wife. "Why don't you tell them?"

"Well," began Kathleen, "we never really had a major crisis in our marriage like a lot of our friends have had. It was more that, about a year ago, I felt like we were in a rut. Dennis was into his work, and I was into the kids. Life was OK. We were getting along pretty well, but we weren't connecting with each other like we did in the early days."

"Like how?" I asked.

"We only talked about things we were doing: work, kids, money, church, vacation. We needed to talk about those things, but we never really connected with each other on an emotional, real level. I finally told Dennis that I wanted more and needed a better connection to him."

"How did that go?"

Dennis smiled sheepishly. "I responded with the usual guy thing. I told her I thought things were pretty much OK the way they were. We weren't fighting, and the family was getting along, so I figured why rock the boat?"

"What happened then?"

"I nagged Dennis about it for a while," Kathleen responded, "and then I gave up. I was a little angry with him, but I thought maybe I wasn't grateful enough for what we did have, so I tried to be happy and resigned myself to life as it was. Like I said, life was OK, so I stayed with OK."

"But that didn't work?"

"Not at all. I kept feeling more and more distant from him. And Dennis could tell. He tried to be nice and asked me about my day, and he took me on date nights. But I just didn't feel connected to him in the way I wanted."

"So what did you do then?"

"Well, I didn't really know what to do. It's more like some things happened, rather than me planning anything. I made other attempts at getting him to understand what I needed, and I even started crying, which I don't do often. Dennis was concerned, but he still didn't commit to working on our relationship." She put her hand on his to let him know she wasn't trying to sound critical.

"So I told him that I wasn't mad or blaming him for anything. But I needed a deeper relationship. Apparently he was choosing not to go that way, for whatever reason. So I started meeting with a small group at my church that had a focus on connection and intimacy. If I couldn't connect better with him, at least I would have a connection of some kind."

"Dennis, how did that affect you?"

"I liked it. I thought maybe that would make her feel better about her life."

Kathleen continued, "I started meeting with some really cool people, and we got pretty close. I got my focus off the marriage and started feeling connected to the group. That began a change in me toward Dennis, but not one I expected. I realized I was asking him to do something he had no clue how to do. When I said I wanted more intimacy, he didn't know what I meant. So I started being more intimate and vulnerable with him, taking risks about my feelings and fears and dreams. I poured out my feelings, but without insisting that he do the same. I gradually began to ask him how he felt about things, encouraging him to talk about his feelings."

Dennis interrupted. "That's when things started opening up for me. I think it was the combination of Kathleen's trying to reach me on a deeper level, showing me how, and helping make it safe. This sort of thing has never been easy for me. Like I said, I'm a guy. What did I know about the world of feelings? I was pretty clueless. She started being nicer to me, but she was still direct at the same time.

"And gradually, I started opening up to her. I started trying to think and talk in emotional terms. I found I had feelings I never knew I had. And we really finally started to connect. It was weird for me at first, like a foreign language or something. But now I can't imagine not relating to Kathleen at this level. It's like we're getting another chance at marriage."

"Wow!" I said, captivated by their story. "Kathleen, was it difficult for you to do all that work?"

"At first it was," she replied. "I thought I was carrying most of the weight of the relationship. But things changed once I realized that *whether or not Dennis responded, the steps I was taking were good for both of us.* I wasn't as resentful after that. Now that I look back, it was totally worth it. I have appreciated his willingness to do some risk-taking. He's shown me parts of his feelings that have been hard, but it has made us much closer. I feel like we're both carrying the weight now."

## Start with the Right Focus

Sure, Dennis was dumb for not responding to Kathleen's requests for connection. But it would have been seriously dumb for Kathleen to keep trying to change him. Instead, she went the higher route and looked at her own contributions to the marriage. She changed herself, not her lover.

Your marriage may be like Dennis and Kathleen's: it's OK, but it lacks the closeness you want. Or your marriage may be in trouble—or even in crisis. Perhaps you have become resigned to not having the intimacy you want in your marriage. Whatever your situation, the best thing you can do right now to rescue your love life is to focus on yourself, not on your lover. As Kathleen discovered, good things can happen to the relationship when you start working on yourself.

You might think, *This is depressing. I'm supposed to settle for the way things are, adapt to them, and try to be happy anyway.* That's what Kathleen thought at first. However, nothing could be further from the truth. Changing your own attitudes can do great things for you and your marriage.

## Health Breeds Health

For years, I (John) had chronic lower back pain due to a sports injury. The traditional treatments of rest, stretches, massage, and cold and heat didn't help. But one day, at a backyard barbecue, an engineer told me, "Your back is like a suspension bridge. To strengthen it, you have to strengthen the supportive structures around it—the muscles that hold it together." He suggested a regimen of daily sit-ups. I followed his advice, and within a few months, my pain was gone.

I don't really understand the engineering behind it, but I do know that when I concentrated on improving one part of my body, the other part improved too. In the same way, your marriage is like that body system. Things you do individually matter to the relationship. And generally speaking, *you can do more to improve your relationship than you think.*

The Bible explains this in terms of being a person of light—that is, one who follows God's light of love, relationship, and growth. "In the same way, let your light shine before men, that they may see your good deeds and praise your Father in heaven" (Matthew 5:16). Light tends to cause a response in other people, including your spouse. Let's look at the three key things you can do yourself and bring good light to your connection.

You CAN ADD HEALTHY INGREDIENTS TO THE MARRIAGE. Notice how Kathleen made herself vulnerable to Dennis instead of resenting and nagging him. She was introducing some good ingredients of growth into her marriage. By working on herself, Kathleen was making openness, trust, and safety easier for Dennis. She was also getting rid of negative ingredients such as distance, stonewalling, and blame. And her involvement in a small group gave her connection, meaning, and support, which flowed into her marriage.

When you shine the light on your own life and attitudes, you add growth and health not only to yourself, but also to your marriage. You may not see instant results, and that's OK. Taking antibiotics doesn't produce instant results either; but over time, you see improvement. Start making healthy and growing choices in your life. Get to know yourself, others, and God in a deeper way.

You CAN INFLUENCE YOUR MATE. Not only does changing yourself bring good things to your marriage, but it also helps you influence your mate to change and grow. For instance, Kathleen modeled personal vulnerability and then directly encouraged Dennis to open up with his own feelings. He responded to her example and her direct influence.

Sometimes we try to control our spouse and force him to change. But the reality is that you cannot make anyone change; your mate always has a choice. And on a deeper level, you don't want someone to love you because he *has* to. You want him to love you because he *wants* you. So give up control. Influence is much more helpful. You model, give information, make requests, and be vulnerable and safe—and you always respect your spouse's choice.

As we have seen, this kind of influence can go a long way. So don't be afraid to put the *right kinds* of pressure on your spouse. Talk to him; let him know that you love him and that your growth as a couple is important to you. Healthy pressure is growth-producing pressure.

YOU CAN RECRUIT YOUR MATE TO HELP YOU. The healthiest marriages are those in which both partners are committed to growth and change, working on themselves as Dennis and Kathleen now are. In these contexts, each of you paddles your own side of the boat and contributes to the progress of the marriage.

Recruit your mate to the team concept. Have some conversations about what you both want together: more connection, more safety, more emotional intimacy, more vulnerability, more honesty, more authenticity, a greater sense of being a team, and a more satisfying sexual relationship. Talk about how you affect each other, ways you let each other down, and what you want from each other. Then shoulder the burdens of changing in the right ways. That is how couples rescue their love lives and experience great marriages.

**A Lifeline:** BE LIKE KATHLEEN: WORK ON YOURSELF FIRST, AND THEN EXPECT GOOD THINGS TO HAPPEN!

# Love Grows When Dependency Goes

"I need you."

"I'm incomplete without you."

"I'm lonely for you."

"I can't make it without you."

Sound like things you've heard before? Like lyrics from a love song? In certain romantic contexts, phrases like these will arouse feelings of closeness and passion in couples, and that can sometimes be a very good thing. That's why songwriters keep using them. Statements like these make couples feel that they belong to each other. They make couples feel dependent on each other, complete, and glad they aren't alone. Dependency and love seem to merge as one.

Once you get past your favorite love song, however, and enter the land of real relationships, it is a different story. Sometimes dependency can be a problem in love. Now, there is certainly a kind of need and dependency that two people in love should have with each other, a dependency that is healthy and satisfying. For example, we all need to know our partner will be there with us and for us when we are down and stressed. That kind of dependency is part of support, empathy, and care. But another kind of dependency can smother romantic love. In this chapter, we will show you the difference and give you ways to overcome the dependencies that might be killing your love life.

## Love and Dependency

For many people, *love* and *dependency* are synonyms. Yet there is a world of difference between them, and that difference can have an enormous effect on your marriage. Let's define the two terms.

LOVE. Love concerns itself with reaching out to another person.

At its essence, *love is taking a stand for the benefit of that person.* Our love for another is a product of the love that God generates for us, and it defines how we are to approach each other: "Let us love one another, for love comes from God" (1 John 4:7).

When you try to understand what your spouse goes through and how to help her have a better life, you are demonstrating love to her. You are extending yourself out from your own perspective and attempting to enter hers so that you can be a benefit to her.

DEPENDENCY. Dependency is different. *Dependency is a state of needing the other person, so that you will become complete and secure.* It is about you more than about the other person. It perceives the other as a need-meeting resource rather than as a person in his own right, with his own viewpoint and needs.

Dependency is not a bad thing in an appropriate context. In a technical sense, dependency is the first stage in learning what love is. The dependency of a baby is a wonderful thing to experience, as she takes in and receives the safety, warmth, and nurture of her mother. During that stage of life, the infant's sole task is to learn to depend and need.

Over time, the experiences of love and constancy become internalized in the baby's mind, and she begins to need less, as she is now using the love she has received. As the process continues, children ultimately grow up and become independent of their parents, which is what adulthood is all about.

Yet even in adulthood we are still dependent people. We depend on God for His love and power. We depend on our supportive relationships for grace and encouragement. And our spouse is a part of that supportive system.

However, that dependency is a different type than we had as children. Adults do depend on adults, and partners do depend on their partners. *But one adult no longer takes primary responsibility for the other. Rather, they walk together as partners in life and growth.* A marriage is comprised of companions who depend on each other as equals, not as a needy person depends on his provider. Each is still responsible for his own life and welfare, which is different from the added responsibility a parent has for a child.

While there are certainly times and situations in life when we are truly dependent on others—such as a crisis, health issue, emotional breakdown, or financial catastrophe—the norm for committed relationships is for each person to be independent in terms of responsibility for one's soul and dependent in terms of being helpful companions in life.

## The Source of the Problem

Though love and dependency are very different, they produce the same result, which can be confusing. *Love and dependency both serve to draw two people together.* People are attracted to each other, seek each other out, and marry because of love, dependency, or a combination of both. You've seen it happen many times. A couple connects, thinking they are in love—only to later discover that one person needed the other for some emotional emptiness or unfinished business, and problems quickly ensued.

Where does this sort of dependency originate in a person? Most of the time, it is a result of some disruption of the childhood developmental process we described earlier. Some pattern may have occurred in a significant relationship that prevented the person from entering the adult world of autonomy and responsibility.

For example, some people will suffer from an insufficient amount and quality of love. They may have had caretakers who were cold, distant, preoccupied, absent, or depressed. So their "love tank" was never full. These people will often live in a state of deprivation and longing, constantly searching for a connection that will fill the tank.

Other individuals will experience warm and loving relationships with their caretakers, but ones in which choice, freedom, and autonomy were discouraged and even punished. That is, their primary connections might have resisted their attempts to stand on their own. The message that imprinted on these individuals is that being dependent and childlike is good, and being a separate individual is not good.

There can be other sources of the problem of dependency, such as inconsistent love from caretakers, or trauma. Whatever the source, these issues will manifest themselves in a person's inability to be his own person. And his relationships will be greatly affected by this inability.

## Dependency in the Love Connection

Several problems can emerge in a relationship in which a partner's dependency has not been resolved.

INABILITY TO LOVE. True love is impossible when a person is dependent on his spouse. He is unable to perceive his spouse as having feelings, values, or a life outside his own need for her to be constant, stable, present, validating, or supportive of whatever he is without. His need is so great that he must be more concerned with his survival than he is about her. So she often begins to feel that the relationship is one-sided, especially when she has needs of her own.

Sometimes the dependent person begins to take care of his lover in some ways. He might provide a measure of safety, structure, comfort, rescue, or financial help. While these can be good things, they can be attempts to draw the lover closer *for the purpose of being able to live in dependence on her.* This is not love; it is unhealthy dependency. When the lover doesn't respond by taking care of the dependent one, the dependent partner then feels unloved and unfairly treated.

ISSUES OF SEPARATENESS AND DIFFERENCE. Dependent people often resist the experience of being separate from their partner. They will not enjoy differences of opinion, conflict, arguments, and the like. For people who are dependent, these experiences threaten the love they need. They see love as merging and fusing with the other person. Therefore, being separate from their partner makes them feel abandoned and alone. The dependent person will often interpret his lover's separateness as a lack of love and concern for him, rather than something they both need.

POWER SHIFTS. Often, the dependent person gives enormous power to his partner, which affects the balance and mutuality of the relationship. She feels desperate for the connection, so to avoid distance, she will let her lover take control, make decisions, and take charge of the relationship. For the dependent person, this often feels like a fair exchange—that is, until she begins to feel safe in the relationship, and her need for choice emerges. Then greater problems happen.

FREEDOM PROBLEMS. The dependent lover is threatened by his spouse's freedom and perceives her choices as removing her love and constancy from him. Feeling threatened by the other's freedom often manifests itself in resentment, jealousy, and insecurity. The dependent spouse often becomes more desperate and clingy, while the other mate may feel controlled or imprisoned.

This often occurs after the honeymoon. At first, the couple can't get enough of each other, and they want only to be in each other's presence. For a period of time, this is a good thing, as they are cementing their attachment. However, once the newness of marriage has worn off and they are back in real life with their routines, friends, and work, the dependent partner will resist that reentry, and the other will feel smothered. What was first perceived as love is now experienced as a prison.

PASSION CONFLICTS. Couples who have a dependency issue often experience problems with sex and romance. The passion they first experienced will wane. This makes sense, because dependency creates a parent-child connection in the marriage. The dependent child wants to be cared for by the caretaking parent. Yet God did not design romance and sex for child and parent, but for two adults. So until the dependency issue is dealt with, the couple often experiences intimacy problems.

## Growing Out of Dependency

If dependency issues are sinking your love life, you need not despair. You can begin to rescue your marriage by applying workable solutions. Here we will give you several keys to success in growing through dependency into secure and happy adulthood.

FIND PLACES FOR DEPENDENCY TO MATURE. You can't just tell unfinished childhood dependency to stop being there. It must be resolved and completed, just as kids must go through a process to grow up. However, unhealthy marriages tend to keep one person stuck in that immature state. So the solution is to find contexts to help the dependent person grow. A good small group, support group, or counselor might be the answer. In this way, the person who struggles with dependency can find help and encouragement to learn how to become more complete, whole, and independent in his own right.

ENCOURAGE RISK AND AUTONOMY. When the dependent person steps out on her own, affirm and support that decision. This might mean allowing her to speak her mind, confront, be angry, or do things without you. Whenever this occurs, let her know that you do not love her any less. In fact, her attempts to be less dependent draw you closer to her, as now you feel the space between you that two people need in order to experience love.

CONFRONT THE PATTERNS. When one of you notices the warning signs of dependency, such as "You don't love me anymore" statements, control issues, and resistance to freedom, take action. In a gentle but direct way, say, "When you got mad and withdrew because I wanted a night out with the girls, I felt smothered, and I don't want that with you. That's not good for either of us. I want you to have nights with the boys, and me with the girls. Let's talk about how that can happen."

STAY OUT OF THE COMFORT ZONE. Often, without being aware of it, couples will get into a type of parent-child connection in which the dependent one goes to the perceived grownup as a source of safety, instruction, and grace. This can become comfortable in a sense, because it may keep you and your partner from disagreement or conflict. But you must get out of this comfort zone and address the issue, because your parent-child connection can cause the relationship to become boring, unhealthy, stifling, and controlling. Genuine marital love comes when two people with independent minds and opinions get together for each other.

DON'T BE AFRAID OF NEED. At the same time, don't think that saying, "I need you" is wrong or unhealthy for the marriage. It's really good for you to need each other. You simply should understand what need you are referring to. Problem dependency says, "I need you to survive/be happy/not be lonely/feel good about myself." But a supportive, healthy dependency says, "I need you to be my loving partner/be there for me as I will be for you/help me grow."

**A Lifeline:** DON'T GET DOWN ON YOURSELF IF YOU HAVE DEPENDENCY PROBLEMS. INSTEAD, REALIZE THAT THE TIME HAS COME TO FINISH THE GROWTH AND MOVE INTO MATURITY—AND ACT. YOU CAN DO IT!

## But I'm Not the Immature One

"I didn't expect a psychologist to say that," Dave said as he and Stacy sat in my (John's) office. He looked surprised and somewhat irritated.

"I'm sorry, Dave, but I think this is the major issue keeping you and Stacy apart. I don't mean to sound critical of you, because I'm really here to help you. But yes, I do think you're an immature person. And if you want the marriage I think you want, you're going to have to take a hard look at your immaturity and deal with it."

Dave eyed me skeptically. "What do you mean by 'immature'?"

"Well, for example, I don't see that you put a great deal of effort into seeing Stacy's side of things. But at the same time, you expect her to see yours. That's the stance of a young child. You, however, are a man. So that's why it's immature."

"When did I do that?"

"A few minutes ago, when we were talking about Stacy feeling disconnected from you because you bought the boat without consulting her."

"I told you," Dave replied, "Stacy did the exact same thing with the furniture."

"Yes, but that was several months ago. She felt bad about it and has made herself accountable to you for financial decisions since, which you haven't done. What you really need to do is listen to Stacy tell you how she feels when you don't hear her side of things. Don't interrupt or make excuses. Just listen and look her in the eye."

Dave agreed, and Stacy turned to him. "I am so scared," she said. "I'm not mad at you anymore. I'm just frightened that I am losing you. When I try to tell you that the boat makes me feel like we're going to be financially unstable, and you get mad at me for bringing it up, I lose all hope that we'll make it. I just don't know what to do." Stacy choked up and stopped.

Dave's face changed. He had been ready to protect his freedom and territory after my seeming assault on his self-esteem. But Stacy's vulnerability took him by surprise, and his eyes filled with tears. He leaned toward her and said, "Honey, I didn't know you were scared; I thought you were just upset with me. I'm so sorry."

Stacy recovered a little and looked back at him. At that point, I said, "Dave, that was a good step. You just entered Stacy's world."

Our conversations continued in subsequent sessions. Gradually, Dave became more aware of his immaturity and made progress in resolving it. The key was in seeing how deeply his immaturity affected Stacy. That helped him to keep moving ahead.

## What Is Immaturity?

Most people are like Dave; they would resent having the label "immature" slapped on them. Yet most of us qualify for it at some level. Immaturity is another of those dumb things that can sink a marriage. But it's also something we can overcome, and growing out of it can bring closeness, intimacy, and passion to your marriage.

To be immature is to be incomplete or undeveloped. In terms of emotional and personal growth, immaturity has to do with certain attitudes that show that an individual has not yet become an adult in the full sense of the word. These attitudes affect one's ability to love, relate, care, and build good relationships. Here are some of the most common attitudes that indicate immaturity.

DETACHMENT. Have you ever been with someone who was physically present but a million miles away emotionally? His body was in the room, but his mind was elsewhere. This describes detachment, which is the tendency to disconnect from a relationship. The detached partner either distances himself mentally or focuses on something else, causing the other person in the relationship to feel alone and disconnected.

Detachment is a sign of relational immaturity. Grownups need to have the ability to connect at deep and emotional levels with themselves and others. This is the basis of love itself. When you tend toward detachment, you are not mature and complete in the ability to love and connect fully.

CONTROL. When one spouse resists the freedom of the other, the issue is control, which is also a type of immaturity. We are designed by

God to control ourselves, not each other. Mature couples support and enjoy each other's freedom and choices. However, an immature partner attempts to make her spouse do things her way, often by using intimidation, aggressiveness, manipulation, or guilt.

Trying to control your partner is a dumb attitude that will sink your love life. When one partner feels that he has to choose what the other wants, he does not feel free. And people who are not free cannot love. Love grows only when it has the freedom to make wholehearted choices.

IRRESPONSIBILITY. One sign of a mature marriage is that both spouses are responsible and faithful in the relationship. That is, they do what they promise. They take initiative to solve problems. When they make a mistake, they own up to it and make changes. Responsible spouses carry their end of the weight in the marriage.

A partner who fails to own her part of the responsibility in marriage is demonstrating immaturity, like a Peter Pan who doesn't want to grow up. She may be charming and loving yet undependable and unreliable. Irresponsibility is another sign that a spouse isn't fully an adult yet.

SELF-CENTEREDNESS. Grownups should be able to step out of their own point of view and enter the world of others' feelings, values, experiences, and opinions. Maturity is when you can put yourself aside temporarily and feel what the other person is feeling.

When a spouse does not readily engage at this level, it is generally the immaturity of self-centeredness. (Sometimes it can also be detachment, but a detached person is more disconnected than self-absorbed.) This was Dave's type of immaturity, and he had to learn to get into Stacy's world and heart.

## What Immaturity Does to Your Relationship

As you may have realized firsthand, immaturity causes imbalance, loss of safety and love, and negative feelings in marriage. It's as if you were a business partner with a twelve-year-old. While he might be a good person and highly motivated, he is still twelve; so he does what twelve-year-olds do. In a marketing meeting, he pays attention for a couple of minutes and then walks around the conference room. When you are working on finances, he wants to spend money on video games. Instead of sharing responsibilities, he wants you to do the work so he can play.

Some marriages are like that partnership. When one spouse is immature, the other feels like a burdened and resentful parent of a selfish child. Then the immature one feels smothered and controlled, and he wants to get away from this resentful person.

It is also harder to connect on a vulnerable emotional level with an immature person. If you are not on the same adult wavelength, it is difficult to let go, to trust, to open yourself up, and to take emotional risks. For example, there are things I talk about only with my wife, not my kids. Sometimes one of our sons will walk in the room when we are having these discussions, and I will say, "Sorry, it's grownup talk time. Can you come back in a few minutes?" There are places you just can't go with a child, only with a mature person. What you want is a partner you can share your heart, mind, and soul with, and know you are with an equal.

## Deal with It Now

The one good thing about immaturity is that it's not an incurable disease. The right treatment will get rid of it. The sooner you begin, the sooner you will have the kind of love life you really want. Here are some ways to deal with immaturity.

LOOK AT YOUR OWN IMMATURITY FIRST. You may have been reading this chapter and thinking, *My spouse needs to deal with some immaturity.* But don't go that route. The happiest couples are comprised of individuals who first focus on how they themselves are showing immaturity. As Jesus taught, everyone needs to "first take the plank out of your own eye" before judging someone else (Matthew 7:5).

This step is what love is all about. When you really love someone, you do not want your immaturity to hurt her. You want to preserve, help, and grow the relationship; and you will do whatever is necessary to stop contributing anything that gets in the way of love.

People who understand and apply this are well on the way to letting go of their immaturity, for that is a mature and loving stance to take. When Dave saw Stacy's fear, he started getting out of himself. That is a great first step. See how simple it can be?

As a couple, you need to agree that whoever does not first look at his own issues is disqualified from judging the other's immaturity. This is important. Say to each other, "I want to talk about our love life and how to make it better. I want to know what you feel I am doing to contribute to the problems."

DETERMINE HOW SEVERE YOUR IMMATURITY IS. Sometimes immaturity is a minor thing, like a wife withdrawing when she is upset. The solution is apparent: she can learn to speak up instead. Sometimes immaturity is major, as when a spouse shuts down, sinking your love life for days or weeks.

How severe is your immaturity? Ask your spouse and other people you trust. Humbly listen to their feedback, remembering that we have a tendency to minimize our effect on others. Start working on the problem.

If your immaturity is minor, simply making yourself aware of it may enable you to stop it. For example, suppose you are a somewhat controlling person. It could well be that asking your mate how this disconnects her from you may provide enough awareness and incentive for you to restrain the urge to control her.

If you have a deeper immaturity, the two of you may need to keep discussing it as a process, not as a one-time event. Take the initiative to say, "I want you to let me know when my immaturity affects you and gets between us. Our relationship is more important to me than what I want."

Your immaturity may be severe enough that you need outside help to resolve it. For example, a person who has rage attacks when his spouse disagrees with him is clearly out of control. In these cases, you need to seek help in the form of a support group or therapist.

### What If My Spouse Doesn't See His Immaturity?

Unfortunately, sometimes immature people are unwilling to acknowledge their problem. Actually, that is often part of the immaturity problem itself. An immature perspective is one that is more about self than about the marriage relationship.

If that is the case, take the time and effort to help your mate become aware of how his attitude affects you and the marriage. This can come in the form of certain appeals, requirements, boundaries, and consequences, which are often very helpful in both people getting back on the same page. (Both of us have written books that deal extensively with this issue: see John's book, *Who's Pushing Your Buttons? Handling the Difficult People in Your Life*, and our book, *Boundaries Face to Face: How to Have That Difficult Conversation You've Been Avoiding*.)

**A Lifeline:** THERE'S NO NEED FOR IMMATURITY TO SINK YOUR LOVE LIFE. IT MAY BE HUMBLING TO CONFRONT YOUR OWN IMMATURITY, BUT HAVING A FIRST-RATE LOVE LIFE IS WORTH THE EFFORT. FACING YOUR IMMATURITY IS A MATURE THING TO DO— AND IT'S THE FIRST STEP IN OVERCOMING IT.

# You Make Me Crazy

In the first section of this book, we've focused on the important idea of rescuing yourself first. Sometimes, however, it's obvious that something is wrong in your marriage, but you can't put your finger on what. If you have certain repeating, crazy-making patterns that do not change or resolve over time, that's a sure sign that there's a problem somewhere. It may be a repeated emotional disconnection, a pattern of arguments that go nowhere, or chronic troublesome behavior. Often these patterns are so painful that couples avoid addressing them, hoping that they will just go away. But avoidance is another dumb attitude that can sink your marriage, or at least keep it so waterlogged it can't sail. Unaddressed, these patterns tend stay the same or even get worse. In this chapter, we'll show you a way to identify and solve these elusive problems.

The crazy-making patterns in your marriage can be a source of diagnostic information. They point to something consistent going on behind the scenes that is creating and driving the problem. When you identify that something, you can resolve your issue and see the pattern vanish. Couples who have great marriages are actively involved in this process of discovering and getting to the root of problem patterns.

### Brian and Lori Deal with an Unresolved Issue

Brian and Lori thought they had a great marriage, except in one area. They could not argue well. Whenever they disagreed on any matter, whether it was parenting, finances, sex, or in-laws, things would quickly go downhill. One would get too angry, the other would get defensive, and they would disconnect from each other. The problem would never get solved, because they could never get back to it. This pattern repeated over and over again.

Brian and Lori hated their inability to solve problems. They didn't like feeling so distant from each other. They tried to stop it, using several approaches. They committed to each other never to fight again. They tried to communicate their feelings better. They tried to be more loving. They felt that they made some progress over time, but not as much as they wanted. The bad fights kept emerging.

Finally, they came to me (John) for help, and what was going on underneath became quickly apparent. Lori was afraid of all personal conflict and had no skills to handle it. When Brian was upset, angry, or even direct with her, she felt attacked and unloved. She felt OK with him when he was supportive and compassionate, but those secure feelings disappeared when he wanted to talk about a problem. Even when Brian tried to be kind while being honest, Lori couldn't take it. Her parents had always avoided negativity, anger, and conflict. So when she married Brian and inevitable conflicts occurred, she didn't know how to deal with them.

Lori realized the problem pattern wasn't because she and Brian weren't communicating or didn't love each other. She just had an unresolved issue. She learned how to give and receive feedback while staying connected and feeling positive toward Brian, and her marriage grew much more complete and satisfying. They no longer had to tiptoe around conflicts. They could just take life as it came and deal with it.

The point is this: Brian and Lori could have continued to communicate, to be positive, and to be loving with each other, but if their conflict issue remained unresolved, it would have kept coming back. That is the nature of being human. *If you do not deal with the underlying issue, you can be sure that you will see it again.*

It's like having a plant in your backyard that is drooping because of a deficiency in some nutrient. You can keep it in the sun, water it, and protect it from insects, but if the nutrient deficiency is not met, the plant will still not flourish, because *the real problem is not being addressed.*

Dealing with unresolved emotional baggage is a major key to rescuing your love life. All the good intentions, date nights, and positive affirmations in the world won't get rid of an issue. The negative patterns will continue until you face the problem and apply the solution.

## Many Causes, Many Patterns

There is not enough room in this book to list all the issues that can cause repeated negative patterns in a marriage. But here are a few of the common ones—and all are fixable.

TRUST ISSUES. When one of you has trouble opening up and being vulnerable, it gets in the way of your connection. Trust is necessary for closeness, as it requires the ability to let someone in to a deep and fragile part of you.

Unresolved trust issues can lead to many problems, such as difficulty in emotional intimacy, long periods of inexplicable silences, seeing the spouse as unsafe, and sexual conflicts. If you see any of these patterns in your marriage, explore the possibility of one of you having a trust issue.

RESCUING. Sometimes a spouse will enable bad behavior and attitudes in other people by rescuing them from the results of their bad behavior instead of confronting the issues leading to the behavior itself. This has to do with an inability to distinguish love from rescue, a tendency to be overresponsible for others, or an inability to cope with their disappointment in others. A marriage with a rescuing partner will often manifest repeated patterns that include one mate's persistent immaturity, acting-out issues, alienation of love, and financial problems. One mate apologizes for the other's behavior, takes responsibility for the financial problems, and feels ownership for the other's selfish attitudes.

PASSIVITY. A passive person waits when initiative is required. He will avoid approaching his partner, waiting instead for her to approach him. He will avoid conflicts, hoping they go away. A marriage with a passive mate will often have recurring patterns of emotional distance, with one partner always chasing the other to get love and connection or the active spouse feeling like he has to solve all the problems in the marriage.

LACK OF INTEGRATION. Integration refers to the ability to see others as both good and bad, and being able to live in that reality. Spouses who are not integrated will often be unable to appreciate their mate's good points when they experience the negatives. To such a person, his spouse is either great or horrible. Sometimes this lack of integration also leads to a long-term perception of the spouse as a bad person after she has failed in one area, even though she has changed. Marriages with this problem will often exhibit unresolved conflicts, intense emotions, and sometimes one spouse using other people to take sides with him.

The list could go on and on. The point to remember here is that often, *the recurring pattern is not the problem.* It is more often the symptom of another unresolved issue.

## Address Your Issues

It may seem hard to address issues that repeatedly divide you, but we can assure you that you are likely to find great relief in the process. You will be glad that finally you are not avoiding something you both knew was creating distance in your marriage. Instead of retreating, you are facing the issue head-on, ready to deal with the issues so you can get back to your loving emotional connection. Here are a few suggestions that will help you confront and overcome the underlying issues in your marriage.

OBSERVE THE PATTERNS OBJECTIVELY. It helps to get a little distance on these issues so that you won't get defensive or withdraw. You are the surgeons; the marriage is on the operating table. Agree that you both want to look at the patterns that you see between each other, with neither blaming the other. You are observing your marriage like doctors observing a patient and trying to diagnose the real disease, so you can treat it. Be gracious and forgiving with each other.

TALK ABOUT WHAT PATTERNS ARE BEING REPEATED. Identify the patterns you and your partner enter into. Suppose when one partner wants to be close, the other feels overwhelmed and distanced. The first partner feels hurt and rejects the "rejecter." The second gives up and distances even more. And on and on.

OWN WHATEVER YOU ARE DOING THAT KEEPS THE PATTERN GOING. Realize your contribution to the pattern. Get beyond the problem. If you are not aware of your issue, ask your spouse to pinpoint what you are doing. Be humble and listen.

Marriages that truly succeed are marked by this attitude: *each spouse is more concerned about how his own issues affect the marriage than about his spouse's issues.* Both are determined to look at themselves without excuse or blame. There is no limit to what a marriage that takes this approach can accomplish.

ENTER THE PATH OF GROWTH TO MAKE SURE THE ISSUES ARE RESOLVED. Work on your issues with love, communication, and positive attitudes. These may be enough to resolve many issues. However, if an issue has been plaguing your love and intimacy for some time, you may need to try some other things. Ask your spouse for help and support. Have her remind you when you inadvertently repeat the behavior. Read about the behavior, pray about it, and ask people you know for help and wisdom. Growth comes in many forms. The important thing is to get moving.

BE AWARE OF REPEATED PATTERNS. Awareness of these problems lets you know your progress. As your pattern of withdrawal, anger, distance, or anxiety goes away, it shows that you are improving your issues. If the pattern is not going away, either you are addressing the wrong cause or one of you is disengaging from the process. If the pattern is getting better but remains a problem, ask a wise friend what you might be missing.

**A Lifeline:** NO ONE IS PERFECT, AND NO MARRIAGE IS PERFECT. YOU WILL BOTH CONTINUE TO MAKE MISTAKES AND SLIP UP IN YOUR ATTEMPTS TO MAKE A GREAT RELATIONSHIP. BUT YOU CAN GO A LONG WAY TOWARD SAFETY, CLOSENESS, AND INTIMACY WHEN YOU ROOT OUT THE PROBLEMS UNDERLYING THE REPEATED PATTERNS IN YOUR MARRIAGE. WHEN YOU RESOLVE THE ISSUE, YOU SHOULD SEE GREAT CHANGE AND PROGRESS.

## One Person Can't Change Everything, But . . .

Glenn and Nancy had the classic detached husband–nagging wife situation. Glen was emotionally disengaged from Nancy and showed little interest in connecting with her. "I'm just that way," he would say. Nancy would nag him, hoping he would become more connected, which never happened, because the nagging would drive him even further away. He would escape by working late and spending too much time on-line or watching TV.

While both had their own roles to play in the problem, Nancy was much more concerned about solving it. Glenn was passive and disengaged, which, of course, was part of the problem in the first place. It made sense, then, that Nancy came to see me (John) alone, without Glenn.

She was really discouraged. "I am pretty much all alone in this marriage," she said. "He's a good provider, and he doesn't have any really bad habits. But he just doesn't show up to connect with me.

Look around; I'm the only person in your office. There's not much I can do when he isn't here."

"It is certainly a problem that Glenn isn't here," I replied. "But don't ignore the fact that 50 percent of the relationship is in my office. That's a lot better than zero." We started working on the issues and came up with a plan.

A few evenings later, Glenn came home from work a couple of hours late. He said hello and went straight to the computer. Normally at this point Nancy would launch into a tirade about his distance, giving Glenn the excuse to say that his biggest problem was a nagging wife.

But this time was different. Nancy went to him and asked how his day was. Surprised, Glenn told her. Then she said, "I wanted to apologize for being so critical of you with the distance thing. I know it doesn't help you, and it just makes things worse. So I am going to stop all that."

Glenn started to perk up. This was sounding pretty good to him.

"But at the same time," Nancy continued, "I do have a problem with the distance. I get lonely and I miss you. I need connection, but for whatever reason, you are choosing not to connect. So I have found some things to do outside the home several nights a week that will help my loneliness. I'm joining a small group at our church, some gals and I will be getting together for a movie night, and I've signed up for a Spanish course at the community college."

Glenn was in shock. "That's three nights a week!"

"I know. I'm not mad about this. I just wanted to let you know."

Nancy followed through, getting a life and letting Glenn have what he *said* he wanted. I wouldn't have suggested this for everyone, as some couples are so alienated and fragile that there is no connection to leverage, but I thought there was enough connection with Glenn and Nancy that this might work.

Fortunately, I was right. (Whew!) In a few weeks, Glenn started missing Nancy. He didn't like being without her warmth, her interest, and her energy. He got tired of eating dinner, watching TV, and being on-line with no one else at the house.

Nancy tried not to sound vindictive when she was home. Instead, when she was there, she connected with him, was loving and attentive, and gave him a lot of grace and interest. In a way, that made Glenn miss her even more.

Finally, Mr. Disengaged made his move. He asked Nancy if she would stay home more. She answered, "I would really like to, but I can't if we're going back to the same detached marriage."

"What do you want?"

"I want you to be home at a reasonable time. I want us to talk about our day and about ourselves and our experiences. And I want us to do things together as a couple. You're my first choice, but I just can't go back to nothing."

Glenn finally agreed. It wasn't easy for him to get out of his detached comfort zone and connect with Nancy, but with her encouragement, he moved out of the cocoon. They now have a much better relationship. She helped transform her marriage with an unwilling husband, and that helped him to become a willing partner in growth.

## One Is Almost a Majority

You may have a partner who is unwilling to deal with a problem, but there is a lot you can do all by yourself to help and change. First, identify the problem. Is it a problem with connection, as with Glenn and Nancy, or a problem with irresponsibility, selfishness, or some other bad attitude or behavior?

You may feel helpless and alone in your marriage. You may be thinking, *Nothing can change until my partner wants to change.* Fortunately, that is not true at all. There is a lot you can do all by yourself to help and change. You don't have to wait until your lover is ready to get moving. There are some moves you can make to help him get moving. Let's understand why this is true.

A scientific theory called *chaos theory* says, in simplified form, that a little change in one part of a system can make a big change in another. An example of this theory is the *butterfly effect,* which says that from the beating of a butterfly's wings in one part of the world, a tornado can be caused in another part of the world. The idea is that changes ripple throughout a system, affecting lots of parts.

This applies to your emotional connection. You and your partner are in a system called a relationship. Your lives intersect in many places: physically, socially, financially, emotionally, domestically, spiritually, and others. As one person makes changes, those changes affect the partner in some way, because your lives are connected. If one person changes, the relationship changes.

Nancy didn't try to control Glenn. She changed her patterns in a healthy way that didn't work against the relationship. But her changes affected him, and he responded. That is what this is all about.

Basically, the chaos theory says that you must not give in to hopelessness and helplessness because *you can affect things.* (For more information on realizing and using your own leverage, please refer to John's book, *Who's Pushing Your Buttons?*) As you bring light, love, truth, and health to the relationship, it exposes problems and helps make changes (Ephesians 5:13–14).

## How One Can Do a Lot

Here are some ways you alone can make good changes that can do a great deal to resolve your relationship conflict in positive ways.

SAY WHAT YOU WANT AND NEED. Be clear and specific about what you need that will help end the problem. For example, you may need to state clearly that you want emotional connectedness, honesty, sharing of time and experience, freedom, respect, affirmation, or comfort. This gives your partner clarity about what you are really after.

It's easy to miss this step, especially if you have what are called passive rescue wishes. That is, some people define *love* as clairvoyance. If they have to spell out what they don't want, they don't feel that their partner cares about them. It sometimes comes out in the baffling statement, "If you don't know, I'm not going to tell you." And just as often, one of you will be very vague about what you want to help the problem, which isn't helpful at all. Statements like "I just want you to get it/to be normal/to stop being a jerk" are less than helpful. Don't fall into this trap. Educate your partner on what you need, and be clear, direct, and specific.

SAY WHAT IS NOT OK. This is the flip side of the coin. Does your partner know specifically what attitudes and behaviors hurt you, bother you, distance you, and will no longer be tolerated by you? These might include withdrawal of love, passivity, control, irresponsibility, self-centeredness, or deception.

These are the things you are bringing in to the light so your partner knows what will solve the problem, meet your need, and bring you closer to her. Remember, if you don't draw a line, your partner has a point when she says she never knew she crossed it. The New Testament says, "Where there is no law there is no transgression" (Romans 4:15). You can't cry "foul" unless you first tell your partner what is not OK.

OWN YOUR TRIGGERS. Your reactions are your own reactions. Your partner may certainly affect and influence you, but he doesn't dictate or control how you feel and react.

For example, if he tends to put off things like bills and projects, that is a problem and needs to be addressed. But if you get panicked and overanxious about it, your reaction is triggered by something within yourself. Perhaps you came from a family that was unstable, causing you to feel insecure easily. Or maybe being dependent on another person is hard for you.

Whatever the cause of your emotional reactions, if you blame them on your partner, you force him to defend himself, rather than focusing on the problem. Instead, face the problem. Own that you do have extreme reactions to that problem, acknowledge that these extreme reactions aren't his fault, and get moving.

INITIATE SOLUTIONS. One person can make a great difference in resolving conflict by coming up with ideas, suggestions, and solutions. Take the initiative and be positive. Don't wait for your partner to have the lights come on. Talk to people in the know, learn some concepts, and say, "I have a couple of ideas of how we can deal with our conflict . . .". You may not come up with the perfect idea, or even a good idea, on your own. And that's OK. Taking positive initiative to problem-solving gets both of you thinking and moving.

BE THE HEALTHIEST PERSON YOU CAN BE. Become a healthy person. Grow personally, emotionally, and spiritually. Get to know yourself, God, and others in ways that transform and change you. Become loving, caring, defined, honest, responsible, and humble.

A healthy person inspires a very strong incentive for the other to change. Being a growing individual, a person of light, will help your partner get off the fence. It forces him either to become a person of light or to move against the light. Either way, you are better off.

**A Lifeline:** TAKE ADVANTAGE OF THE TREMENDOUS POWER AND EFFECT YOU HAVE IN YOUR RELATIONSHIP, AND BE AN AGENT FOR CHANGE AND REDEMPTION. ULTIMATELY, YOU CAN BE ON YOUR WAY TO MOVING PAST CONFLICT INTO LOVE, RECONNECTION, AND INTIMACY.

# "My Lover Should Make Me Happy"

From the time children watch their first animated movie with a prince and a princess, they begin forming ideas of what love and romance look like. Girls think that someday a knight in shining armor riding a white horse will come for her, and his unfaltering devotion will make her happy for the rest of her life. Guys think that someday he will rescue a damsel in distress, and her unparalleled beauty and passion will make him the happiest man on earth. Little do they know that real life isn't exactly like that.

And, as any marriage counselor will tell you, some of the expectations and demands that adult couples have for each other are pretty lofty as well. Couples forget, at times, that they each are married to a real human being, and all honeymoon stages ultimately have to face reality. If their marriage is going to experience real joy and bliss, they will have to release their childhood fantasies and embrace reality.

Lest that sound too depressing, read on. We believe in joy and marital bliss. We believe that love does not end when the honeymoon is over. We think that marriage is an incredible creation of God that is designed to provide some of the most amazing experiences that a human can have. But getting to those requires a step into adulthood.

Children have unrealistic fantasies that can only be realized in fairy tales. The good thing about growing up is that if people are willing to get out of the storybooks and into the real world, they can find lasting, fulfilling, and even intoxicating love. Join us as we take a look at how that kind of love is only found in the real world of real expectations. You may even find out that you have not been expecting enough!

## The Real Scoop About Happiness

"When I was single, I was unhappy and insecure. Then I married Ron and became married, unhappy, and insecure." So said my friend Denise, whom I (John) had not seen in several years.

"Even though at first it was depressing to realize that," she continued, "it really helped me to understand that my failure to be happy was my own problem. If I expected to be happy, I had some growing up to do."

### The Fantasy of Marriage

As you focus on rescuing your love life, it's important to recognize that many couples have a dumb attitude that can put an intolerably heavy burden on their marriage. Here's the dumb attitude in a nutshell: *my spouse should make me happy.* In other words, you think that if your partner is sufficiently loving, caring, passionate, dependable, strong, brave, and so on, you will be a happy person in a happy marriage.

The converse of that idea is this: *my spouse is the reason I am not happy.* In this thinking, your partner is either not providing the good things you need or providing toxic things you don't need, and therefore you are not happy.

In my experience, many couples will not actually express the first fantasy, but they will admit the second one. The problem is, however, if one is true, the other is also. It's an issue of dependency on the other person, which we will help you deal with in this chapter.

Before we splash cold water on this fantasy, we want to validate the profound effects spouses do have on one another. Since marriage is the most intimate of relationships, spouses do have the power and influence to bring joy, love, and encouragement to each other. The same is true about pain, hurt, and disappointment. Mates do affect each other, in big ways, for good or for ill.

Saying your spouse affects you, however, is a very different thing from saying that your spouse can, or should, make you a happy person. That task and responsibility is for you, and only you, to achieve. You can have the best spouse in the world and still be a totally miserable person. The truth is that your happiness is your problem, and it is also your opportunity.

## The Secret of Happiness

You may be thinking, *If my marriage can't make me happy, then how do I get happy?* This sounds like a reasonable question. The answer is that *happiness is not a good life goal.* A much better life goal is *growth*, and one of the byproducts of growth is happiness.

There is certainly nothing intrinsically wrong with happiness. It's a good and positive thing, and a gift from God. Psalm 68:3 says, "May the righteous be glad and rejoice before God; may they be happy and joyful." However, people whose life goal is to be happy are acting like children. Children don't like pain, frustration, rules, or delayed gratification. They want to feel good all the time. Yet we wouldn't consider them as great role models for what we aspire to be.

The spiritual and emotional growth process, designed by God, is about discovering what we lack inside, where we are empty, and where we are broken. We find out how unfinished we are and how much we need God and others. But it doesn't stop there. The next step is experiencing the many ways we can be filled, matured, and healed. When we begin addressing our needs for growth, we find happiness.

## Placing Growth Before Marriage

Let's get the pressure off the marriage! Don't ask from marriage what only personal growth can provide. Instead, put the pressure on growing out of whatever is keeping you from being the fulfilled and complete person you need to be. The end result is that your marriage, freed from a burden it cannot bear, can become a wonderful haven of love, connection, intimacy, and passion.

It's a little like how I (John) try to learn Spanish. My wife, Barbi, is bilingual; and from time to time she will speak Spanish to me, so that I can become conversational. I listen to her and try to follow her, but just hearing Barbi speaking another language isn't enough. I need to get the home study course, do the exercises, and practice. When I do that, I improve.

Suppose I were to complain that I can't speak Spanish because Barbi doesn't help me enough. That would simply not be true, and it wouldn't help me learn. The real reason that I can't speak Spanish is that I haven't made it a priority and don't do the necessary work.

Growing people create growing marriages. People who aren't growing tend to look toward their spouse and want more of what they aren't getting enough of. Ask yourself what you are demanding from your marriage that you should be achieving in the growth process.

For example, you might have a tendency to feel empty and unloved. Marriage provides love indeed, but marriage alone doesn't fill that hole in your heart that yearns for love. That is filled through the growth process, with God, other people, and grace.

Or you might be depending on your spouse to give you a sense of purpose and strength. Often, someone who lacks structure and confidence marries a person who has a lot of both, hoping to receive these qualities through some kind of transfer. Instead, the weaker one becomes dependent on the stronger, and the stronger one becomes resentful and sometimes controlling of the weaker. That is not how people become strong. Purpose and strength come when we learn what we want, work through why we have been afraid to go after what we want, and then take the necessary risks to achieve it.

You will not move from an unloved to a loved state, or from a weak to a strong state, simply from having the right spouse. Even if your mate has the necessary qualities to facilitate the move, it would unbalance the entire relationship. *In essence, your spouse would be fulfilling the role of a parent, not of a lover and an equal.* Marriage is about two adults loving, growing, failing, and forgiving together. When one becomes the parent and the other becomes the child, no one is better off.

## Growth Within Marriage

Another benefit of taking the pressure off the marriage and pursuing your own growth is that *growing people tend to be attractive people.* When a person becomes compassionate, she can show compassion to her spouse. When she becomes honest, she can give and receive truth with her spouse. When she has hope for change, she can give that hope to him. When she has experienced that it is OK to be real and imperfect, she can accept reality and imperfection in him. When she can look into deeper parts of her own soul, she can help make it safe for him to reveal his deeper self to her.

This kind of personal growth frees the partners from feeling responsible for the happiness and fulfillment of each other. That is a huge weight to bear—and a good one to get rid of. I remember a friend telling her husband, "I'm sorry for making you responsible for making me happy. That is my problem, not yours. I do want things from you, and I want to give you good things too. But I'm taking this one over for myself." His jaw dropped. He couldn't believe it wasn't all his fault anymore. And their relationship improved dramatically.

## How to Start a Growing Marriage

Here are some ways to begin the process of rescuing your love life from the dumb attitude that makes your spouse responsible for your happiness.

ASK EACH OTHER IF THE MARRIAGE IS BURDENED WITH THE "HAPPINESS FANTASY." Has one of you been expecting the other to make him happy and fulfilled? Also, is one of you blaming the other for her unhappiness? You will often find that the unhappy one is not even aware that this is going on, while the one being blamed is very aware of it! If the "happiness fantasy" is alive and well in your marriage, agree together that the fantasy must die so that real love can live.

COMMIT YOURSELVES TO THE GROWTH PROCESS. As a couple, decide that you will both find ways to deal with your own emptiness and unhappiness. Many resources are available to help you, such as books, seminars, and professional counseling. The important thing is to commit to personal and spiritual growth, which will take time, energy, involvement, and probably the help of other people. For example, many couples find that a small group becomes a center point of growth for them. Because you are individuals, you will have differ-ent issues, hurts, weaknesses, and pasts. Find the best settings and context for yourselves. And by all means, budget your commitments to be sure you allow time for each other.

People who commit to marriage growth also commit to individual growth. How can you repair a house if you don't consider the condition of its individual parts? The frame, plumbing, foundation, roof, and floor must all be in good shape for the house to be considered sound. No one will be successful in making a marriage grow who is not also invested in personal growth.

BECOME COMPANIONS TO EACH OTHER'S GROWTH. The best attitude couples can take is that of two companions: *I will support your growth, and you will support mine. We are not responsible for each other's growth process, but we will help and encourage each other in it.* If only one of you wants to take this step, don't be discouraged. Good things can occur when one person gets the pressure off the marriage and concentrates on her own growth. Sometimes it even inspires the other person to get on-board. Remember, a growing person will be an attractive, interesting, encouraging, and passionate person. As you grow, your spouse should become aware that he is getting a really good deal.

**A Lifeline:** KISS THE FANTASY OF THE PERFECT MARRIAGE GOOD-BYE, WITH EACH MATE POURING ECSTASY AND COMPLETE-NESS INTO THE OTHER. DO MARRIAGE THE RIGHT WAY, AND TAKE OWNERSHIP OF YOUR OWN HAPPINESS.

## Are They Needs or Desires?

"So you think I ought to just love him unconditionally and live with his behavior," Ally said, pouting.

"No, I didn't say that," I (Henry) responded. "Yes, I think you should love him unconditionally, as that is the only kind of love there is. But I did not say that you should just live with things as they are, not saying anything about what is wrong."

"Yes, you did," Ally insisted. "You said that I should just accept the fact that Ben doesn't express love in the way I need it."

"No, I didn't say that. One of the most important things that partners in a relationship must do is to work hard on expressing, understanding, and meeting the needs of each other. That is *key*, and I would not want you to give up on making that happen.

"What I said was this: the way you have decided that you 'need' love is not a true need. It is more of a wish that is unique to you, yet you speak of it as a universal demand that a husband must fulfill.

"I said that you should examine what you think you need from Ben and see if those things are truly needs. I want the two of you to increase love, but some of the things that you are defining as 'needs' get in the way of your feeling loved."

Ally didn't like hearing it, but it could save her relationship. She was perpetually unhappy with Ben because she believed that a man should do certain things in a relationship and that those things were her "needs." For example, she had a "need" for Ben to manage their finances in a certain way. When he did not do that in the way that she "needed," she was devastated and withdrew from him, thus damaging their connection. But Ally was not talking about a real need at all. She was talking about a wish that she *felt* was a need.

Interpreting wishes as needs is another common but dumb attitude that can sink your love life. But rescue is fairly simple if you know what to do. It's a matter of getting straight about what is a true need and what is not. If lovers fail to distinguish between wishes and needs, they will either disconnect over issues that should not be connection breakers, or they will put energy into the wrong things and thereby ignore the true needs that make a relationship thrive.

## Needs, Preferences, and Wishes

What does one truly need in a marriage? *A true need is something that, if missing, results in damage.* For example, you need food and water for physical survival. You need shelter or you could die in the cold or heat. If a genuine need isn't met, destruction occurs.

There are many things that we wish for but do not really need. They may be essential to certain kinds of fulfillment, enjoyment, or quality of life, but we can live without them and not suffer any injury. That is the difference between needs and wishes.

Preferences are like wishes. They have to do with the way we would ideally like things to be, but they are not always the way we find things to be. For example, when I go to a restaurant, I *need* food. I *wish* for pizza on the menu. I *prefer* to sit in a booth. The reality is that I won't suffer much if they only have hamburgers and I have to sit at a table. Nothing bad happens to me; I get what I need, and I just have to wait to get pizza another day.

Mature people make sure their needs are taken care of, and they also try hard to find what they wish for and prefer. They cover the foundational things first and then build fulfillment on top of that.

In marriage, a loving, honest, and responsible spouse is someone to be grateful for. But Ally felt entitled to more than that. She felt that she "needed" more than a good, loving person. She needed her husband to be a financial wizard as well. That, she felt, provided the security that she "needed" and felt that she deserved. As a result, she was very dissatisfied with her husband when he did not perform as she expected a husband to.

Now we don't want you to be bored, unfulfilled, or have a relationship that lacks luster or interest. Nor do we want you not to push for what you desire from each other. We are saying that relationships truly have certain universal needs, and the focus should first be on those things. Wishes and preferences fall further down the list.

One of the biggest tragedies today is that people feel entitled to have their wishes met. And when that does not happen, they feel victimized and shortchanged, like they somehow deserve more than they are getting. So they either get angry with spouses they should appreciate, or they believe the lie and leave to find the fulfillment they feel entitled to. The reality is that the things they are seeking are not true needs.

## What Are Our True Needs?

If you focus on the true needs of your relationship first, you can pursue those other areas of fulfillment as extra benefits, for you and your partner will have the kind of connection that enables both of you to grow to greater heights. What are those needs? Here are the ones we have found.

EMOTIONAL CONNECTION. Empathy, support, care, listening, understanding, and trust are all parts of what creates an emotional connection. It comes through the ability to hear and understand each other. Emotional connection is the basic sense of being present with each other in a way that ends isolation, alienation, and aloneness.

FREEDOM. Love only thrives in an atmosphere of freedom. Where there is control, manipulation, or an inability to have an identity apart from the partner, love dies. You have a real need to set each other free from any and all kinds of control. This means you don't punish each other for time apart, choices you don't agree with (as long as they are not immoral, illegal, or unethical), tastes you wouldn't choose, and so on. Enjoy each other's individuality and differences. Invest in each other becoming the best individuals you can be, even when it has nothing to do with the relationship. A good relationship serves not only the needs of the relationship but also the individual needs of each partner. So give each other the freedom that is the foundation of love itself. And act responsibly with the freedom you are given.

FORGIVENESS. Dare we say it? All of us are sinners. Sin means that we miss the mark of perfection and create an offense to someone. It's going to happen in every relationship—that's reality. If a relationship is not strong enough to handle sin and failure, then it's not strong enough to handle reality. Our sin and failure create a huge need for forgiveness. If you punish each other for failure and do not forgive, your relationship will suffer damage and die.

ACCEPTANCE. Similar to our need for forgiveness is our need to be accepted regardless of our imperfections. Ever since the Garden of Eden, we all have been less than we should be—physically, spiritually, intellectually, emotionally, and every other way. As a result, we tend to hide who we really are. But for intimacy and love to occur, we need to reveal our true, naked selves. We'll do that only when we have the assurance of being totally accepted.

LIMITS. All of us get out of line, even when we don't intend to. Sometimes we do not see when we are wrong. At other times we do see, but we do not care. In both of those situations, we need limits from each other.

Correction and discipline are two of the greatest gifts that we can give each other, and a good relationship provides those for us. As Proverbs tells us, "Better is open rebuke than hidden love. Wounds from a friend can be trusted" (27:5–6). In a marriage, limits are essential to keeping love alive.

A good relationship does not allow hurtful behaviors to gain more ground, because these negative behaviors destroy love. Good lovers confront them and limit their ability to take over. Express limits, and let each other know when something wrong is happening. And do it in love.

SECURITY. We need to know that our partner's love is not going away. That is one of the biggest reasons for the Bible's commitment to marriage for a lifetime. For love to grow in a marriage, we need to know that our spouse's love is secure, unconditional, and forever. A secure commitment, one that preserves the connection through all sorts of times, is essential.

EQUALITY AND MUTUAL RESPECT. Romantic love is based on mutual respect and equality. The kind of love that builds a marriage cannot thrive if one person dominates the relationship and the other is overly submissive and not respected. Equality values the contribution, talents, ideas, gifts, perspectives, and uniqueness of each partner. In such a connection, both spouses become more of who they are supposed to be. This mutuality spills over into other settings, where each shows validation and respect in front of others instead of criticism and put-downs.

DESIREDNESS. From infancy, we need to know that we are desired by the people whom we are with. Otherwise, we feel like intruders in our most significant relationships. In your marriage, it is important that each of you communicates your desire for the other. This is done in many ways, some of them universal and some highly individualistic. Learn what causes your partner to feel desired, and then act on what you learn.

PHYSICAL EXPRESSION. Humans need to be touched, hugged, caressed, and nurtured physically. Your relationship needs physical contact that expresses all of the needs we have mentioned. Desire, equality, security, and acceptance are all expressed through physical contact.

In addition to normal human touch, marriage needs a fulfilling sexual relationship as well. Sexual fulfillment is a big part of God's design for "becoming one." In fact, the Bible tells husbands and wives not to deprive each other sexually (1 Corinthians 7:5). And like the other aspects of touch, sex is intended to be respectful, mutual, accepting, desirous, secure, and free.

TIME. Love needs time. No relationship ever perfectly met the needs of each person from the get-go. It takes time to develop love, to develop maturity, and to grow a relationship. For you to have all of these needs met in increasing measure, an investment of time is essential.

## Keep the Important Things Important

Like Ally, most people want it all. We want our marriages to meet not only our real needs but also our every expectation, preference, wish, and desire. Wouldn't that be nice? The truth is that it's not going to happen, except in some fantasy. And we've already shown the dangers of fantasy.

Demanding that our wishes and preferences be fulfilled is a dumb attitude that will sink a marriage. However, at the same time we must realize that some needs are truly essential. If these real needs are not met, a relationship will suffer.

Don't get caught up in fighting about your wishes. Work on those and try to fulfill as many as possible. But *do get caught up in focusing on your needs.* Learn to communicate them, educate each other about them, meet them, stand up for them, nurture them, grow in your mutual ability to meet them, and do whatever you can do to make sure they are being met.

Collectively, these needs are the things worth fighting *for*, not about. If you fight *about* these needs, you are probably violating one of them. But when you fight *for* them, you get closer to having them met.

**A Lifeline:** YOU CAN KEEP YOUR LOVE LIFE ON COURSE BY NOT DISCONNECTING WHEN YOUR WISHES ARE NOT MET AND BY ALWAYS WORKING TO MEET EACH OTHER'S REAL NEEDS. MEETING EACH OTHER'S REAL NEEDS WITHIN A SAFE CONNECTION WILL BRING YOU MORE FULFILLMENT THAN YOU EVER THOUGHT POSSIBLE!

# Stop Looking for Your Other Half

I (Henry) listened as Faith told me about her fiancé, Daniel. She was excited about their relationship and their upcoming marriage. I was excited as well, until she said something that revealed a dumb attitude many people have about relationships: she expected her fiancé to be her other half.

"We are such a good balance for each other. I am the people person in our relationship, and he likes to get out there and accomplish things. It feels so good to have someone who will fight all my battles for me, and I help to draw him out and express himself. So we are a great team!"

I hate to be the bearer of bad news in a thriving relationship, but as her counselor, I had to do it. I could see a lot of potential problems in their relationship if the division of labor was exactly as she described.

Here was the issue: Faith was doing the age-old math problem the wrong way, but the way so many people try to do it when it comes to relationships. Like this:

$$1/2 \text{ person} + 1/2 \text{ person} = 1 \text{ whole person}$$

Here is the dumb attitude stated another way: "I am incomplete as a person, and you are lacking some big things too. So let's merge our strengths, and we will make up for each other's weaknesses. Together we will achieve the happiness that each of us lacks alone."

This strategy feels right to people. They find someone who embodies all that they are not, and they feel complete when they are together. And that makes sense. We always feel more alive when we get near what we don't possess but need. It brings parts of us to life that have little chance of emerging on their own.

But something happens when this formula is applied to marriage. When two incomplete people marry in hopes that merging their strengths will make up for each other's weaknesses, the result is not the happiness they hope for. In fact, what happens is that each partner slowly comes to want from the other the things that that person does not possess.

Let's look at how this will happen with Faith and Daniel. She wants him to be more relational, so that the part of her that is such a people person, as she put it, can have someone to talk to and connect with. She starts to feel lonely and pushes him to open up. He feels overwhelmed and withdraws, not knowing what to do. Why? Remember, he is not a people person. He is the conqueror; that's why she liked him so much. But now she is awakening to her need for something that he doesn't possess. And they begin to tear each other down.

Likewise, he wants more performance from her—more attention to tasks, more responsibility in dealing with finances, and the like. He gets frustrated with her disorganization, her procrastination, and her inattention to detail. When he expresses his frustration with her inefficiency, she feels misunderstood, because he is not a very good communicator, at least emotionally. Faith and Daniel no longer love the attributes that first attracted them. In fact, they now resent them. "All he thinks about is getting things done," she will say. "She is always nagging me to 'connect' more," he says. "What is she talking about?"

## Do the Relational Math

Looking to your spouse for the strengths and the traits that you lack is another dumb attitude that can sink your marriage. But like most self-defeating attitudes, this one is common and highly fixable. So don't feel alone or discouraged. First, let's understand what happens in this situation, as it happens to everyone who encounters it.

The problem is that wrong expectations were set up in the beginning because the wrong formula was applied. Relationships are not *additive* in nature. In other words, one-half plus one-half does not equal one in relational math. Relationships are *multiplicative*. Remember? "The two shall become one," God said (Mark 10:8). So when you take a whole person and multiply his or her strengths by the other whole person, you get a unified, mutual relationship that is incredibly strong.

The problem is that when you multiply one-half of a person times one-half of a person (which is always what happens in every relationship, as none of us is totally whole), you get one-quarter of a person. That's less than you started with! And struggling couples will often tell you that. They bring each other down by demanding that the other "half" display more than the original half that he or she brought to the relationship. As is often said, they are attracted to someone because of a certain trait, and then they fight about that trait for the next forty years. So what's the answer?

The key to breaking that pattern or blocking any tendency for it to appear in your marriage is realizing that *everyone* is incomplete, including you and your lover. Your first task is to lower your expectations for that "half-baked" person to be "done." Realize that your mate is still in the oven, and God is at work making him into the complete person that both you and God desire him to be.

## Hints for Living with a "Half-Baked" Person

Accept the fact that you and your mate are not yet fully complete, well-rounded people, even in the areas of need that we talked about previously. Give up the demand that your mate be other than he is, and start dealing with it in a better way. What does that mean? Here are some hints on living with a half-baked person—and how you can overcome being one.

ACCEPT YOUR SPOUSE AS AN INCOMPLETE PERSON, JUST AS GOD HAS ACCEPTED YOU. There are areas where your partner truly is more of a "half" than a "whole." So accept that reality *lovingly*. Stop protesting with rage, nagging, shame, condemnation, and any other way that you do not like to be treated yourself.

LOOK AT THE AREAS WHERE YOU ARE INCOMPLETE BEFORE FOCUSING ON YOUR MATE'S INCOMPLETENESS. Get the plank out of your own eye first (Matthew 7:5). Ask your partner where you need to develop more. Ask what incomplete areas of your personality affect him the most, and begin there. Be a model for change.

BECOME SUPPORTIVE CHANGE AGENTS FOR EACH OTHER IN THE AREAS OF GROWTH YOU NEED. Talk about those things together, not with nagging or judgment, but as teammates. Create a safe space in which you can talk about them in love—no judgment, no shame, no guilt, no anger allowed.

FOCUS ON THE THINGS THAT ARE IMPORTANT FIRST. Address each other's real needs, as we discussed previously. Helping each other grow to completeness in those areas is more important than some of the stuff you may tend to fight over.

BE PATIENT. This is important: be patient with your partner just as God is patient with you. Want to see how it works? Think of your most incomplete issue as a person (such as procrastination, emotional vulnerability, completing tasks, sharing feelings, or being assertive). Got it? How long have you been aware of that issue? How long have you been working on it? How long has God been patient with you? How has He loved you unconditionally along the way? That is the way you have to look at this issue in your partner.

## Don't Push the Process

You must face these issues, or your relationship will not improve. Even push for change if needed. But you cannot expect your relationship to change overnight. You *can* expect your spouse to hear you and face the problem, but you can't expect immediate maturity. Some things take time. What you want is to be on the same page, working on your spouse, investing in him, and delighting in improvement.

Accept what the marriage is, work on it lovingly, and give each other time to grow. Suppose that when baking a cake, you opened the oven when it was half-done and demanded that it be ready right now! That stance with a mate is one of the most common ways to break a connection.

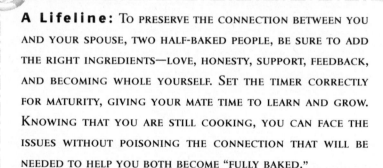

**A Lifeline:** To PRESERVE THE CONNECTION BETWEEN YOU AND YOUR SPOUSE, TWO HALF-BAKED PEOPLE, BE SURE TO ADD THE RIGHT INGREDIENTS—LOVE, HONESTY, SUPPORT, FEEDBACK, AND BECOMING WHOLE YOURSELF. SET THE TIMER CORRECTLY FOR MATURITY, GIVING YOUR MATE TIME TO LEARN AND GROW. KNOWING THAT YOU ARE STILL COOKING, YOU CAN FACE THE ISSUES WITHOUT POISONING THE CONNECTION THAT WILL BE NEEDED TO HELP YOU BOTH BECOME "FULLY BAKED."

## Self-Denial? You're Joking, Right?

"So how are the newlyweds?" I (John) asked Ted at dinner. I was referring to Ted's brother, Bob, and his new wife, Diane.

Ted smiled and said, "Really good. It's fun watching him adjust to marriage."

"Like how?" I asked.

"For instance, the other night I called Bob to ask if they could meet us for dinner. He said, 'Sounds great; no problem.' And I had to say, 'I think this is one of those things you'd better check out with Diane."

I chuckled. "What did he say?"

"He sort of hesitated, and then he said, 'Oh, yeah. Right. I'll ask her and get back with you.'" Ted laughed. "I'm sure I enjoyed that a little too much. I said, 'Hey brother, welcome to marriage.'"

Welcome indeed. Bob had to adapt his habit of deciding what he would do for dinner to include Diane's wants and needs. If you remember those days before the two of you were married, you can probably relate to this story. Remember the freedom of doing whatever you wanted, when you wanted? Your schedule, money, friendships, and habits were all yours. You answered only to yourself, and that was pretty much it.

Then you fell in love.

All of a sudden, you found yourself having to say no to yourself with respect to freedoms, choices, and preferences that you enjoyed in your previous life. You now had to consider someone else's feelings and desires, which can be a painful way of life.

This way of life is called self-denial. And while self-denial may indeed be painful, it is literally your only hope of connecting at the deep, intimate, and passionate levels you have wanted and waited for. Couples who understand and engage in self-denial never look back at the old days because what they have gained is so much better.

Simply put, self-denial is *the practice of postponing, or even giving up, activities and attitudes that block love and connection.* In healthy marriages, self-denial is a daily way of living, relating, and thinking. And it is one of the most important keys to love.

### Contrary to Our Intuition

On an intuitive level, what we just said may not make sense. Many of us think of love as being in the form of the person we have waited for, prayed for, and finally have found. You may have endured long years of loneliness and hoping. It makes sense to think that when you find the person you fall in love with, your needs, wishes, longings, and hopes will all be fulfilled.

Isn't love about feeling better inside—more fulfilled, more connected, more encouraged, more energetic? That is certainly one aspect of love and relationship. Love is indeed a transfer of grace, acceptance, comfort, and empathy between two people.

Yet that is only part of the entire story of love. It is love at a beginner's level, an immature form. True lovers go far beyond the idea that giving and receiving should be an easy, uncomplicated flow between two people.

As most couples discover after the honeymoon, relationship becomes complex. Though you feel deep love for the other person, you become aware that you are two separate and different people, and this brings conflict. The two of you have varying viewpoints, wants, needs, desires, values, and feelings.

When many couples experience this reality, they begin to question the authenticity and strength of the relationship. They think, *This is too hard; it doesn't feel like real love.* And they start to doubt that they have the genuine article.

## Shut Down the iPod

Expecting your partner to meet all your needs without you giving up anything is another dumb attitude that will sink your love life. But the solution is simple: *self-denial creates the space you both need for love to grow.* The more you understand healthy self-denial, the more you will truly love and give to your mate. And don't be surprised when your lover responds in kind!

Think of it this way. Suppose you want to talk to your mate about something, but he's wearing his earphones, listening to music on his iPod. You ask your question, and he looks at you quizzically. He can't understand a word you are saying because there is no room for you.

His mind is filled with the music, and there's no place in it for your words. But when he sees that you want to talk and shuts down the player, you can communicate and be together.

In the same way, we are all focusing on our own feelings, opinions, dreams, hurts, needs, and wants. These aren't bad, but there are a lot of them. And when we can only attend to those things in our own world, we make no room for the other person's world. Our own internal iPod shuts down relationship and love.

Self-denial is the mechanism that helps you shut down the iPod in your head. It allows you to say no, sometimes temporarily and sometimes permanently, to things you are focusing on. As a result, you create space to hear and respond to your lover's wants and needs.

When couples learn to deny themselves, they experience a wonderful and transcendent mystery of love: *when I deny "me," I connect with "us."* To let go of a wish or demand for the sake of the relationship puts you into a new level of life: the life of "us." This life is far superior to the life of "me." It is the essence of why you left your unattached status to cleave to another person. "I" serves "we" and is the better for it.

This self-denial should not go unnoticed by your mate. Can you imagine how it feels to be married to someone who says, "I have decided to let the extra money go for something you want. I just feel like letting you have something good"? You cannot help but feel trusting and open to a partner who denies himself. Conversely, it is almost impossible to feel open and vulnerable to someone who cannot practice self-denial. He is not safe. You can love him, but it is much more difficult to trust him fully.

Recently, my (John's) wife, Barbi, let our sons and me convert a room in our home to a music room, as we each play instruments. She had wanted that room for another purpose. At the same time, however, she knew that music is important to us, and it also brings our kids' friends over, which we feel is valuable. Someday she may get her room back. But for the time being, she shut down her iPod on that desire and sacrificed it for a greater good. That self-denial has brought us much closer, because it caused me to feel much gratitude and love for her.

## Having a Self to Deny

Some people become concerned that they are denying themselves too much. They feel that in their relationship they have been denied freedom, love, and respect, and they have very little left.

This is an important issue to clarify. Certainly in some connections the love is in trouble because one person gives too much and gets too little. But the more common problem in self-denial is not having enough of a "self" to deny. That is, the one who gives too much (generally, this is more rescuing and enabling than true wholehearted giving) is doing so because she does not yet possess the love and internal structure she needs before she denies herself. As a couple, you may want to determine if you need to do some recovery or personal growth work in order to feel full enough to lovingly empty yourself.

## What Self-Denial Looks Like

A loving and well-thought-out attitude of self-denial will mean giving up things like these.

THE COMFORT OF DETACHMENT. Love requires the effort of making an emotional connection, even when you least feel like it. It's very natural to disconnect when you're stressed, tired, or upset with your spouse, and at times you do need "me" time. But more often, you need to deny yourself the choice of being away from relationship. Getting out of your comfort zone and connecting on the relationship's terms, not your own, helps generate love and close feelings.

YOUR DREAMS AND DESIRES. At times, one partner will need to postpone some good dream or legitimate desire for the sake of the connection. For example, a wife might delay developing her career track while she raises kids. Or a husband might live in a city that is not best for his career, but best for the marriage and family.

THE RIGHT TO DEMAND FAIRNESS. When both partners insist on playing fair, they enter a legalistic, scorekeeping, loveless emptiness. Give more than you receive in your love life, and deny yourself the demand for fairness. Don't get put out if you end up going to more of his basketball games then he has gone to your musicals. Love gives up keeping score in order to gain connection and compassion.

SAYING WHATEVER YOU WANT. Learn to deny the strong urge to say to your mate exactly what you feel when you feel it. Neglecting this discipline can sink your love life. Lovers hurt each other deeply when they feel *carte blanche* to say anything to each another. Then they sometimes justify their hurtful statements by saying, "Well, it was true." Just because something is true does not mean it is the most loving thing to say. Instead, when you want to say something to the person you love, ask yourself, "How would I feel if he said that to me?" This sort of approach also includes denying yourself the privilege of confronting every little thing your mate does. As Proverbs 19:11 says, "A man's wisdom gives him patience; it is to his glory to overlook an offense."

THE "NOW." Love, romance, and marriage require that you often give up an immediate good for a longer-term better. Instant gratification is for children; adults practice patience, timing, and waiting. Taking time to connect from the heart and listen to each other before having sexual relations is a good example. Putting off a decision until consulting with your partner, as Bob was learning, is another. It is like the economic laws of saving and investing money: those people who can be patient and wait will always reap the greatest payoffs in the long run.

> **A Lifeline:** Love is certainly free; it is a gift of God. But its full experience is costly. Freely deny yourself the things that would be an obstacle to the love both you and your lover want. Love lives are rescued every day when one or both parties say no to the "I" for benefit of the much greater "we."

# Lopsided Relationships Take On Water

As you work on rescuing your love life, ask yourself these very important questions: "Is our relationship lopsided, or is it balanced? Is there a balance of choice and power? Do we tend to make decisions as a team? Does one person do more relational connecting than the other?" The extent to which there is a balance of love and power in your relationship is the extent to which both of you will feel valued, safe, loved, and ready to move into deeper intimacy with each other. If your relationship gets too lopsided, tilting too far one way, then your love boat will take on water and eventually sink.

## What Lopsidedness Looks Like

Marriages can become one-sided in relationship and in power. Let's look at each of these.

LOPSIDED IN RELATIONSHIP. How many times have you heard one of your friends say, "He doesn't care about me as much as I care about him"? This generally refers to some perceived inequality in the emotional investment in the relationship. The wife, for example, may feel that she is more committed and cares more. As a result, she feels unloved and not a part of his life.

Sometimes this inequality is a reality, and sometimes it's only a perception. Either way, it is a problem that must be addressed. If you are the person who perceives the problem, it is always helpful to give grace to your mate first. Find out if perhaps his style of showing love and commitment is different than yours. An undemonstrative and reserved husband may be madly in love with his wife, but because his communication methods fly under her radar, she may not feel it.

If that effort isn't fruitful and your partner remains passive and withdrawn for some reason, confront this as a real problem. Work on why he is not forthcoming in holding up his part. Is he afraid, disconnected, or dealing with angry feelings that he thinks, if expressed, will ruin the relationship? Get to these problems, as resolving them will help reestablish balance.

Lopsided in power. Often, one-sidedness results when a controlling partner is matched with a more compliant one. The controlling one is more dominant, takes charge, and makes the decisions. The compliant one adapts, fits in, and supports. These relationships may look OK from the outside, but all is not well. Inside the relationship, the compliant one often simply checks out and disconnects. He doesn't feel valued or respected, but he stays quiet because he doesn't like the fights. Or he is afraid to take risks and responsibility for decisions. So he gives in to his dominant partner to avoid conflict and continues to distance himself emotionally.

The dominant one will often sense this withdrawal and become even more controlling. She assumes that since asserting control worked with finances and vacations, it should work with matters of the heart. So she will escalate, badger, and sometimes manipulate. Ultimately, however, that will fail. The compliant one just burrows deeper inside himself, and his real feelings become even more inaccessible. Neither person gets what they need from each other.

## Alan and Karen Right the Imbalance

As a psychologist, I (John) have seen many examples of this imbalance. Fortunately, I have also seen how much connection and love can be created by couples who understand and value a "both-sided" relationship. For example, Alan and Karen had been dating for a while and became engaged. They wanted me to help them work on a relationship problem.

Their concern was that, as they became more serious with each other, Alan's feelings of desire, romance, and passion were diminishing. He didn't want them to; he wanted to be in love with Karen as he had been before the engagement. But he couldn't make himself feel what he had felt. Karen was especially concerned. She really cared about Alan and was confused as to why he no longer felt what he had felt for her before.

We began talking about their connection. One thing that quickly came out was that Alan tended to be a people-pleaser with Karen. He gave a lot of power to her that he should have kept for himself. In the beginning of our sessions, for example, when I waited for one of them to begin talking, Alan would always look to Karen first, either to see if she had something to say or, it seemed, to ask her permission to speak. On her part, Karen tended toward being somewhat bossy and controlling, though she saw herself as being clear and assertive. And the truth was that Karen did have pretty good judgment about things, so it was easy for Alan to give the steering wheel of the relationship to her. So their connection tended to go in whatever direction Karen steered it.

I thought that might be key to the problem. When you don't possess your half of the power equation, your passion and desire shut down. They only come out when you have self-control and freedom. In some marriages, a woman will be unable to respond sexually in the way she would like because she feels controlled by her husband.

Once I saw the pattern, I said, "OK guys, how badly do you want Alan to get his feelings back?" They both nodded in vigorous assent. Then I said, "I think I know how it can work, but it will cost both of you. Karen, you will have to back off and shut up sometimes when you don't want to. And Alan, you will have to stop being dishonest with Karen about how you resent her controlling you and start taking the lead sometimes."

They gave me a surprised look, as if to say, *Is this guy joking?* This wasn't their expected talk about spending more quality time together. But the more we went over it, the more Alan and Karen began to understand that they needed to develop a balance of power. I told them not to worry about the passion problem for now, but to work on the power and honesty factors and see what happened.

They did that. Alan started taking risks with Karen. He began to disagree, to bring out his own opinions without first checking them with her. And he stopped trying to read her mind to make sure things were OK. I was proud of Karen also. She bit her lip and let Alan make some bad choices. She truly loved him and was willing to give up some control in order to get back the love she once had from him.

Within a short time, Alan reported success. His romantic desire and feelings of being "in love" with Karen had returned, as he felt the one-sidedness change to mutuality. They married and now enjoy a great connection with each other.

### Where's the Power?

When you talk with your partner about the power balance in your relationship, you will probably conclude that it's not exactly 50/50. Few relationships are. In most, one person tends to take more initiative, and the other is more responsive.

This doesn't necessarily indicate a lopsided relationship. Nor does it mean that the more dominant one is a mean person. Sometimes one person has a natural tendency to take initiative, be assertive, and make decisions. Others have a tendency to reflect, respond, and fine-tune those decisions. A corollary to this in the corporate world is when a marketing person has a zillion-dollar idea, the accountant trims it down to fit the company's budget.

If this is your situation, it doesn't necessarily mean you have a major problem. But you both need to look at the pattern. The less assertive person should ask herself and her partner, "If I did want to speak up more, do I feel the freedom and support from you to do that?" That is the central question. Many couples do very well with this style. The healthy indicator is that the initiative taker is always looking for, asking for, and truly open to the feelings and opinions of his partner.

In other couples, one partner may truly be dominating and not allowing mutuality, while his lover feels controlled, unloved, and dismissed. As we saw with Alan and Karen, this will disconnect you from each other, and it needs to be addressed and resolved.

Many couples who are trying to rescue their love lives struggle with the one-sided problem. Some people follow the motto "peace at any price." What they generally get is not true peace, which brings warmth and vulnerability, but more of a truce. While a lopsided relationship may seem calm and without conflict on the exterior, underneath, where it matters, there is often a sense of alienation, disconnection, hurt, and even anger.

## Moving Back to Mutuality

Whether you have a slightly or seriously lopsided relationship, you can take some steps to rescue your relationship from taking on water. Here are some ideas.

SLAVES GO FIRST. The partner who feels controlled—the "slave"—is generally the one who needs to make the first step. Often, the more dominant partner will not be as aware of the problem, as he is not experiencing the loss of choice and therefore doesn't feel as deprived.

If you are the slave, break out of your shackles! Tell your lover that you want to feel all the love, passion, desire, and longing for him that is in you. You want to give him everything you have. A mate would have to be pretty dumb to argue against that! At the same time, tell him that, in order for you to experience those feelings, you must have more of the power and decision-making in the relationship's choices and directions.

ADMIT YOUR PART OF THE PROBLEM. Often, the "slave" has brought this issue of passivity and compliance into the relationship. The lopsidedness may be more about her and her fears than about her partner. Because of her past, she may even be afraid of taking charge with a reasonable, mutual, and noncontrolling lover. It is not always because one partner is overly dominating. Admit your contribution: your fear of conflict, your fear of responsibility for decisions, or your fear of failure. That will help your partner to know that he is not being seen as the ogre.

The lover who has more control also needs to see his part in the problem and give up some territory. Sometimes he will find that he just hasn't been paying attention, and that awareness will spur him to bring his lover into balance with him. Others may find it hard to allow the partner to have choices, because he will feel helpless and out of control. Others may have a self-centeredness issue. The dominant one may be resistant to his partner's power because he feels entitled to have things go his way. He may need help to see how his dominance is hurting the thing he values the most: his relationship and the love he needs.

COME BACK TO RELATIONSHIP. As you and your partner work on your balance of power, you must remember keep the main things the main things: relationship, closeness, and love. It is easy to get sidetracked into focusing simply on choice and decision. These are important. But choice and decision must serve your need to give and receive love. Tell your partner, "I want us both to be in charge of this relationship. This isn't simply about me wanting more choices, though I do. This is more about how sharing decisions will help me feel closer to you and more a part of 'us.'" Appeal to what you both want most: the connection. And that connection can be rescued and strengthened.

SET LIMITS. If the control problem does not resolve itself—if your mate continues to be too controlling—the relationship may require setting limits. Some patterns may not be easily broken, and there are situations in which you may need to establish boundaries. The resulting consequences can help you maintain your stance that you insist on being able to make choices in the relationship. Good relationships and struggling relationships all benefit when defined by clear delineations of power, choice, and respect for each other. (Our books, *Boundaries in Marriage* and *Boundaries in Dating,* are resources for more information in the area of establishing self-control in your love relationship.)

**A Lifeline:** YOU BOTH NEED CHOICES. YOU BOTH NEED POWER. YOU BOTH NEED SELF-CONTROL. AND WHEN YOUR CONNECTION PROTECTS AND SUPPORTS THE BALANCED, TWO-SIDED RELATIONSHIP, LOVE HAS ROOM AND ENCOURAGEMENT TO GROW. AND PASSION, DESIRE, AND INTIMACY ARE OFTEN THE FRUITS OF MUTUALITY. GIVE UP SOME TERRITORY FOR THE GREATEST GIFT GOD PROVIDES: A TRULY SATISFYING RELATIONSHIP. IN VIEW OF THE RETURNS, IT IS NO REAL SACRIFICE.

## DUMB ATTITUDE #3

# "My Lover Should Be Perfect for Me"

So here you are in your relationship. You're learning to look at your own issues and live in reality with your spouse. You may be tempted to tell him, "OK, I'm doing my part. Now get your act together and become the perfect lover I have always needed!"

But that's another dumb attitude that can sink your love life. Your next move isn't to stand back and wait for him to transform into the perfect mate. Instead, you are to help each other grow through each other's needs and weaknesses. He needs you to assist him, and you need him to assist you. Couples who accept each other's needs and weaknesses and help each other grow are well on the way to rescuing their relationship.

Both of you have needs and weaknesses. And when it comes to love, you are always on better footing when you deal with what is, rather than what should be. You and your partner need to know each other on a real-life level.

When you connect with and help your lover's frailties in order to help him overcome them, you are giving grace at a deep level. And that grace always brings forth good things in a connection. It is also beneficial in the other direction: when your spouse helps you in your own weakness, you then experience love, acceptance, safety, and gratitude.

So don't run from your partner's needs and weaknesses. They won't go away anyway. Be a redemptive, healing force for your mate, and you will bring love and intimacy to your marriage.

## There Are No Perfect 10s

Ryan was one of those guys whom women sometimes describe as "commitment phobic." These men are good at dating, pursuing, wooing, and romancing; but after the chase, they just seem to stall out. Walking down the aisle is a step they just can't seem to take.

Ryan came to me (Henry) for counseling because his current girlfriend was getting tired of his not delivering the ring. They were at a place in their relationship where it was time to put up or shut up. So he wanted help figuring out what he should do.

"Do you love her?" I asked.

"Yes, I guess," he said. "I mean, I care about her. I am just not sure that she is 'the one.'"

"And why is that?' I asked.

"Well, she is just not all the things that I always envisioned in the woman I would marry," he said. "She doesn't fit the list."

"What list?" I asked.

"The list of things I always wanted in the woman I married," Ryan replied.

"Like what?" I asked, thinking that he would reel off a few qualities, and then we would talk about the problems in his relationship related to those.

"Here, I'll show you," he said.

Then—would you believe it?—he pulled out a real list. I had never seen such a thing. He was not talking about a list of wishes in his head. He actually had a hard copy of the characteristics his future wife would have to possess. On it were qualities from isolated physical attributes ("legs like Angelina Jolie") to personality traits ("kindness like Aunt Laura"). The list included achievements like education and career standing, and spiritual issues such as how theological astute she would be. I was flabbergasted.

One interesting thing about Ryan's list was that it included traits that are essentially mutually incompatible. For example, he wanted someone spontaneous and creative, yet highly organized and structured. Have you ever known anyone who was high on both ends of opposite continuums? Such a person is rare indeed. For the most part, highly creative people do not tend to be organized and ordered. You have to pick one or the other and live with it.

I gazed for some time at Ryan's list, fascinated at how unbelievably extensive it was.

"So, what do you think?" he asked.

"If this is what you are looking for, I think you had better get used to being single," I said.

"Why? Those are really important things."

"I understand," I replied. "But I have never seen anyone like this. I have never seen anyone who has every good trait of all feminine humanity combined in one body. And *what a body!* Even in your physical description, you take one part from one supermodel and another part from someone else. You like a certain famous model's face, but her hair color isn't good enough for you. That's what I mean when I say, 'Give it up.' This isn't going to happen. Is this what's wrong with your relationship with your girlfriend now? She doesn't match this list?"

"Well, pretty much," he said. "I just thought I should know what

I was looking for and go for it. I started dating Jen, and she wasn't all of these things. But I liked her, and we kept going out, and now we've gotten really close. I feel a lot for her. I love her, but I guess I want more."

"What is it that you like about Jen?"

At that moment something happened. It was like someone else climbed in Ryan's body. His face changed, his expression got lighter, and his eyes sparkled when he talked about her. As he described Jen and the times that they had together, he was obviously really excited. It seemed as if I was talking to a man in love.

"So, right now, as you think of her, what are you feeling?" I asked.

"I'm feeling all the things I always feel about her. She is great. I really like being with her," he said.

"So what's the problem?"

"Sometimes I feel like I do now, like I like her. But then I think of all the things she *isn't*, and something happens inside, and I just want out of the relationship. I feel like I don't like her anymore," he said, the life draining from his face.

"Well, you're right. That's a problem," I said.

## The Problem of the Ideal

One of the biggest relationship killers around is *comparing the person you love to a fantasy.* The truth is, a real person can never match up to the fantasy. Even if the fantasized person is a real person, the fantasy of being with that person is far from what actually being with them would really be like. We see evidence of that in the high divorce rate in second marriages. People think that if they could just "find a better person," then they could really be in love. The truth is that what they are fantasizing about does not exist, and the comparison often inhibits their ability to love the person they *are* with.

What Ryan discovered as we continued was that his love for Jen was real. He had very real feelings for her and a growing commitment for who she was and the connection they shared. But he also found that comparing her to the fantasy had to die in order for love to live.

As we worked, Ryan began to see a pattern. Every time he got very close to Jen, or when they encountered a difficulty or a conflict, the fantasy would emerge. He would begin to see things about her that did not match up to what he wanted, and his heart would move away from her. He would just go through the motions of relationship but not feel close to her. At other times he would tell her that he was not sure that he loved her.

But Ryan saw something else also. He saw that it was the comparison to the ideal, what she did *not* have, that was creating his loss of connection with her. As he began to see that, something good happened. He became more assured of his love for her, and the connection between them began to grow as well. He found that when the "other woman" was not in the picture, the woman he actually had was very fulfilling. He loved Jen. Not long after, he proposed to her, and they have been happily married for years.

This could not have happened if Ryan's wish for the ideal had not died. As he realized, *either the ideal dies or love dies.*

Real love can only exist with a less-than-perfect person, since the world contains no other kind. The fantasy of finding someone perfect to make you happy is just that—a fantasy. There's a lot of love out there waiting to be found. But to find a solid love connection, the fantasy of the perfect mate has to die.

Lovers engage in this kind of fantasy every day with disastrous results. They may be attracted to someone who possesses a quality that catches their attention at work or in their circle of friends. That person or quality becomes the standard to which they compare their spouse, and the connection is spoiled. The partner does not measure up in that area. The fantasizer's heart moves away, and love has broken down. The real does not compare to the fantasy.

But those who indulge in this kind of fantasy don't realize that the image in their mind is not a real person, but rather an ideal image that does not exist. They do not realize that the quality they admire in the person they are fantasizing about is not seen in the context of a real relationship, with real problems involving all that person's inevitable imperfections, conflicts, selfishness, and the like. They focus only on the fantasized ideal, and it destroys what they could have with the real person they are with. Sometimes they not only fantasize and diminish their relationship and love life, but they actually leave the marriage to chase an empty fantasy.

See if you can identify with any of the following:

- You look at your spouse's body and see more of what is wrong than what you like. The result is that you feel indifferent or turned off.
- You notice some talent or trait of another person, compare that to your spouse, and get a sinking feeling.
- Your spouse interacts with you in some way, and you go away wishing that you were married to someone who is not like that.
- You have a "partial" relationship with someone, such as a co-worker, that does not involve interacting with the whole person in a real relationship, and you fantasize that being with that person would be better than being with your mate.
- You look at fantasy material in magazines, the Internet, or the movies and wish you had someone like that. Or you read romance novels or watch romantic movies and wish your husband were like the hero in the story.
- You look back at a teenage love or the one that got away and longingly compare your mate to that person.
- You look at who your spouse is not, or who she is in comparison to your expectations, more than who she is in terms of the things you love about her.

A relationship is a connection to a real person, just as he or she is. Real love is found with real people, all of whom possess both beauty and flaws, good qualities and imperfections. If you chase a fantasy, you are going to hate reality. But reality is the only place you can find real and satisfying love.

Don't allow a fantasy to interrupt building real love with a real person. Certainly, you could always look at your lover and see how someone else would be better in some way. But you are not in a real relationship with someone else. You are just in a fantasy with a specific part of that other person, such as physical beauty or an isolated personality component. If you were married to that person, you would also be in relationship with the rest of him, including his presently invisible flaws and imperfections. The fantasy would pop like a bubble, and you would not be happy there either. You would soon be comparing his flaws to someone *else* who has that "part" you desire in a better way. So throw away your list of ideals. It is getting in the way of loving the real person you are with.

## This Is Not Disneyland, So Grow Up

I (Henry) love Disneyland. I will never forget when I first went there as a five-year-old. I thought everything was magical and truly believed that I was in the place "where life is a fairy tale and dreams really do come true." It's a place where little boys and girls can dream of life happily ever after. And the magic is real—if you are five years old.

As 1 Corinthians says, "When I was a child, I talked like a child, I thought like a child, I reasoned like a child. When I became a man, I put childish ways behind me" (13:11–12). If you are a child, you can dream of the perfect mate—a prince or princess with no issues and no faults—and the two of you will live happily ever after. But when you're a child, you're not allowed to marry!

When you become an adult, you are allowed to marry, but the

preacher will make you take a vow that has little to do with Disneyland fantasies. Part of the marriage vow is "for better or for worse." Perhaps the vow ought to say "for better *and* for worse," because the truth is, there's no "or" involved; the better *and* the worse will certainly come in marriage. It is an adult vow for an adult relationship. And when two people go into marriage as adults with the goal of producing an adult love, not a childish fantasy, the results are better than they could have ever dreamed.

**A Lifeline:** So BECOME THE HERO AND RESCUE YOUR LOVE LIFE FROM FANTASYLAND AND THE RESIDENT VILE KILLER— COMPARISON TO THE IDEAL PERSON WHO DOESN'T EXIST IN REALITY AND WHOM YOUR MATE IS NOT AND NEVER WILL BE. WHEN YOU DO, YOU CAN FIND THAT A PRINCE OR PRINCESS HAS BEEN WAITING FOR YOU ALL ALONG. IT ONLY TAKES THE KISS OF YOUR LOVE TO AWAKEN HER. IF YOU STOP THE COMPARISONS AND LOVE THE ONE YOU ARE WITH, THEN YOUR DREAM CAN COME TRUE. YOU CAN LIVE HAPPILY, THOUGH IMPERFECTLY, EVER AFTER.

## Pour On the Grace

Here is a dilemma every couple who wants to rescue their love life must solve:

1. You and your partner both need copious amounts of grace and love.

2. It's your responsibility to give large amounts of grace and love to each other.

3. You probably don't have enough grace and love to give.

This is a tall order. The first item speaks to how deeply each of you needs to be loved. The second is the task all loving couples must take on. And the third expresses the reality that we don't possess enough grace and love internally. Couples who go outside the relationship to replenish their supply of grace find their connection with each other strengthened and steadied.

One of the most profound examples of this that I (John) have witnessed is Will and Megan. When she found out about his Internet porn addiction, she was deeply hurt, and she questioned their entire marriage. She felt that Will had betrayed her, and she didn't know if they could ever recover.

On his part, Will was not defensive or blaming at all. He was remorseful and repentant, and he told her, "I am so sorry I hurt you with this. It's not at all about you; it's something in me. I will do anything to resolve this and to win your trust again."

Megan listened to him and decided to try to slowly connect with him again. Will got into a men's group and begin getting support for the problem, as well as the underlying issues that drove it. He worked hard, and things got better for him.

After she observed his changes for a while, Megan began to feel more secure. Then she did something that showed her own capacity to dispense grace to help her husband. She told him, "I really hate this stuff and the behaviors. But I am ready to know more about your struggle and where it came from. Tell me about it."

Will was blown away that Megan wanted to know about the shameful habit that had almost torn them apart. He couldn't believe she wanted to understand this problem. But she did, because, as she said, "It is part of him. It's not a part I feel good about, but I want to know as much of him as I can, so I can help him and love him."

Will started telling her about his own childhood of living with a controlling mother and a passive father, and using porn to comfort himself in secret. He hated himself for this pattern all his adult life, including his married years. Megan listened and understood. While she didn't condone his behavior, she understood the reality that Will needed truth and grace. She told him, "Let me know how you're doing in the process. I will be praying for you, and you can talk to me. I may not always be able to handle it, and that's why you have your group. But I want you to know that I am facing this with you."

Megan's attitude made a world of difference. Will felt so much gratitude, love, and grace from the one he had damaged. As a result, things are much better for them now.

This kind of reconciliation isn't always possible in a marriage. Sometimes the wound is too deep. But it is an illustration of the importance and power of grace in rescuing a love life.

## You Need More than You Think

Grace, as you will remember, is undeserved favor. It is not an enhancement of your relationship; it is your very survival. We want to help you focus on how the need for grace is experienced and understood, so that you can learn to provide it for your lover.

Most of us don't realize how much grace we need in our marriage relationship. We have an enormous empty place inside that only grace will fill. Life is hard, and love relationships take work. Every couple needs a big helping of grace to go deeper, reconnect, take risks, forgive, accept, be truthful, and help each other reach intimacy.

Not only is our need for grace great, but most of us have negative and critical voices in our heads that fight off grace: "I shouldn't be that way;" "I should be stronger;" "I'm a loser;" "I don't deserve to be treated well after what I've done." Grace is the only thing that can defeat these voices and allow us to let each other inside.

Couples who are aware of their deep need for undeserved favor are starting at the right place. *The need that both of you have for unde-*

*served favor can draw you together emotionally, personally, and spir-itually.* Conversely, those couples who try to go it alone or to live with-out their dependency end up disconnecting. Where there is no need, there can be no needs met. The relationship becomes a nonevent.

Don't make the mistake of thinking you only need to give grace to each other during bad times and struggles. Divinely bestowed grace is not just for broken things like problems, hurts, and failure. It is also meant for the sustenance and maintenance of life and love. It is some-thing that is ongoing, regular, and a part of life. Grace should be the norm of a relationship, not the exception.

So the best place to start in rescuing your love life is for both of you to come to the ends of yourselves and admit to each other that you need each other's grace—not today, not once, but every day and in every way.

For example, my wife, Barbi, and I (John) are your basic, garden-variety active and busy people. We have work, kids, and all the expected responsibilities of life. We have found that when we get into our "doing" zones of tasks and responsibilities, and we neglect the grace we each need from each other, things go OK for a while. But at some point, we detect friction, disconnection, and misunderstanding.

When this happens, we try to use the disconnection itself as a signal that one or both of us needs grace. And we will sit down and open up with each other about what is going on inside. Often the act of doing that will bring us back in sync with each other, as we feel the other person's stress, overwhelmed emotions, or frustration. So stop and experience the need. Grace cannot be administered until the need is admitted.

## The Task and Responsibility to Give Grace

Take on the task of being alert to your lover's need for grace. Though ultimately each partner is responsible for getting her needs met, the best couples are always concerned about meeting the needs of the other.

BE GRACIOUS IN YOUR CONTENT AND TONE. We administer grace to each other by both the content and the tone of what we say. *Content* has to do with letting your spouse know in words that you care, the extent of how much you care, and what you value about him. For example:

- "I love you."
- "I want to know you better."
- "I need you."
- "My life is better because of you."
- "I want to be with you."
- "You are the most important person in my life."
- "I want us to be closer."
- "I forgive you."
- "I'm sorry I hurt you."

These are a few of many ways you can give grace and favor to your mate. It's important to tell your lover how you feel about her. Don't assume she always knows. You refuel your car regularly, because gas burns up. The same is true with grace.

*Tone* is the way you speak. How you convey your words is as important as what you say. Your tone should be caring and warm, consistent with the grace you are providing. Your tone should draw your lover in, not distance her.

Listen to yourself, and pay attention to your content and tone. You may find it helpful to put yourself in your spouse's place and listen to yourself. How would you feel if you were on the receiving end of the grace you're extending? Would you feel dismissed, cold, and misunderstood? Often, we are not as lavish and warm with the other as we ourselves would need.

BE A STUDENT OF YOUR LOVER. Grace is a universal need, but it is often administered in a highly individual and personal way. Observe your lover and get to know her so that you can give her the grace she needs. Ask yourself, "Could what I say to her be applied to any other person, or does it fit only her?" This may be a little more work for men, because we are often not acutely aware of all our spouse's characteristics. But becoming aware is worth the effort. Here are some things to watch that can improve the way you dispense grace to your lover:

· What is she insecure about?
· What makes her happy?
· What scares her?
· What does she feel is wrong with her?
· What does she need to hear often?
· What does she dream of?
· What does she want from the relationship?

Affirm and support her in these areas, and give her grace tailored to her life and ways.

## Undeserved Means Undeserved

Grace—in the Christian faith, in a marriage—cannot be earned or merited (Ephesians 2:8–9). In the same way, you and your partner qualify for each other's grace on a need basis, not on a performance basis.

Our natural tendency is to give love when our spouse acts lovingly toward us and to withhold love when he disconnects from us. However, this is not what love is about. This tendency puts your relationship under the law, and a law-based connection will never experience grace. Though it often isn't easy, one of the most connecting things couples learn is to provide grace even when the partner has neither earned nor deserved it. That is a hallmark of a truly intimate couple.

For example, when she is being selfish, you might say, "What you are doing feels selfish to me, and it distances me. But I want to deal with this and get through it, because I want us to be OK." Or if he has been hurtful or critical, you may say, "What you said really bothers me. Part of me wants to walk away right now. But I know we need to talk about this and get it straight. I don't want it to come between us."

It is easy to do the opposite and protest, "I am the injured party here. It's her job to apologize and change." That stance will screw up your connection. Get out of the law orientation, and give your lover grace by taking the first step to move toward her. Be for her, be for the relationship, and face the issue so that you can resolve it and move on with each other. You may need to grow thicker skin in order to give her the favors that she and your connection need.

This is not about creating positive feelings in a struggling relationship. Feelings don't come because we want them to. The path that works is to be *for* you and her and the relationship, to connect as much as you can, and to be in the process of growth. These steps will create the feelings you want. Don't try to make yourself feel things; you can't do it. Create a context of grace that will grow the feelings.

## Get Grace from the Outside

As we have said, you don't possess all the grace you need for yourself and for your partner. You both need more grace than there is in the relationship. A couple who exists in a bubble, without others supporting them, is a couple who will be in trouble at some level.

There will be times that, through no one's fault, you won't have enough grace for each other. You may be drained from work, fatigue, or stress. There will be other times when you are feeling alienated and disconnected from each other. This is normal and expected; it is part of love. During these periods of disconnect, don't pull away and don't pretend to feel things you don't feel. These approaches don't work.

The real solution lies in humility. Admit your need and get more grace from the outside your relationship. God gives grace in your relationship with Him. Other people are also a major source of the grace we need for our relationships, as we engage in "faithfully administering God's grace in its various forms" (1 Peter 4:10).

This is why the most connected couples are not just connected to each other, but also to others who are caring, safe, full of grace, and supportive of your relationship with your partner. You don't weaken your marriage by having other relationships; you infuse it with the grace you want to lavish on each other.

I cannot tell you how many times I (John) have experienced this in my marriage. After connecting with people who love Barbi and me, I come back to the relationship with a renewed desire and love for her. Sometimes it is because I am now more filled up inside. Sometimes it is because I can see her more clearly through the eyes of my friends. Sometimes it is because I can see her as God sees her.

Admitting our need and filling our emptiness from good sources is a far cry from our natural tendency to "try harder," "suck it up," and "commit more." It's much better to receive, experience, and lavish grace.

**A Lifeline:** STOP AND EXPERIENCE YOUR NEED FOR GRACE. GRACE CANNOT BE ADMINISTERED UNTIL THE NEED IS ADMITTED. ALSO, MAKE IT A HABIT TO BE GENEROUS WITH GRACE. YOU CAN NEVER OVERGRACE YOUR RELATIONSHIP. GRACE WILL GO A LONG WAY IN RESCUING YOUR LOVE LIFE.

# Sometimes Your Lover Needs a Nudge

Couples who do well in closeness, attachment, and love have experience with something I (John) call *the nudge*—a healthy and balanced confrontation intended to push each other to be more than they are. Nudges tend to produce really good relational results.

To illustrate, consider the case of Ross. For some time, he had been in an executive role in his job. His position was stable, but he was getting bored and restless. Ross's wife, Anne, believed in him, and she thought he could do better. So she began bringing up a dream they had shared that one day he would start his own business.

She would say, "I want you to think about doing this. I'll get a part-time job to help. We have our savings. I think this is the time." Ross would counter with, "But what if it doesn't work? We've got the family to consider."

Anne didn't nag or belittle Ross, but she didn't back off either. She would just say, "OK, just think about it. If you want to do this, I am 110 percent behind you."

In time, Anne's support and nudging resonated with Ross, and he set out on his own. It was a little scary for a couple of years, but then his business became successful. The competency that Anne saw in him paid off, and now they are doing very well.

We all need nudges in our relationships, especially with our lover. The person who knows you best should be able to see not only who you are, but who you can be. She needs your permission to help you get there, for that is a great part of what relationships are all about.

When nudging (not nagging!) is acceptable in a relationship, and when nudging works, you both get the reconnections and intimacy you want and need.

## Expectations Are OK

Nudges have to do with seeing that each of you can be more than you are and helping each other on that path. They have to do with our *expectations* of each other. *You are to love each other enough to expect your partner to grow into more than he is right now.*

You want your partner to be a better person—more loving, responsible, real, spiritual, and honest. You want him to connect to you better. You want him free of bad habits and addictions. Your love for him drives you to desire these things. They are good wishes for his best. They are also for your best and for the reconnection and depth of your intimacy.

Having higher expectations does not mean that you don't accept your mate as he is. No one grows or truly changes from the heart unless he is first accepted as he is. There is really no conflict between acceptance and expectations. In fact, they are partners in intimacy.

Sometimes one partner will think the other is being critical or unaccepting because he has standards, requirements, or expectations. He may say, "If you love me, love me as I am." The answer to that is, "I do love you as you are. But if I didn't want you to be more than you are, I would not really be loving you." Expectations, challenges, and rules are good for you and good for your love. When you have reasonable and good standards, you are defining what you want and need. You are establishing a healthy structure for love to grow. You are letting your partner know what will help you two be together and happy.

## Why You Need Expectations

John Lennon and Paul McCartney wrote many great songs, but they were wrong about "all you need is love." You do need love, and lots of it, but you also need to be honest, to confront, and to have expectations of each other. None of us grows and blossoms without both. Why is this? Here are some reasons.

EXPECTATIONS GET YOU OUT OF THE COMFORT ZONE. When two people become committed to each other or married, they almost always start regressing into comfortable and nongrowing patterns. You stop working out and start gaining weight. You drop some of your work or personal growth interests. The home gets a little sloppy. You stop listening to each other the way you used to and get into your own world more.

Some of these things happen simply because relationships require an investment of time and energy. Some activities must move to the back burner in order to keep the connection going. It takes time to find out about your partner's day and how she feels about life and your relationship in general. You cannot leave that undone.

On the other hand, this regressive force can create a real problem if it leads you to think, *I have my love and she accepts me, so I'll just be me.* If the "me" you regress into tends to be unloving, self-involved, disengaged, lazy, controlling, or irresponsible, you have fallen into the comfort zone.

The comfort zone is also where fears live. When we are afraid of failure, conflict, or change, we stay in a state of paralysis and become comfortable with that. That isn't laziness; it's fear. But fear can be dealt with, and you can help each other out of it.

Whether the comfort zone is from regression or fear, lovers should give each other permission to nudge each other out of it. When expectations and requirements are given lovingly and not harshly, they can be welcome and effective.

EXPECTATIONS HELP YOU SEE YOUR BLIND SPOTS. We are often unaware of when we aren't being our best. Who better than your mate to point out something you are doing that is hindering your own growth, development, and success?

For example, one of you may have a tendency toward compliance and passivity. Like Ross, you may be a successful person, but not aggressive in your growth. When things aren't in crisis, it's easy to be satisfied with the status quo. What if your partner said, "I want you to push more, take some risks, and stop being satisfied with the average"? Would you be hurt? Confused? Or would you be energized with new vision?

What if you have a long-held dream to pursue or a talent that you're not aware of? Your partner has a duty to see it, to know it, and to let you know she wants you to follow the dream or develop that talent.

We can be blind to problems as well as to dreams and talents. Specifically, we are often unaware of things we do to hurt each other and ourselves. Your partner might say, "I'll always love you, no matter how much you weigh, but I have to be honest: I am really scared about your health. And I think I am being reasonable to say that it's hard to be romantically drawn to you at this size. I want you to get a checkup and begin a fitness program. When can you do this?" That is not being critical, mean, or judgmental. It's an attempt to deal with a blind spot and rescue the love life. It is an act of love, not of control.

EXPECTATIONS HELP YOU AND YOUR PARTNER GROW TOGETHER. When you grow as individuals, you grow as lovers. Partners who encourage each other to be all that they can be and see positive results in each other tend to be closer, more romantic, and more interested in each other.

This is true because growth and love can't be separated. Love is a part of growth. If you are becoming a better and more developed person personally, emotionally, and spiritually, your heart is being enlarged. You are learning to receive and give love. You have a greater capacity for love and empathy. And that translates to a direct benefit for the connection.

## Where to Start

Here are some things you can do to "nudge" your love life along.

WALK OUT OF THE COMFORT ZONE. Talk about how the two of you want to be safe, accepting, and unconditional in your love. But at the same time, humbly submit to each other in growth areas and problems. Give each other permission to say, "I see things in you that are undeveloped, and I want to help you develop them. I see problems that disconnect us, and I want to help you solve them." With grace, love, and healthy expectations, couples become better individuals and better lovers.

BECOME A TEAM. Work together on what each of you wants for yourself and your mate. Do you want him to become a better listener? How would you describe that desire so he can get on the same page with you? Show him what it means, what to say, and when to say it. Be a partner, an encourager, and a coach. Make it something for the two of you.

CELEBRATE CHANGE. When one of you makes a few moves in the right direction, celebrate it! Change is not easy. It takes time to deal with stagnation and sameness. When your lover makes the effort and takes the risk, even a small one, affirm and reinforce him.

The best gift for change is yourself. Give him your love, your admiration, your respect, and your attention. Let him know that his steps to be all that he can be will bring him even more of you than he has now.

**A Lifeline:** LIFE IS NOT MEANT TO BE ABOUT SETTLING FOR THE STATUS QUO. IT IS A TEMPLATE FOR EACH OF US TO BECOME SOMETHING MUCH BETTER THAN WE ARE, AND RELATIONSHIPS CAN PROVIDE THE GROUNDWORK FOR THAT TO HAPPEN.

# Vive les Différences

I (John) was speaking at a conference on love relationships recently. During the question-and-answer time, a man asked, "What if you and your mate are just too different from each other to be compatible?" I hear this question a lot. "I would put it this way," I answered. "If you insist on similarity to make a relationship work, plan on spending most of your quality time by yourself."

Differences should not be a problem in your relationship. In fact, the opposite is true. Differences are a necessary component for finding, keeping, and sharing the love life we all want. When one partner resists the other's differences, she risks losing the love she would like to develop.

## Differences Help Create Love

Everyone has been around a couple so alike that they seem to be two sides of the same coin. Their interests, personalities, views, and even clothing styles are in sync. However, even those twinnish couples are different from each other in some ways. That's the nature of individuality. So the attempt to make a homogenous relationship is futile in the first place.

People are intricately designed and formed. The Bible illustrates the point this way: "You made all the delicate, inner parts of my body and knit them together in my mother's womb. Thank you for making me so wonderfully complex! It is amazing to think about. Your workmanship is marvelous—and how well I know it" (Psalm 139:13–14 TLB).

Given that reality, how can differences help two people rescue their love lives? The answer lies in the contrast between immature and mature love. Immature love seeks sameness and similarity. When you first met your lover, for example, you liked the fact that you had some things in common. The early stages of the growing connection focused on your similar interests, likes, dislikes, and preferences. This is not a bad thing; it is just the nature of how love begins, with alliance and similarity. These likenesses are the early glue that begins to make a bond between two people.

As the relationship develops, mature love should supplant immature love. That is, while the two of you maintain and enjoy your similarities, your differences begin to emerge, as they should. In mature couples, this is also a positive thing. Your life and perspective are enhanced and stretched by your partner's varying views and experiences. Love seeks out growth. It isn't threatened by differences; it enjoys them. Because of his differences, you see that other person as interesting, sometimes challenging, and able to show you new ways of relating to life.

Couples are different in a lot of ways. Here are just a few examples.

FEELERS AND THINKERS. The feeler lives in emotion first and analyzes later. The thinker lives in the world of logic and sees relationship through that filter. Often the feeler is perceived as childish and the thinker a grownup. But that is not accurate. Feelers can also be mature, highly responsible adults who simply have an emotional nature. They often sense things in a relationship far sooner than the thinker does.

EXTROVERTS AND INTROVERTS. The extrovert draws energy and life from people—lots of them. The introvert, in contrast, gravitates toward solitude and fewer people. My (John's) parents are classic examples. My mother never met a stranger, while my dad is more of a loner. Yet after more than fifty years of marriage, they still get a kick out of their differences. He likes to watch her make her rounds at a party. And she enjoys his insightful thoughts about life, God, and the universe.

ACTIVE TYPES AND REFLECTIVE TYPES. Some people are into aggression and initiative, while others are quieter and would rather relax. One of you might love bungee jumping in Africa, while the other may be more into summer novels and hammocks. Couples often will find ways to compromise on their vacations, so that both partners get what they need. The active partner learns how to relax, while the reflective one learns the value of taking a few risks.

Nurturing each other includes encouraging, appreciating, and connecting with each other's differences. This kind of connection is never boring. More than that, your partner will feel great value, love, and understanding from you. A large part of empathy comes from connecting with differences. When you support the individual styles and preferences of your lover, he truly feels that you know him for who he really is. This is the opposite of feeling criticized, put down, or shamed for simply being yourself.

## Don't Moralize Your Differences

Be aware of the tendency to make your own opinion a moral issue, rather than an apples-versus-oranges preference. There is no one "right way" between feelers and thinkers, extroverts and introverts, or active and reflective types.

This "right way" thinking is an immature perspective, and it needs to be resolved and ended. There are certainly right and wrong behaviors, and we will deal with them in this chapter, but these matters of style and preference aren't in that category. As a couple, do not tolerate moralizing the styles of either of you, but move toward accommodating them. Stay open, appreciative, and even protective of your partner's individuality.

## Get Rid of Destructive Differences

Certain types of differences that are not just matters of style or preference are actually problems, and they cause negative things to happen in relationships. As a couple moving toward closeness, you need to be aware of these, so that you can identify and deal with them successfully.

Destructive differences are not the same as style differences. They come out of a person's brokenness, baggage from the past, immaturities, or character issues. Healthy, growing couples will always have style differences. But they will have a minimum of destructive differences.

For example, I (John) have a friend, Michele, who is now divorced from her husband, Stan. I knew them when they were married, and it was never a good marriage. Stan had little or no interest in relating to Michele on an emotional, personal level. He wasn't a mean guy, but he wouldn't connect with her. When he got home from work, he would watch TV or go online until bedtime. And that was the pattern in most of their years of marriage.

When Michele told him that she wanted more of a connection with him, Stan's answer was always the same: "That's just the way I am." He had always been a loner; it was who he was and the way he would always be, as he told it. Michele bought that excuse for a while, but in time the estrangement became too much, and the marriage eroded and ended.

I don't believe that Stan was right about his difference. We are designed by God to be relational beings and to connect with Him and with each other. I could understand Stan's introverted tendencies, but his pattern was much more severe than that. I knew that he had come from a dysfunctional family with no consistent attachment and a lot of manipulation. So I had sympathy for him. But I disagreed with his view. Chronically disengaged was not "the way he is." It was baggage he carried that cut him off from the grace and love that his marriage offered and that Michele needed.

Apparently Stan had become comfortable with his detachment from Michele and the world. He was neither interested nor willing to see it as a problem to improve. Had he done that, perhaps they would be together now. It's sad, because they are both good people. But Stan's lack of connection was not merely an acceptable apples-versus-oranges difference. It was hurtful and destructive for both of them.

Pay attention to these hurtful sorts of differences, for they can do a lot of damage to the love you are trying to create. Here are a few more differences that are truly destructive: irresponsibility, control, criticism and judgment, manipulation, self-centeredness, rage, guilt messages, deception, addictions, and violence. If your marriage exhibits any of these behaviors, you need to take action. Confront your partner. Ask for change—and insist on it. Get help from a third party if necessary. But don't ignore these issues.

Compare this list to the personality differences discussed previously. It should be very apparent that these are not the same in nature. Here are some ways to identify these destructive differences.

THEY CUT OFF LOVE AND TRUST. Destructive differences destroy intimacy and sink your love life. You cannot trust, be safe with, or be totally vulnerable with someone who is not honest, dependable, or in control of himself.

THEY REDUCE FREEDOM. Destructive differences don't leave the other partner feeling free to make choices and speak the truth. The person often feels that she is walking on eggshells around her partner, because she doesn't want to upset him for "being who he is," at least in his words. So her freedom to be herself and say what is on her heart is greatly diminished.

THEY ARE ABOUT "ME," NOT "US." Destructive differences also tend to cause one partner to focus on dealing with the person who has them. The other partner finds himself worrying about them, trying to fix them, or having to protect himself from them. This is a far cry from the fun of observing and interacting with your lover's quirks and individuality.

Stand up to these destructive differences. Tell your partner that you won't tolerate how they affect the relationship. It is a good sign if he becomes concerned about them and wants to work on them, for there is a lot of help available, such as small groups, healthy spiritual growth contexts and churches, and therapy. And the problem is quite fixable; so don't give up, but ally with your lover in treating the disease.

In some cases the person will, like Stan, show little ownership or accountability about his destructive differences. He may excuse, blame, or deny their existence. In those cases, you may need to become more strict and direct, and even seek help. (John's book, *Who's Pushing Your Buttons?*, is a guide for dealing with a partner with this issue.)

**A Lifeline:** LET'S END ON A POSITIVE NOTE. *VIVE LES DIFFÉRENCES!* EMBRACE AND ENJOY THE LOVE THAT COMES FROM STYLE DIFFERENCES. BUT DON'T FALL FOR THE DUMB ATTITUDE, "THAT'S JUST THE WAY I AM" AND PUT UP WITH THE DESTRUCTIVE DIFFERENCES THAT CAN SINK YOUR LOVE LIFE. BE A GUARDIAN AND PROTECTOR OF LOVE, FREEDOM, AND GROWTH IN YOUR CONNECTION WITH YOUR PARTNER.

## Getting to the Heart of Feelings

One of the most powerful keys to an intimate and passionate love life is also one of the most unnatural and counterintuitive things you will ever do. It is called *validation,* and it refers to your ability to understand and empathize with the feelings and experiences of your lover, *especially when your view is not his.*

Validation is even more important when your mate sees something negative in your own behavior that you fail to see in that way. It has to do with drawing him out and help him feel that you truly hear him on a deep level. It's making him know that you really understand his feelings. Proverbs 20:5 says, "The purposes of a man's heart are deep waters, but a man of understanding draws them out." As you help him express his heart and be understood, you are drawing him out.

## Why Validation?

Validation is necessary for couples to navigate successfully through conflict because we all need to be heard and understood. We really don't move forward to resolve conflicts when we do not feel we have been understood.

Think about the last fight you had with your partner. When you were trying to get your feelings across, did your partner minimize, dismiss, or simply not understand what you were saying? What was that like for you? How did that affect your ability and desire to hear his side of things? Most likely, not receiving validation from your mate disconnected things even further.

A lack of validation essentially puts your heart in prison: you have expressed your views, but you feel that you have not been heard. You are left all by yourself with your viewpoint, feelings, and experiences. Yet you are required to hear your partner's side—the bad things you have done. This imprisonment generally results in disconnection, guilt, false external compliance, anger, and a host of other reactions that will tear a relationship apart.

When couples learn to validate each other's experiences, they feel that their partner is part of their life again. They no longer feel alone.

A good example of this is how to handle those times that you make the common mistake of joking about the wrong thing at the wrong time and unintentionally hurt your lover's feelings. Suppose, for example, your husband's hair is thinning. He jokes with you about it from time to time, so you think it's no big deal. Then, at a backyard barbecue, he says something self-deprecating about his hair to your neighbor, and you chime in on the joke. That evening, he comes to you very angry and says, "I can't believe you. In front of the neighborhood, you put me down about my hair. Thanks so much for the embarrassment."

You can think of several responses that might have truth to them but are useless at best, because they are not validating:

- "You joke about your hair all the time. How am I to know I'm not supposed to?"
- "Nobody even cared; it was no big deal. You're overreacting."
- "What about the times you joke about me in front of our friends?"
- "You know I don't think your hair is all that bad; you still look good to me."

Some of these responses are better than others, but none are validating. They don't attempt to understand your husband's point of view. Validation would sound something like, "I'm really sorry, honey. That must have been awkward, especially in front of our friends." There are other ways this could be said, but the essential element is present: he knows that you are attempting to understand what the experience was like from his perspective.

The above example brings up another important point: *validation has nothing to do with whether you agree or disagree with your partner.* Validating your mate's feelings as being important and real to him does not mean you accept his view as truth and reality. A viewpoint is one thing; reality is another, and they need to be dealt with separately. But you need to deal with them in the right order. Validation comes first, and then reality. People are much more open to hearing facts after their viewpoint has been validated.

So when things start to get hot, validate. That should help the other person calm down and be more receptive. Then say, "Are we OK on this?" If so, then clarify the truths and realities: "You know, you joke about your hair all the time, so I just assumed it was all right with you. So I guess it's better for my jokes to be just between you and me, right?"

Sometimes validation can help pave the way to resolving the problem and resuming connection. And sometimes validation is the resolution itself. Simply being heard is often enough. I (John) was recently bugged about a scheduling problem our family was having. It was one of those times when we had planned too many sports, social activities, and church events in one weekend. We were rushed and late to everything, and nothing was going right. I wasn't mad at anyone, just at everything.

When I complained to Barbi about what a rotten weekend it was turning out to be, she just listened and then said, "Yes, I guess it really is a pretty crummy weekend for you, not being able to relax and enjoy anything." I felt better, because she got it. Nothing about the circumstances of the weekend changed. We still had to play out the weekend schedule. But we were connected, because we were together in the weekend.

## The Work of Validation

Validation is unnatural; it takes work. Here we will list for you the kind of work that will help you and your partner validate each other.

GET OUT OF THE WAY. Learn to suspend your own point of view, to put your way of seeing things aside in order to leave room for your partner's feelings and experiences. Give up the attempt to be seen as good, innocent, or right, and be willing to endure some angry feelings from your lover without responding to them in kind. Getting out of the way means caring more about hearing him and helping the relationship than justifying your own position and correctness. And it is totally worth the work.

GO FIRST TO EMPATHY. When you know your partner is upset, angry, or hurt, think first about figuring out and understanding how he is feeling and why. This is an act of grace and love: "Do to others as you would have them do to you" (Luke 6:31). Of course, you also need to be understood for who you are, right or wrong. But don't make the mistake of insisting on being heard but not really hearing your partner. Empathy must go both ways, or it doesn't work.

ASK; DON'T ANSWER. When you validate your mate, ask him more about his experience. Get to the pain and emotions. Don't try to answer the problem or fix it. That can come later. Open things; don't close them. Instead of saying, "Well, you'll feel better later," say, "That sounds awful; tell me more." You are building a bridge with your lover, not only for resolving this conflict, but future conflicts as well. When you validate consistently, you gradually create a strong, adaptable, and safe bridge to a lifetime of love.

CHECK IT OUT. When your lover explains her viewpoint, ask if you are understanding her experience. She can guide you and let you know if you are way off base. And even if you are off, she is likely to appreciate that you are making a real effort to connect with her experience and perspective.

LIVE WITH THE TENSION OF UNHAPPINESS. We all have a tendency to want a happy ending, and quickly, especially when our partner is upset with us. Couples who love well and deeply learn to sit with the unhappy feelings of their partners. Feelings take time to resolve, and they cannot be rushed. You may need to validate some hurt emotions concerning the same event several times before it is resolved. Go ahead and do it. You are investing in a better relationship for the future. Be patient, present, and empathetic. Your mate's unhappy feelings won't last. Stay for the long haul.

**A Lifeline:** VALIDATION REACHES INTO THE HEART OF YOUR LOVER SO THAT THE TWO OF YOU CAN RECONNECT AND DEAL WITH THE PROBLEM BETWEEN YOU. WHEN YOU REACH THE POINT WHERE YOU BOTH FEEL YOU HAVE BEEN HEARD AND UNDERSTOOD BY EACH OTHER, THEN YOU ARE READY TO GRAPPLE WITH THE PROBLEM. WHATEVER THE NATURE OF THE CONFLICT, USE VALIDATION TO MAKE YOURSELVES ALLIES, NOT ADVERSARIES, AS YOU DEAL WITH WHAT YOU NEED TO DEAL WITH.

# "My Lover Should Never Hurt Me"

**T**hink about the last time you looked at your mate and thought, *I really don't like this person very much right now.* Perhaps he said something to you that hurt you deeply. Or you've just had an argument that didn't end well. Whatever it was, you couldn't shake it off by thinking positive thoughts or denying the reality.

What do you do? Marriage is supposed to be about love and wanting to be with someone, yet at this point you may not be feeling those things at all—especially if your mate has hurt you in some way. Many couples don't know the next steps to rescuing their love life, because *they don't feel drawn to rescue it anymore.* If you feel like this, don't panic. This is not time to throw in the towel or to resign yourself to a D-minus marriage. In fact, it is a pretty normal experience at some point for most couples.

As wonderful as he or she is, your spouse will fail you at times, and it's going to hurt. The reality is that all of us are imperfect people, and we all love imperfectly. So you are in good company if you are struggling in your marriage in this manner.

There is a lot you can do to rescue your love life from the dumb attitude that says, "My lover should never hurt me." The task that we will show you in this section is to use *the power of your love to reestablish your connection*. That is, your actions and attitudes can go a long way toward making a reconnection that will bring about attachment, intimacy, and positive feelings toward your spouse. Rescue is at hand.

## Hurt Happens, But You Can Handle It

I (Henry) was doing a marriage seminar and asked the crowd to take a moment to think about their spouses, bringing to mind all of the wonderful qualities about them and the reasons that they married them. I asked them to focus on their spouses' strengths, the special things about them, and to feel how they are drawn to them.

"OK, everyone there?" I asked. I could see many couples turning to each other, smiling, some poking each other, others being playful in different ways as they got in touch with the love they had for each other. The room was filled with lighthearted giddiness.

"Now, here is what I want you to do," I continued. "Turn to your mate, who is totally enraptured with you, and say the following: 'Honey, I promise I will hurt you."

You could sense the jolt in the room. They gaped at me in disbelief. "Just do it," I said. "I'll explain in a moment." They turned to each other and said it to each other, some laughing, others seeming a bit nervous.

"How was that?" I asked. "Feel a little strange?" Many nodded in agreement.

"Here is why I wanted you to do that: *because it is true*. That wonderful person whom you love so much, need so much, and desire to be with so much, is an imperfect person and will do things, mostly unintentionally but some very intentionally, that will hurt you. That is reality. You have married a sinner—one who 'misses the mark,' as the Bible says. As wonderful as he or she is, your spouse will fail you at times, and it's going to hurt. That is the nature of human love. It isn't perfect, and it sometimes hurts. But that's OK, because the good stuff is worth all the pain, and there are ways to resolve it well. The sooner you learn that, the more you will be able to love and enjoy each other."

Realize that not only is your mate far from ideal, and immature, as we have seen, but he or she *will* hurt you. Sometimes these hurts are minor; sometimes they are major. Some marriages have small scars; others have very big ones. From bad attitudes to betrayals and all points in between, the best of lovers hurt each other.

The more fully you accept that reality, the better your relationship will be. You will not be crushed when your spouse hurts you, and you will likely have the tools to resolve the hurt. Mature, good marriages are *not* ones in which there is no pain, but in which pain is accepted as part of the package. As a result, the couple consciously focuses on getting better at processing pain and resolving conflict.

### False Expectations

Many people never find the wonder and joy that marriage *can* provide because they look for something it *can't* provide. People set themselves up for failure by expecting a good marriage to be one without pain, and that expectation comes in at least three forms.

THE WISH FOR A CHILDHOOD FANTASY. Children dream of marrying a fantasy prince or princess who will always make his or her life fun and happy. *Marriage should be all fun,* they think. *It should always make me happy. It should not hurt.* And especially their fantasy prince or princess should not be the one to hurt them!

Some adults enter marriage with this childhood fantasy. So when those hurts do come and the marriage is not fun anymore, many cut and run. They want a relationship that makes them feel good all the time. They forget the vow "for better or for worse," and they refuse to acknowledge, as children do, that sometimes the "worse" does indeed show up in marriage. Only when people set aside childhood fantasies about marriage can they grow up and find the pleasure of genuine, adult love—the only kind that is real.

THE WISH FOR A PAIN-FREE LIFE. No matter how much you wish it were otherwise, the reality is that we live in a fallen world, and bad things happen. People we love die. Accidents happen, and people get hurt. Financial setbacks hit us. As Jesus said, "In this world you will have trouble" (John 16:33).

In a good relationship, partners not only face the reality that they will hurt each other, but they face and process the general pain of life together. They cry together, grieve together, go through loss and sickness together, and face failure and setbacks together. They face together the hurts they cause each other as well.

You cannot choose to have a pain-free life. The only choice you have is whether the two of you will lean into the pain together or avoid it. If you avoid it, then you will encounter more pain in the end as the infections of unprocessed pain eat away at your connection.

THE WISH TO MAKE UP FOR PAST HURT. When the past has held substantial hurt and pain, a person may dream of a relationship that will one day make it all better, of being with a man whose love will heal all her past hurts. But even when she finds a really good relationship with a good man, he does disappoint her at times. There *are* hurts and pains, and this person experiences a double hurt—the hurt itself as well as the greater hurt of being disappointed that the longed-for rescue did not happen. She feels abandoned, hurt, and betrayed in her present relationship just as she did in the past.

## The Reality

Each and every one of us will hurt other people, even the people we love the most. We all get it wrong sometimes, and that will often cause hurt. Partners in good marriages realize this, and as a result they develop the following attitudes and practices that preserve the connection, even when one has hurt the other.

ACCEPT THE FACT THAT YOUR MATE WILL SOMETIMES DO THINGS THAT HURT YOU. When you accept this fact, you'll be able to deal with the hurts when they come, and those hurts won't destroy the connection and the love you share.

HANG ON TO THE THINGS THAT YOU LOVE ABOUT YOUR MATE, EVEN WHEN HE DISAPPOINTS YOU. Do not label your mate as "all bad." He gets it wrong at times, of course, but he is still a wonderful creation of God with extraordinary qualities. Don't let the hurts blind you to his good qualities.

WHEN HURT HAPPENS, FACE IT WITH HONESTY AND DIRECTNESS. Good marriages do not deny problems; they face them. When you are hurt, tell each other. Speak the truth, but do so in love, not anger (Ephesians 4:25–26).

WHEN YOU ARE THE ONE WHO HAS HURT THE OTHER, APOLOGIZE. Confess your wrongdoing—do not excuse it!—and empathize with the hurt you have caused. The worst thing you can do is rationalize it or explain it away. Just realize that this was one of your moments to blow it. Confess your offense, and ask for forgiveness.

WHEN YOU ARE HURT, GRIEVE IT AND FORGIVE. Forgiveness is as vital as your digestive tract. It is the way that we metabolize and remove waste from the system of a relationship.

IF THE HURT IS SEVERE, GET SUPPORT AND HEALING, AND PROCESS THE PAIN. Grieving the hurt and letting it go may be impossible without outside help if a major hurt has been inflicted.

GET STRAIGHT ABOUT WHAT IS WORTH BEING HURT OVER. Some things simply are not worth bringing up or making into an issue. One of the most annoying things in life is to be around someone who is annoyed by everything. If you find yourself hurt continually by much of what your mate does, you may need outside help to correct your perspective.

WORK TOGETHER ON HOW YOU PROCESS PAIN AND HURT. Talk to each other about how to let each other know when you are hurt. Discuss what you need from each other at those moments. Grow in your communication, listening, and conflict resolution skills. Take a class or a workshop. See resolving hurt and conflict as one of the most important skills you can develop.

**A Lifeline:** IF YOU FOLLOW THESE SUGGESTIONS, YOU CAN BE MARRIED TO A PERSON WHO HURTS YOU AND YET HAVE A WONDERFUL RELATIONSHIP. THE TRIALS IN YOUR MARRIAGE AND IN LIFE WILL ONLY MAKE YOU STRONGER AND MORE MATURE IN THE END. THEY WILL BUILD YOUR CHARACTER AND MAKE YOUR RELATIONSHIP STRONGER THAN IF YOU HAD NEVER GONE THROUGH THEM. BUT THAT CAN HAPPEN ONLY IF YOU SEE HURT AS PART OF THE PACKAGE. THEN YOU WON'T BE SURPRISED, BUT EQUIPPED.

## Past Hurts, Present Problems

You may have heard someone say, "The light at the end of the tunnel is a train headed toward you." We're going to twist this saying into a description of something that often occurs in love relationships: There may be times when the light at the end of the tunnel really is love, but you may mistake it for a train and swerve to avoid it. When you do, the good that could have benefited you and your mate never occurs.

Swerving to avoid what looks like an oncoming train can mean the loss of many satisfying, intimate, and enjoyable times of love and connection. Missing out on those good things may seem dumb, but it can happen to the best of us. In this chapter, we'll show how you can recognize the true light of love for what it is and not try to dodge it.

## A Good Marriage Transfers Love

Just as a good cell phone transfers information, a good marriage transfers love. And that love has many voices, many ways to be heard and received. It can be the voice of grace, affection, comfort, encouragement, or passion, to name a few. And that "voice" is not always audible; it can come in many forms—a glance, a word, a conversation, or a touch.

Even though love comes our way, we all have a tendency to misunderstand what our mate wants to provide for us. And we often swerve out of the way, causing disconnection, alienation, and hurt between two good people who actually do love each other.

Why would we avoid the very thing that we desire and need from our lover? In a nutshell, we miss the voice of love in our spouse because *old messages drown it out.* Past hurts and unresolved issues can distort the true meaning and emotion that is coming your way in your marriage. The following example will show you what we mean.

## Is It Love, or Is It a Train?

Debbie and Kevin had only been married a couple of years when they found themselves in a pattern that was not satisfying to either one. It went like this: whenever Debbie approached Kevin on a vulnerable and emotional level, Kevin would withdraw or even be negative toward her. In one instance, Debbie had taken a risk to tell Kevin that sometimes she felt she was unattractive to him, and she was afraid that the more he got to know her, the less interesting he would find her. It was one of her deepest fears and very hard to talk about. Yet she wanted her husband to know this part of her.

Kevin's response was not comforting. "Well, I'll tell you what," he said. "I'll let you know if that ever happens." It was meant to sound humorous, but clearly it was the wrong joke at the wrong time. Debbie was really hurt, and she shut down from Kevin for a while. When she did try to talk to him about it later, she was still hurt and didn't address it the right way. They got into a blaming argument which distanced them even more.

Debbie came to me (John) with the problem. As she explained things, I began to see what had happened. So I coached her on how to approach Kevin about the issue. I told her to tell him that his response had put her off. And then she was to go further, saying, "I don't think the way you sounded reflects the way you really feel toward me—at least, I hope not. I hope you were being sarcastic to protect yourself in some way. So I want to solve this between us. Can you tell me what it was like for you when I told you how scared I am of being unattractive to you?"

Debbie did as I suggested, and what happened then was instructive. She told me that Kevin thought a minute and responded, "I think I wanted what you said to feel good, but it didn't. It felt more like you were setting me up."

"Like a trap?"

"Yes, like you were saying something good to get me ready for the next thing you would say, which would not be good."

As they talked, something became clear. Kevin began remembering his mother's relational pattern with him. She suffered severe mood swings, and often Kevin got the worst end of them. She would be kind and affectionate toward him; then, within a few minutes, she would become critical and cold, for no apparent reason. This kept Kevin the child confused and bewildered. Eventually he learned to cope with his mom by not trusting her. When she was warm with him, Kevin would become guarded and careful, preparing himself for the storm that was sure to follow.

Kevin had learned that the light of love was really a train coming to run him down, and he had developed a survival skill to defend himself against it. He never really thought about it much, though he was aware that he had difficulty becoming close to people. But when he met and married Debbie, he wanted to be part of her in a way he had never felt before.

When Debbie shined the light of love by saying a kind thing to him, his past experiences conditioned him to see it as a train, so the survival skill he had developed kicked in and he jumped aside. His past experience warned him: *you'd better distance yourself from Debbie's love; it's a trap.* Thus the couple suffered a sense of alienation from each other.

However, when they became aware of the source of Kevin's reflex, they faced it squarely and took steps to resolve it. Debbie worked on not taking his distance as a personal affront. She now realized where it came from. When it happened, she would say, "You just put up a wall between us. Can we get through it?" That helped Kevin know what had occurred. He learned that his wife was a much healthier and warmer person than his mom had been, and gradually he grew able to stay present and connected with her.

### Get to Know Your "Train"

There are other "trains at the end of the tunnel" besides Debbie and Kevin's. See if any of the following is a train in your life.

IF YOU TELL ME THE TRUTH, YOU DON'T LOVE ME. Many couples encounter this misconception. One partner confronts the other with an issue, and the other feels unloved. Her feeling could be due to past experiences of harsh judgment with little compassion.

IF YOU COME CLOSE, YOU WILL DRAIN ME. Some mates feel drained by the needs and approaches of the other. Instead of feeling filled, he feels emptied. This is often the result of a family system in which a child had to take care of the dependency needs of a parent.

LOVE MEANS CONTROL. Sometimes when one partner attempts to draw close, her mate feels that he is being smothered and his freedom taken away. Any form of intimacy is experienced as a way to tie him down, and he must escape by distancing.

YOU'LL LEAVE ME. Somewhere in the past, one spouse has suffered abandonment by someone she loved. She has learned not to trust in the goodness and stability of love. As a result, the closer her lover comes, the more she distances herself, to protect her feelings from the terrible pangs of abandonment.

There are many more of these messages and issues. (For a more complete listing, see John's book *Hiding from Love: How to Change the Withdrawal Patterns that Isolate and Imprison You.*) The point is, it's a good time to take a look at your connection and sort out all the lights that could be mistaken for trains.

## The Bottom Line

The bottom line is this: *couples committed to rescuing their love life will search for, identify, and deal with whatever is getting in the way of the voice of love.* They won't tolerate old hurts from the past screwing up the opportunity for full, rich, and exciting love for the rest of their lives.

Do old messages and hurts make a difference? Certainly they do. You can't just ignore them and hope they will go away. That would be like hoping a bacterial infection will go away by simply powering through it. Most of the time, the condition gets worse without intervention. Just as you must take an antibiotic to clear up the infection, you must administer treatment to overcome past hurts.

## Learning to Hear the Voice of Love

There are some good things you can do as a couple to administer the right antibiotics.

DISCUSS RESPONSES THAT DON'T MAKE SENSE. Talk to each other about any times when one of you approached the other with a good and positive message, but your spouse withdrew, shut down, felt hurt, or became irritated. As Debbie did with Kevin, explain what your intent was, and help the other person discover the source of the reaction. *Don't be satisfied with simply identifying the reaction.* There is almost always something driving it.

UNEARTH THE PATTERNS. Using the examples in this chapter as a starting point, help each other discover what sorts of patterns you have as a couple that get in the way of love, connection, and passion. Is one of you afraid the other will leave? Is one still struggling with childhood abandonment? Is one still attempting to protect her freedom from her parents? Get to know the patterns.

VALIDATE EACH OTHER'S EXPERIENCE. Don't say to each other, "I'm not your dad; get over it." Getting over it is not an instant thing, but a process. Instead, say something like, "I understand that when I confront you, it's hard for you to feel that I love you at the same time. I know those feelings are real, and I don't want to make it worse for you." Validation helps your spouse see that you are different from her past experiences. You are not a train; you are a true lover.

SEPARATE PAST FROM PRESENT. You and your mate need to help each other make a distinction between the old and the new, so that you can hear each other's voices of love. Say, "I want you to know that when I do confront you, I am not wanting to hurt or control you. I just want to solve a problem so we can get back to being close and safe for each other."

SET UP FEEDBACK. Memories of past injuries and issues need to be addressed over a process of time and given the right ingredients of love, safety, and reality. So give each other permission to bring up the "train" when one of you notices it. That helps to break the grip of the past on your present connection.

For example, you may say things like, "When I told you that I had had a bad day and I needed to talk to you, you flinched. Did it seem to you that I was going to drain you with my needs? Actually, I do have needs, but not like the old days. In fact, I want to hear about your day too. OK?" Or, if the shoe is on the other foot, say, "You were just really nice to me. I know I'm being paranoid, but do you have some bad news to tell me?" You can get a laugh out of this if there's no bad news!

STAY IN CONFESSION. You and your mate may sometimes truly be "trains" for each other. At times, you may not be very loving when you approach each other. You may be angry and not balanced with your love. You may be manipulative in your approach. You may be blaming your partner for something he doesn't deserve.

In these instances, don't hide or pretend. Confess your negative behavior and tell the truth. Confession is good for the soul, and the marriage. Your lover will appreciate your vulnerability and honesty, and you can move on. If you don't do this, it is likely that your mate will sense the "train" and not be able to separate you from his past. In effect, you will be part of the sick system he came from. This is no way to have a healthy love life. Clear it up, and get back to love.

**A Lifeline:** LOVE BRINGS US CLOSER TO EACH OTHER AND GOD. LOVE KEEPS US ALIVE. LOVE KEEPS US GROWING. HELP EACH OTHER NOT TO SWERVE AND AVOID LOVE WHEN IT COMES YOUR WAY.

# Accepting Without Approving

I (John) was having dinner with Dan and Stephanie, friends who have been married for a long time. They have always seemed close to each other. The conversation turned to their early days as a couple. They talked about the challenges they had resolved, which resulted in the good place they were in now.

Stephanie said, "I was so mad at Dan for a long time. I thought he was the most unaccepting, unloving, critical person I had ever met, and I wondered how we ever got together."

Dan laughed. "I remember those days. I was such the bad guy."

"So what was the deal?" I asked.

"When we were dating, he seemed really caring and compassionate. But after we got married, all of a sudden he started talking about things that were wrong with me."

"Like what?"

"Like it bugged him that I spent so much time with my mother. Or that the apartment wasn't kept up. Or that I wasn't keeping to a budget in our finances."

"These don't really sound critical and unloving to me," I said. "They sound like real concerns."

"That's the point," Stephanie replied. "Dan was pretty much right about these things. I came from a family that never required me to clean up, pick up, or have any real responsibilities. My mom did it for me. She thought that was her job. So when I got married, I had no clue about these things. It bothered Dan, and he didn't use the kindest words to tell me about it."

"I was really bugged. I wasn't nice," said Dan.

"Nope, you weren't," she agreed. Stephanie didn't have a problem being direct. "I thought that Dan didn't accept me for who I was and didn't really love me for myself. If he really accepted me, he would live with these things—that's what you are supposed to do if you love someone, right? But after a lot of talking about it, I finally realized that it wasn't about accepting me. It was about expecting things of me. I saw those two things as the same. But I finally got it that they were different, and things got better."

## Acceptance and Love

Stephanie and Dan's early days are a good starting point to understand what acceptance means in love and romance. Acceptance is one of the primary bases for healthy intimacy, yet there is a great deal of misinformation and dumb attitudes about it. Let's begin with what acceptance looks like between two people who love each other.

*Acceptance* is a term often used to mean that your love is so great and so deep that there is nothing the two of you can do that will really disturb or distance each other. Where acceptance exists, all can be forgiven and forgotten in the service of love.

This is a little tricky, because in some ways it is true. Acceptance does have to do with a great and deep love. And if you want to rescue your love life, acceptance will play a large role. *In fact, the extent to which you love your partner is the extent to which you accept him.* But there is more to acceptance than that.

When we accept someone, we receive that person into our heart. We take in all parts, all aspects, all realities, good, bad, and green. That is the meaning of the acceptance God gives to us, and that we in turn give to our partner. In response to acceptance, we "accept one another, then, just as Christ accepted you, in order to bring praise to God" (Romans 15:7).

Acceptance is important because no one can love, trust, or grow without knowing that they have been received, warts and all, by another person. If your lover feels that some part of him isn't good enough for you, he will disconnect, get angry, or pretend to be someone else. And the two of you will not experience the fullness of love.

Think of some past relationship in which you felt you weren't good enough. You probably did the same things in response: you pulled away, you got mad, or you tried harder to be what the other person wanted. But the relationship most likely failed, and it should fail because of the nature of acceptance. *If you have to earn it or be good enough, by definition it cannot be acceptance.* Acceptance is based on the acceptor's love and the acceptee's need. It has nothing to do with performance, working hard enough, or being good enough. (For more information on the nature of acceptance, please refer to our book, *How People Grow*.)

The two enemies of acceptance in a couple are *denial* and *judgment*. Let's say your lover has a problem staying organized and structured, as in Stephanie's case. It bothers you. So first you go into denial—that is, you act as if the problem doesn't exist and hope it goes away. But, as the old saying goes, an elephant under the rug is still an elephant. It doesn't go away, so then you judge her on the basis of her weakness, being harsh, critical, and condemning whenever it appears. Not only will you probably see no progress in her messiness, but you are almost guaranteed that the love, passion, and intimacy you want will not be there either. Denial and judgment are lose-lose approaches.

Needs and weaknesses are usually at the top of the list of those things a couple should learn to accept in each other. But we can't accept each other's faults and failings, immaturities, and undesirable habits if we're denying that they even exist. Besides, acceptance and love are the only way that those parts of you two will ever have a chance to grow, heal, change, and mature.

All growth begins with acceptance, for without it we just hide and pretend better, hoping to avoid the disappointment and wrath of our partner. Only in the light and freedom of acceptance can you talk about, process, pray, support, and come up with solutions for these weaknesses and issues.

## Approval and Agreement

Now let's set out what acceptance is *not*. A major misconception about acceptance is that it conveys approval or agreement. The thinking generally goes in the negative direction, something like, *If you don't approve of or agree with what I am doing, you aren't accepting me.* Sometimes a partner will demand that an action, speech, or attitude must be approved for the other to be seen as an accepting person. This is not true, and it doesn't work in relationships.

If you approve of or agree with something that is bad, immature, or wrong, you are contributing to more of the same, which is what you will most likely experience. For example, suppose your partner has friends you don't approve of. They aren't supportive of the relationship, and they aren't good for him. They bring out his negative aspects. For you to approve of or agree with these friendships is to give license to something that could hurt your connection and intimacy. You may accept that they are his friends without denial or judgment. But you shouldn't approve of what could be bad for you as a couple.

## Feeling Attacked

Some people respond to disapproval by feeling hated, judged, and persecuted. Psychologists call this a *persecutory issue,* and it stems from a person's character and experiences in significant relationships.

Stephanie had a slight tendency toward this problem. With others, it is more serious. Sometimes an individual has a history of receiving harsh and hurtful messages. To her, a loving mate who simply attempts to tell the truth may be seen as uncaring. In other instances, a person who has never experienced limits or has been somewhat spoiled will be unable to see requirements as a loving thing and will also feel persecuted.

If confronting a problem you disapprove of destroys your partner's sense of acceptance, work on it with her. Make it a project. Reassure her that you love her. Get other healthy people to help her see that you love her. Help her be aware of past hurts and old patterns that may be causing her reactions, so they can be resolved. Be as accepting, humble, loving, and open as you can be. But whatever you do, *do not give up your position*, as long as it is healthy and reasonable. You want growth and improvement. To love and accept each other totally, you must care enough to confront.

**A Lifeline:** DISAPPROVAL AND ACCEPTANCE SEEM MUTU- ALLY EXCLUSIVE, BUT THEY ARE NOT. IF YOU WANT TO RESCUE YOUR LOVE LIFE, START BY TOTALLY ACCEPTING AND RECEIVING EVERY ASPECT OF EACH OTHER WITHOUT DENIAL OR JUDGMENT. THEN BRING UP TO THE LIGHT FOR DISCUSSION AND CHANGE THOSE BEHAVIORS AND ATTITUDES THAT BLOCK YOUR LOVE FROM EACH OTHER.

## Lovers Can Bring Out the Worst in Each Other

If you have been in your present relationship for any amount of time, you've probably noticed that *your closest relationship can also be your most difficult relationship.* You can experience both the best and the worst of emotions in your connection with this delightful but exasperating person. For example, you may notice that a simple phrase or even a certain look from your mate can profoundly affect your emotions. She can make you feel criticized, misunderstood, unloved, or like an idiot—all with a simple movement of an eyelid. That is power.

Marilyn, a family friend, was visiting our home recently. I (John) asked her how things were going with her boyfriend, Jeff. "I don't know how to answer that," she said. "We're starting to get serious, and I really care about him. But the more serious we get, the worse things are between us.

"For example, Jeff knows I am insecure about other women. I get jealous. He used to try to be really sensitive about it, and that helped. But the other night we were at a party, and he talked to a pretty girl for a long time. When I told him it made me feel insecure, he just said, 'Deal with it,' and he went on like it was nothing."

"That sounds insensitive," I said.

"Really insensitive. The problem is, Jeff didn't used to be that way. It only started happening when we got more serious."

Mark Marilyn's last words: *it only started happening when they got more serious.* That is the key to understanding what happens to couples. The deeper the connection becomes, the more problems you and your partner will encounter. Jeff and Marilyn began to experience more alienation, disconnection, and conflict—not things they signed up for when they began to be interested in each other.

## Making Sense of the Problem

You would think that the closer you get to someone you love, the better things should be. Increased time, vulnerability, experience, and love should lead to increased trust, desire, and satisfaction, right? Of course that is certainly the way it should be, and it does happen. But as Marilyn was experiencing, and you may be also, increased closeness can also bring out dark, intimacy-breaking issues. Let's take a look at how this happens.

LOVE REGRESSES US. Being in love with someone has what psychologists call a regressive pull on us. That is, as you become safer and more vulnerable with your lover, you expose parts of yourself that don't normally come out in everyday life. It is the very safety and security of the relationship that brings out our fragile parts. We stop trying to be strong, to keep things together, to be thick-skinned. God designed love to bring out these vulnerable parts of us at their proper time.

Regression is not a bad thing in and of itself. In fact, it is a good sign. *If love regresses you, you are alive and allowing yourself to be connected at deep levels.* If you love this person, you're not always at your most together and strongest, and neither is she. But if the relationship is safe enough, you can expose these fragile and vulnerable parts to get the grace, caring, and empathy that you need.

OLD PATTERNS ARE REENACTED. Not only do we regress in our deepest love relationship, but we also reenact old patterns that we haven't resolved. For example, one of you may be the "lover" and the other, the "fighter." That is, one values connection more, while the other is more comfortable with confrontation. These are roles that many learned in order to survive their families of origin. So when things are tough, the lover will entreat, comply, and adapt, while the fighter will argue, distance, and provoke. At some level, both parties are replaying mental tapes that reflect patterns from a long time ago and continue to replay, over and over again.

CLOSENESS BRINGS FEAR. Many times, the very presence of closeness and vulnerability can elicit strong feelings of fear and distancing. If closeness in your past relationships meant being hurt, controlled, or abandoned, as you become more intimate with your spouse, that old baggage will often reemerge. As love penetrates the heart at a deeper level, *whatever is there gets activated*—including conflicts, fears, immaturity, unresolved trauma, and the like. This is why some partners will be cold or angry after an intimate time. When he gets close to his mate, he becomes afraid at some level of an emotional danger or threat to himself, and he reacts accordingly.

CLOSENESS PROVIDES AMMUNITION. When you expose yourself to the other person, you give her information about yourself that, unfortunately, she can use against you. When she is angry or self-centered, she can exploit these secrets and truly cause pain. This is a cruel thing to do and a sign that a relationship may need some real work. It's what Jeff did to Marilyn, maybe without knowing the damage he was doing. But she questioned the wisdom of showing him her insecurity after his cruel reply to her.

The natural (not best) result is often that, in retaliation, the other partner then dredges up what she knows about him. Now you have a situation in which two people care, but neither has the tools or maturity to handle the negative aspects of their love. In essence, you have two children in a dual tantrum, which only escalates until somebody gets hurt. Watch any soap opera or reality show, and you get the picture.

## Bringing Out the Best in the Worst

Bringing out the worst in each other is an inevitable problem that can sink your love life. But it's dumb not to recognize it and deal with it—and we have some simple and straightforward solutions for you. But first, remember that if you two are disconnected because the relationship brings out the worst in you, it's a sign that *the relationship matters.* It is powerful enough to make you a little crazy, and that is good news. Here are some things you can do to reestablish the satisfying connection you need.

AFFIRM THE LIFE. In a quiet and peaceful period, not in the throes of battle, talk with each other about the reality that there is a lot of care and love between you. Tell each other, "I don't let anyone make me as crazy as you do. You must be pretty special to me!" This can go a long way toward the two of you reconnecting. Simply recognizing and confessing how much you matter to each other can bring a sense of being valued and loved.

MAKE IT RELATIONAL. When one of you brings out the worst in the other, that is not the time to draw back and shut down. Unless you are in some sort of danger, or you are simply totally depleted and exhausted and need to regroup, *make the issue part of the relationship itself, because it truly is part of who you are as a couple.* Bring into the light what is already true about you, and talk about it.

You might say, "I feel alone and unloved when you bring up my weight in such a critical tone. I know my weight is frustrating for you, as it is for me. But when you say those things in that way, it moves me away from you. You can hurt me more than other people about this, because you know me so well." Doing so can lead to understanding and mutuality.

STRENGTHEN THE WEAK PARTS. When you become aware of what things "get to you" in the relationship, it is a signal to shore up, develop, and strengthen those parts. Those things are often a symptom of some sort of brokenness or injury within, so work on healing and growth. The worthwhile result of such effort is less reactive pain and hurt.

For example, here is the rest of my conversation with Marilyn. "I don't blame you for being hurt with Jeff's comments about your jealousy," I said. "I think you should confront him with how his insensitivity pulls you out of the closeness you both want and how that needs to stop.

"At the same time, I don't think it's good for either of you to stay insecure and jealous. Something has caused you to have those feelings, and I'd like you to become curious about that and find ways to become more open to Jeff's having safe female relationships."

Marilyn did do that. She told Jeff that she would work on her jealous insecurity, which helped him feel more like they were a team. She realized that, as a child, she had an insecure relationship with her mother, which had translated into an inability to feel unconditionally loved. As she worked on experiencing Jeff's steady love and that of others in her life, her insecurity was gradually replaced by a confidence that she had his care and his loyalty.

GIVE YOUR BEST TO THE RELATIONSHIP. As the two of you continue taking vulnerable risks with each other, you will bring immature, broken, and hurt parts into the relationship. But that is not the basis of the entire connection. You also have love, grace, compassion, empathy, guidance, and honesty to give each other. Couples invested in connecting and deepening are actively involved in giving their strengths and best parts to the relationship. When this happens, not only is the relationship better, but you also are able to tolerate and navigate through the realities of the bad parts.

This takes a little attention. It is very easy, as you become more used to each other, to take each other for granted and strut your good stuff only when you're with others. Make your relationship one in which your first thought is to give the best, healthiest, and most adult parts of your heart to your lover.

HONOR YOUR COMMITMENT. It's sad when people fall in love, get married, and then, when reality hits and they see the worst in their spouse, they conclude they are with the wrong person. When your mate exposes the worst of himself and you are tempted to break your marriage vows, you must go through reality and make a choice to love.

The commitment of marriage not only protects us from bailing out when the inevitable comes, but it also ensures that we truly do get to the promised land of real intimacy and love. Genuine intimacy involves all of the heart, and the only way to the real heart is through whatever lies within. Those hidden parts only come out as time and love do their work.

> **A Lifeline:** FACE IT: YOUR LOVE CONNECTION WILL BRING OUT THE WORST IN YOU, WHICH SIMPLY MEANS THAT LOVE IS TAKING ITS NORMAL PATH. REMEMBER THAT THIS IS A VITAL SIGN OF LIFE, AND BRING IT INTO YOUR LOVE LIFE WHERE YOU CAN ADDRESS IT SQUARELY, HELPING EACH OTHER TO GROW AND CHANGE. REMEMBER YOUR MARRIAGE VOWS, AND WORK IT THROUGH WITH PATIENCE AND GRACE.

## Resist the Temptation to Cut and Run

Put yourself in the counselor's chair for a moment. You are working with a couple trying to put things back together after an affair or a spouse being tempted to have an affair. This is what you hear:

"I tried to tell him that I was not being fulfilled in our relationship, but he wouldn't listen. Then, when Rob and I started getting close at work, I felt like there was finally someone who connected with me. I didn't mean for it to happen; it just did because Allan was not meeting my needs."

"She was just not interested in sex. I tried everything, but it always felt like I was making her do it. I was deprived, so you can understand why it was so natural to say 'yes' to Susan. She found me attractive and made me feel like a man again. What's a guy supposed to do when he's not getting anything at home? Kristin forced me into a no-win situation, and I gave in."

"I haven't done anything yet, but I am tempted. I try to get Jack to connect and to make me feel attractive, but it's like he doesn't even notice me. When I travel with my sales team, Dave is so different. He pays attention to me, and I feel so much more alive around him. It just makes sense to want to be with someone who makes you feel better, doesn't it? Doesn't God understand what I am going through?"

## A Common Thread

Did you notice the common thread in these complaints? Each person claimed that the affair happened because their mates did not meet their needs. Oh, there is truth to the claim that things were not going well in the relationship before the affair. Their spouses were not giving them all that they needed, or at least wanted. But that is not why they had the affair. *They had the affair because they chose to solve their misery in that particular way.*

Now, we are all sinners, and no one can stand in judgment of anyone else. Any of us who thinks we are morally superior to people who have affairs must remember what Jesus said when the Pharisees wanted to condemn the woman who was caught in adultery (John 8:1–11). He invited anyone present who was without sin to cast the first stone. There were no takers then, and there wouldn't be any today.

But the issue is not about guilt or condemnation. It is about getting to the real disease behind infidelity. First, we need to understand that deprivation is not what causes failure. Deprivation may provide the motivation to look for comfort, even illicitly. But it does not cause the choice to achieve comfort in a destructive way.

Jesus was the best example of this truth. He was taken to the desert and deprived of everything human (Luke 4:1–13). His basic needs for food, water, companionship, social interaction, and self-expression were all neglected. Yet He did not go the way of immediate comfort. He denied that option.

James tells us that we sin because we are carried away by our own desires: "Each one is tempted when, by his own evil desire, he is dragged away and enticed. Then, after desire has conceived, it gives birth to sin; and sin, when it is full-grown, gives birth to death" (James 1:14–15).

So temptation is not about deprivation in a relationship, nor is it about our own stress, hurt, or need. Those are real and valid needs that call for help and healing; these needs cannot be met by giving in to things that cause death. That is what infidelity does—it causes the death of marriages, children, churches, and many other things.

We want your relationship to be "affair-proofed" so you can avoid these kinds of death. Technically, "affair-proofing" is impossible because no human is above any temptation. But certain attitudes can bring your chances of falling much closer to zero.

### Dissatisfaction Is *Your* Problem

While your mate's behavior may be the cause of your dissatisfaction, your *response* is your responsibility. And you are the only one who can choose your response. You have the freedom to do the right and helpful thing in response to your spouse's failure. Your response can be a redemptive force for change in your marriage instead of a force to take it further down. As Jesus said, even "sinners" love the people who love them.

The real test is how well we love someone who does not love us well. That is the true calling of Christ. Here is how he says it: "If you love those who love you, what credit is that to you? Even 'sinners' love those who love them. And if you do good to those who are good to you, what credit is that to you? Even 'sinners' do that" (Luke 6:32–33).

As we said earlier, that does not mean that you should just endure mistreatment. In fact, the loving thing to do is to take a stand against the mistreatment and confront it in a loving and redemptive way. The loving thing is to make the effort to do what is necessary to turn things around. Sometimes that means you may have to take some tough growth steps yourself in order to do it correctly.

Your feelings of being alone and hurt are very real and need help. But affairs are not healing. They are destructive, like illegal drugs.

They may medicate the pain for the moment, but in the end, they destroy all that's really important. The responsible thing to do is take your pain to good people who can love you, support you, and help you through the process of healing your marriage.

## Attraction Is a Bad Barometer

People get fooled all the time by attraction. First, attraction is based on becoming intoxicated by someone with whom they do not have a real and whole relationship, and they idealize the part of him that they relate to. As a result, they feel magically in love although there is no real relationship to back that up. When most people in affairs think back, they'll remember that they also felt the same way at one time toward their spouse—the one they now want to be rescued from.

Second, affairs are so attractive because they offer a partial relationship that only includes the positive. The spouse in pain directs all the negative stuff—the disappointment and hurt—toward the mate. So all of the "good stuff" goes toward the fantasy love object who is desired for an affair. And that idealized, "all-good" fantasy is allowed to remain intact because it does not have the day-to-day pressures that marriage inevitably has. In an affair, there is little need to work out compromise, conflict, and the like, as it is mainly a rescue mission from the "bad spouse." So the hurt spouse has an inordinately positive view of the rescuer, which he or she mistakes for love.

Many times we have heard the sad story of someone who had an affair, lost her spouse, and married the person she had the affair with—only to find that he was not all she thought he was. And she was miserable in the second marriage, longing for what she had before. That's why research shows a much higher divorce rate for second marriages. History tends to repeat itself.

The bottom line is that attraction is a bad barometer. It gives you false readings of what the other person is truly like, which you can discover only in a full-blown relationship with him. It gives you false readings of what you really need from a relationship, because an idealized romantic state is not what you need long term. The attraction will fade, and then you are left with all the negatives that did not surface in the affair, along with one additional negative, which is to see yourself as someone who betrayed your spouse and perhaps even stole another person's spouse. Using attraction as a barometer gives you a false reading of your spouse as well. The reason for this is simple: the comparison of your spouse to the idealized affair is never realistic, and the spouse always loses to the fantasy.

If you are attracted to someone strongly enough to consider an affair, heed the warning of Solomon about infidelity: "The lips of an adulteress drip honey, and her speech is smoother than oil; but in the end she is bitter as gall, sharp as a double-edged sword. Her feet go down to death; her steps lead straight to the grave" (Proverbs 5:3–5).

The romantic scene may be enticing, but that scene is part of a larger movie with a tragic ending. Play the movie all the way to the end. See your family destroyed, your friends split up, your spouse brokenhearted, your children devastated, and all of the other devastation that will occur. That is the real movie that you are contemplating. So before you raise the lights and lock the theater doors for the night, add another scene to the plot: the one where you get smart and run the other way. Do not succumb to the fantasy of attraction.

## Adultery Is Not About Your Needs

Too often, people claim that they were driven into an affair because their mate did not meet their needs in some way. Related to that is the feeling many people have that they deserve to have their needs met. It is their "right" to get what they want or need in life.

People who have successful lives and relationships hold to a different philosophy. Instead of thinking of themselves as entitled to what they want, they believe that their God and the people they make commitments to are entitled to having them live up to the standards they hold to. In other words, they do not ask the standards to change to meet their needs. Instead, they change to meet the demands of the standards. That means honoring their commitment to the relationship, even when the sailing gets rough.

The paradox is that when we hold to those standards, we are the ones who get what we most want in life. We put commitment first and suffer through the hard times that it takes to resolve problems and make relationships last. As a result, when things are tough, our first thought is not about how our needs are not being met, but about what we can do to redeem the relationship.

This very countercultural truth is exactly what Jesus modeled for us: dying to yourself and picking up your cross (Matthew 16:24). To redeem bad things, we sometimes have to suffer not getting what we need, just as Jesus suffered. But in the end, the good suffering to live up to your values and commitments—in this case, the vows of your marriage—are the ones that redeem bad situations. And if the situation is not redeemed—for example, if a spouse leaves you—your character will be strengthened more as a result of doing the right thing, and you will still benefit in the end. Good suffering always produces good results.

Whenever you feel that your need is becoming more urgent than your values, remind yourself that you have a real and important need for love and relationship that is going unmet. Instead of letting that need drive you into an affair, turn to your godly, supportive friends and relationships to meet that need while you work on your marriage. It will pay off in the long run.

Clearly, "for better or for worse"—the vow you took—is a serious vow and a hard one, especially when your need is going unmet. But if you realize that your commitment is above your need, then you have the greatest chance of reaping the fruit that those values were designed to bring about.

## When the Wolf Knocks, Don't Open the Door

One of the most common dumb attitudes is the confidence in our own will power to resist temptation. If you don't believe it, then look at your dieting history: how many times have you told yourself that you would resist the temptations of pizzas and sundaes after January 1? We humans think we are stronger than we really are, but given the right circumstances—ploys by the devil, our own dependencies, and other factors—we are all subject to falling to some kind of temptation, including the temptation to infidelity.

Many people do not think they would ever have an affair, but they allow themselves to get into situations that become too much to handle. They open the door, never with the plan to get destroyed, but "it just happens." We can all empathize with that common weakness. As the Bible teaches, pride goes before a fall, and we are most vulnerable when we think we are strong enough to stand (Proverbs 16:18; 1 Corinthians 10:12).

This is where good accountability relationships are important. Each of you should have someone in your life who asks you about these issues, someone you can be honest with. Have couple's accountability as well. Keeping out of temptation keeps you out of trouble.

Avoid even opening the door to temptation. The Bible does not say to resist temptation; it says to "flee" from it (1 Corinthians 6:18). If you place yourself in a tempting situation and rely on your moral strength to resist it, you are asking for trouble. Don't rely on a strategy to resist temptation, but avoid placing yourself in it to begin with. As Mark Twain said, "It's easier to stay out than to get out."

Only you know when you may be tempted and when you won't. There are too many variables for us to tell you what you should and should not do. But you know. And you should consider the feelings of your mate. Neither of you should be doing things that the other feels uncomfortable with. Talk it through and avoid any kind of duplicity.

**A Lifeline:** KNOW THAT IF THE LEAST BIT OF THE OPPORTUNITY FOR TEMPTATION APPEARS, THAT IS THE WOLF. WHEN HE FINDS YOU ALONE, HE WILL EAT YOU. THE LONE SHEEP IS THE ONE WHO ALWAYS GETS ATTACKED. SO STAY ON THE PATH WITH THE REST OF THE FLOCK, AND AVOID BEING ALONE WITH THE WOLF OF TEMPTATION. WHENEVER HE KNOCKS, DO NOT OPEN THE DOOR.

# DUMB ATTITUDE #5

## "My Lover Should Read My Mind"

H as your partner ever accused you of saying things you didn't mean at all? Have you ever been upset with your partner for not being able to figure out why you were angry with him? When this sort of thing happens it creates confusion, but one thing is sure: there is definitely a disconnect.

As we have stressed throughout this book, establishing, preserving, and repairing the connection is essential in a relationship. And to do that requires being able to communicate. That means being able to talk to one another in a way that gets the two of you closer instead of farther apart. Sadly, because we are human, that is a very difficult thing to do at times.

If you can absorb some principles about how to talk to each other and how not to talk to each other, as well as how to listen to each other in some ways that you may never have done, you really can connect. Communication can hardly be overrated as a primary key to relationship rescue. In this section, we will find some very doable ways to begin to reconnect with the one you love through specific, clear communication. If you follow these principles, you won't ever again fall for the dumb attitude of expecting your partner to read your mind.

## Don't Hide Your Feelings

"Why didn't you tell me?" she said, referring to the grim financial realities he had been hiding.

"You never told me you were feeling alone," he said, referring to her reason for getting involved with someone at work.

"I didn't know you didn't want to go," she said, referring to his resentment at going to her parents' for the holidays.

"You always seemed happy," he said, referring to her complaint in counseling that her marriage felt dead.

Sound like things you have heard before? Sound like things you have said before? You know the experience of being surprised that someone close to you felt a certain way, and you had no clue. It happens in a marriage! Sometimes one partner doesn't hear when the other is trying to communicate something important. But at other times the communication is not so clear after all. And often when the hidden feelings are uncovered, it is too late.

### Why People Hide Their Feelings

Something happens to the openness and intimacy of a relationship's early seasons. The two people slowly stop communicating what they *really* think and feel, and they slowly get further and further away from each other emotionally. Their hearts either settle into a partial intimacy or a detached relationship, without a total connection between them. For others, the divide takes on more poisonous forms, such as affairs, addictions, or even divorce. Let's examine why the sharing stops in the first place and how detachment occurs in a relationship.

THEY LEARN THAT SHARING IS NOT SAFE. For two hearts to be connected, there must be a place to share feelings where one feels safe. Many couples find that defensiveness, attack, blame, judgment, pulling away, anger, and other bad things happen in their relationship when they share what is in their heart, so they just stop doing it. They have little hope for resolving a conflict or being heard. They give up honest sharing with each other.

THEY HAVE OLD FEARS THAT KEEP THEM FROM SHARING. For some couples, it's not the things they encounter in their marriage that keep them from being direct and open, it's the things they bring *to* the marriage. They carry fears from past experiences that have taught them that sharing is not a safe thing to do and something bad will happen if you are totally honest—such as abandonment, criticism, rejection, abuse, disapproval, anger, escalation, breakdown in connection, withdrawal, attack, or judgment. So they hold back from sharing, and as a result, intimacy suffers.

THEY DO NOT HAVE THE SKILLS OR KNOW HOW TO SHARE. Some people did not grow up in families that communicated well or have not had other people show them what real, honest communication looks like. In the beginning of the relationship, they can share with their partner when there is not a lot of really threatening things to reveal or work through, but as time goes on and the attachment deepens, they find that the sharing requires communication skills they don't possess. They just don't know how to do it.

THEY HAVE HAD EXPERIENCES THAT ARE TOO OVERWHELMING. Sometimes the bad things that happen in life and in a marriage are too painful to know how to deal with. These events overwhelm a mate's system. Some couples, for example, split up after the loss of a child or some other devastating trauma. The pain is too much for them to be honest about, and they shut down and shut each other out.

THEY FEEL THAT THE THINGS THAT THEY WANT TO SHARE ARE UNACCEPTABLE. These can be failures in the relationship or deep secrets about themselves. But whatever it is they would like to share, shame and the fear of loss of love keep their hearts locked up inside. They cannot accept certain things about themselves, and they feel so terrible about them that they are really afraid to open up.

THEY THINK THAT THEIR DESIRES OR WANTS ARE NOT IMPORTANT. Many people have been taught that what they want doesn't matter, is selfish, or has little or no chance of being fulfilled. So they shut down from feeling those things and communicating them. They do not realize that communicating their wants and feelings actually add to the relationship for the other person.

Whatever your reason, hiding your feelings is not only dishonest, but it's a dumb attitude that can sink a marriage in a sea of lies and miscommunication. If this is your problem, you can do something about it. And it's not as hard as you think—read on!

## Whatever the Reason, You Can Turn It Around

If you want to rescue your love life and reestablish connection, you have to start sharing. Opening up your hearts together is what intimacy is all about. As we said earlier, to *know* your mate is the essence of love. Here are some tips on how to reestablish your connection.

STOP LYING. Lying may seem too obvious to mention, but it's a prevalent dumb attitude that we'd better address. If you are outright lying to your spouse, you can't expect to have intimacy. So come clean about the things you are lying about. Your partner will probably find out anyway, but you need to do this even if they won't. One couple I (Henry) worked with fought for twenty years over his not being honest about their finances. She would always find out, of course, and each time, she felt betrayed. Yet he continued to do it. Finally, he realized something. She was going to be angry either way—whether he lied or told the truth. He might as well be truthful and let her vent over that instead of trying to protect her (and himself) by lying.

Their relationship turned around when he got up the guts to stop lying, and was upfront with her about the bad news. He also had to work up the guts to patiently endure her reaction—the anger and disappointment regarding the financial bind. He learned that her finding out about bad financial news was a lot better than her finding out about a lie about bad financial news. Countless spouses have told me that they wish they could just have the truth, no matter how bad it is, instead of the lies. I have never heard anyone say the opposite. Relationships and trust are built on truth.

STOP FUDGING. Most people don't lie outright. They just fudge the truth a little bit to keep the peace or to not make things worse. What does that mean? It means saying things like:

· "Oh, no, I'm fine. Nothing's wrong."
· "No, it doesn't matter to me. Whatever you want is OK."
· "No, I am not angry. It's OK. Really."
· "No, that didn't bother me. Not at all."

For the sake of keeping the peace and togetherness, people fudge on how they really feel and what they really think. As a result, they lose both peace and togetherness. Honesty means not sugarcoating it, but telling it to each other like it is.

BE DIRECT. People who establish intimacy with each other communicate directly. They do not beat around the bush about what they want and feel. Great passion is created when desires, feelings, wants, and the like are communicated directly to each other. Learn to say:

| | |
|---|---|
| · "I want . . ." | · "I feel . . ." |
| · "I think . . ." | · "I hate . . ." |
| · "I don't like it when . . ." | · "I like . . ." |
| · "I don't want . . ." | · "I prefer . . ." |

Learn the power of "I" statements. People who use "I" statements when talking about themselves are far better understood than those who say things like, "Well, you know, you start to feel alone when the person you love doesn't ever call to see how you are doing." Instead, the direct person says, "I don't like it when you are gone for long periods and don't call. I start to feel alone. I want you to call me." Such statements draw the other person in, as they are direct expressions from the heart.

FACE YOUR FEARS. If you are not direct and honest with your partner, then you are probably afraid of something. This fear needs to be addressed if it is in the relationship itself. But if you have your own fears about being direct and honest that show up in your communication with other people as well, your fear is contaminating your relationship. You cannot blame your mate for that.

The principle in the Bible is to take the plank out of your own eye first, and then you will see clearly enough to fix the connection (Luke 6:42). Face your fears, and be truthful with your partner. When you do that, you may even find that you have solved the problem and that your mate is much more able to handle the truth than you had guessed.

SAY MORE WITH LESS. One woman I counseled was having trouble connecting with her boyfriend, causing him to stall in committing to her. I gave her an assignment I like to give to many people: "Say whatever you want to say in one-third the number of words." She was beating around the bush, getting so lost in gobbledygook that her real expression of what she wanted and was feeling was lost. When she began to cut down her words, she became much more connecting and drew him into the relationship more instead of distancing him and overwhelming him. They ended up married and happy. She learned to just say, "I think . . ." or, "I want . . ." Finally, a connection was possible.

LET YOUR MATE HAVE HER OWN REACTION. Many people do not tell the truth because they, like the husband who lied about finances, are afraid of their mate's reaction. You cannot control her reaction, and you are not responsible for it. There are a lot of things that you can do to respond to it, but you cannot allow your fear of her reaction turn you into a liar. There will be no trust or intimacy if you do. Intimacy comes from the risk of telling the truth and allowing your mate to respond.

ADDRESS THE REASONS YOU CAN'T TALK. Sometimes a relationship can't handle honesty. It is like medical cases in which doctors can't do the proper surgery to cure the patient because it would kill the patient. There is often not enough grace in a relationship to face the truth. If that is the case, then address that issue so your relationship can get to the place where honesty can happen. I have also seen relationships in which the issue was not grace, but timing. Sometimes one must wait until the proper time to share something really painful—when the environment is right and the spouse is ready to hear. Waiting until the proper time is a strategic move to strengthen the relationship first.

In most situations, though, the issue of honesty doesn't threaten the entire relationship. More likely, this issue causes fights and disconnects the partners from each other. If that is your issue, talk about why you can't talk. Discuss what happens both in the relationship and inside you when you are direct and honest with each other. Listen to your mate, and try to understand why honesty is hard for him. Look for things that are making honesty impossible, like judgment, defensiveness, contempt, disgust, shaming, anger, reactivity, shutdowns, disengagement, or blame. Address the ways that the two of you respond. Begin with the question, "What do I do to make it hard for you to be honest with me?" Then listen to what you hear.

MAKE THE PROBLEM THE PROBLEM, NOT THE PERSON. Most disconnects could be prevented if couples would just learn one principle: *talk about the issue instead of smearing the character and personhood of your partner in the process.* When you are honest with your partner, be specific. Many frustrated wives, addressing the problem of a husband who does not call when he's working late, tend to say something like this: "You're so selfish and irresponsible. You think I like sitting here all night waiting for you? You don't think of anyone except yourself." That is not a direct, honest statement about what the problem is and how it affects you. And it will cause your connection to shut down. A more honest approach is to be specific and direct: "I need for you to call me when you are going to work late. It helps me plan to use the time and not worry." Addressing a specific problem in concise language conveys helpful information to make your relationship work better.

## To Know and Be Known

Aloneness, dissatisfaction, temptation, and financial struggle are all just part of life. Good relationships can handle them. In fact, research shows that the best relationships are the ones where couples go *toward each other with the most difficult things.*

Good relationships process things continually, almost as a way of being, not as an extra task. The communication is ongoing, similar to a DSL Internet connection as opposed to the slower dial-up system. Couples who practice good communication don't occasionally check in or have a talk. They are talking and checking in with each other all the time.

**A Lifeline:** IN GOOD RELATIONSHIPS, TALKING IS HONEST AND FREE OF HEDGING, HIDING FEELINGS, OR NUANCES. THESE COUPLES LIVE THE TRUTH OF SOLOMON: "AN HONEST ANSWER IS LIKE A KISS ON THE LIPS" (PROVERBS 24:26). WHEN COUPLES DO THAT, THEY FIND THAT THE KISSES ON THE LIPS TEND TO BE A LOT BETTER TOO!

## Choose to Face Reality

Christy and Brian were out to lunch with their kids, and all was going well until their four-year-old, Sophie, began to climb all over the place, getting on Brian's nerves. Christy corrected Sophie a few times, so Brian remained patient, choosing to let her handle the problem. However, he found himself getting more and more annoyed, not just at Sophie, but also at Christy for not enforcing her correction. She just kept saying, "Sophie, sit still and eat," but did nothing about it when Sophie started moving again. Soon Christy's failure to follow through on her discipline was bothering Brian much more than Sophie's behavior.

He scowled at his wife and said, "Do something!"

"Why don't *you* do something!" she snapped. "You always expect me to handle it."

"Always expect you to handle it? Are you joking?" Brian shot back. "You don't handle it. You let her get away with everything. Our kids are totally out of control. Every time I step in, you just let them run to you and get pampered, and they totally ignore me. You make me the bad guy, then they don't want anything to do with me. That's why I asked you to do something about it, so they would finally have to listen to you. You are a total pushover, and the kids don't even listen to you."

"Don't just put it all on me," Christy came back harshly. "I have them all day long, then you just come in, lay down some law, and criticize me when I don't fulfill it. And you don't even offer to help. You make me feel like the 'bad parent.' If you want them to have a consequence, then do it yourself."

Brian stepped in and took Sophie outside the restaurant for a time-out, to which she protested with tears. When she came back to the table, she ran to Mom's lap for comfort. Brian looked at Christy and shook his head, as if to say, *Any questions?* Christy disconnected from his disapproving stare and began interacting with the other children. Brian was quiet throughout the rest of the meal, feeling hopeless about this issue getting resolved. But past that, something worse was happening.

He felt that the connection between Christy and himself was broken, and that made him sad. He felt as if they could not discuss issues. He and Christy could be connected when they were having fun or doing things together, like projects around the house. They talked well about things of interest and had an active social life. But when there was a real *issue,* then there was almost always a disconnect.

Brian attributed this disconnect to Christy's "defensiveness." He felt as if he couldn't bring anything up without her reacting, and it was a long, silent drive home. Christy felt as alone as he did. The sad thing was that before the conflict, they were feeling close to one another and having a great time as a family. What happened? Was there a dumb attitude here on the part of either of them? One that could have sunk their love life?

## The Need for Both Love and Reality

Christy and Brian were feeling very loving and together before the incident, but behind that lurked a reality problem. The reality was the kids needed discipline, and Brian felt he was being made the bad guy whenever he disciplined the kids. That was true, and it was a very *real* problem—a reality that was undermining a lot of the love they shared. It had bothered Brian for some time, but *he felt like that issue and others could not be discussed without a major disconnect following.*

Another reality was bothering Christy. She felt that Brian criticized her and expected her to do the discipline all by herself. She saw him as wanting to remain uninvolved in the nitty-gritty of raising kids and then just swoop in and tell her what to do. She thought that his attitude was unfair and that he was asking her to do all the dirty work.

Brian's motivation, however, was quite different from what Christy imagined. He actually felt true sympathy for her in having to deal with out-of-control kids and wanted to help. But he did not want to do all the discipline himself because he was concerned that the kids were developing a classic "good parent–bad parent" split. He knew that they needed to obey her as well as him in order to grow up secure. That was a real problem. If they could have talked about this issue without all the hurt, she might have seen the validity of his objective and helped him achieve it.

So what was going on here? Exactly what a million couples experience every day: *the problem of facing reality and maintaining love while they do it.*

What causes so many people to lose their connection is that when they focus on loving each other, they do not face the harder realities they need to deal with. Another reason people lose their connection is that, when they do face life's hard realties, they don't do it in a loving way. They do it with contempt, anger, guilt, shame, condemnation, a critical spirit, blame, put-downs, sarcasm, indirectness, and a host of other ways that break the connection. They think that experiencing love and dealing with reality are mutually exclusive. But we all know that the experience of love begins to break down when certain realities are not dealt with in a relationship. Couples must have a way to face reality and maintain love at the same time.

### Grace and Truth: The Absence of Judgment

The Bible's solution to combining love and reality is to speak the truth in love (Ephesians 4:15). Doing so combines both grace and truth. Grace means favor, and truth is what is—reality. This means that a couple must face the realities that they need to face, but with an attitude that keeps the other person in a position of favor. Grace is the opposite of judgment. While judgment is *against* the other person, grace is *for* her.

That means when Brian brings up the problem he sees in Christy, he does it in a way that assures her that he is not against her, but for her. He does it in a way that lets her know he is on her side and not her adversary. Speaking the truth in love means that he does it without judgment, hurtful anger, put-downs, outbursts of rage, shame, sarcasm, or condemnation. Instead, he does it with love.

What this approach does, in psychological jargon, is "neutralize" the reality. The problem is no longer packed with negative emotion. It is just a reality that needs to be addressed for the betterment of the connection or for life itself.

In Brian and Christy's relationship, the discipline problem was an issue to solve, not a connection breaker. It was not really about them and their love for each other, but just a child-rearing reality to negotiate. But because of the way it was communicated, the issue turned into something about their relationship instead of about the kids. *The communication itself became the problem.*

To neutralize the reality would be to do the opposite: to state it in ways that are loving. Then the problem remains the problem, and the couple remains a team, focused on solving it. Otherwise the original problem is no longer the problem, and the disconnect between the couple becomes the issue. They are no longer a team, but adversaries, each feeling hurt by the other.

The attitude necessary to maintain the connection is one of facing reality and communicating the issue in love, with care and regard for the other person. As Paul says, "Do not let any unwholesome talk come out of your mouths, but only what is helpful for building others up according to their needs, that it may benefit those who listen. . . . Get rid of all bitterness, rage and anger, brawling and slander, along with every form of malice. Be kind and compassionate to one another" (Ephesians 4:29, 31–32).

Watch how you talk to each other when facing tough realities. Be honest with yourself. Is it with anger? Malice? Sarcasm? Condemnation? A critical spirit? Or is it done in a way that is "helpful for building others up according to their needs, that it may benefit those who listen"?

Think about how things could have gone had Brian spoken to Christy in that way. She would have felt grace from him, an affirmation that he was *for* her and trying to meet her needs. It might have sounded like this: "It looks like you are feeling alone in disciplining our kids. Let's figure out a good way to do this. I want to help you, and I also want them to see the limits as coming from both of us. Let's talk about how to do that."

It may be that it couldn't be done right there at that moment in the restaurant. Often the situation is one where timing prevents even the most gracious statements from being heard in the spirit they are offered. A mate may feel so overwhelmed at the moment that any comment feels like criticism or a put-down. At those times, grace may require waiting until emotions subside. But when the time is right, move to connect with grace first, then talk about the tough reality. Here are some tips.

AFFIRM YOUR SPOUSE FIRST. "I love you, and I want this to be better for us. Let's take a look at this problem and see what we can do to make it better."

LISTEN TO YOUR SPOUSE'S PERSPECTIVE BEFORE GIVING YOURS. Seek to understand before seeking to be understood. You could say, "Tell me what this is like for you. I want to make sure I understand your side of things."

LISTEN TO YOUR OWN EMOTION IN WHAT YOU ARE SAYING. Are you angry? Are you talking down to your partner? Do you show contempt or disgust? Are you shaming? Are you trying to make him or her feel guilty? Remember, those kinds of dumb attitudes are going to diminish the value of what you are saying and probably keep you from being heard at all. All your partner will hear is the tone, not the words.

AFFIRM THE ISSUE THAT YOU ARE TALKING ABOUT AS AN IMPORTANT PART OF YOUR RELATIONSHIP. What if Brian had said, "I love parenting with you as my partner. I love being a team. Let's think of how we can solve this thing together"? Christy could have seen the reality they faced as being part of a good thing that has meaning for the relationship, not just a problem between them.

TAKE A TIME-OUT. If your emotions keep you from saying what needs to be said in a loving way, take a time-out. Then come back to it when you are more in control of how you are communicating. When you are emotionally aroused, a different part of your brain is in control, and it is urging you to fight or flee. It is looking for ways to preserve and protect you, not ways to resolve issues and draw close to someone else.

DON'T USE DISTANCING LANGUAGE. Stay away from parental language, such as "you should," and from judging language, such as "you always," or "you never." Those phrases do not communicate that you are on your partner's side.

KEEP THE GOAL IN MIND. Your goal is not merely to look at the reality, but to preserve the connection above all else.

LISTEN AND TAKE IN YOUR MATE'S PERSPECTIVE. You do not have the corner on reality. To assimilate and accommodate your spouse's perspective is a huge way of showing your favor and getting a larger grasp on reality at the same time. To remain cut off from your partner's perspective limits favor and shuts you off from a part of reality.

If Brian and Christy had done these things, their lunch might have had a better ending, and the rest of their connection would be better as well. They could have a productive problem-solving session around the reality of disciplining the children, and both could have felt loved and cared for in the process.

**A Lifeline:** LOVE AND REALITY CAN—AND MUST—GO TOGETHER TO PRESERVE YOUR CONNECTION, AND ACTING ON THE EIGHT TIPS FOR CONNECTING FIRST WITH GRACE CAN HELP.

# Are You Saying What You Really Mean?

"If you don't know where you're going, you'll probably get there." Ever heard that? Knowing what we are trying to accomplish before we take steps just makes common sense. Otherwise, we are at best wasting time, and at worst working against ourselves.

When you think about it, a lot of couples would be closer if they just kept their mouths shut. It seems that with each word they say, they move further apart. Often, when I (Henry) am listening to couples as a counselor, I find myself wondering, *What in the world were you trying to accomplish when you said that?* Marriage counselors can see months of work go instantly down the drain because of something one partner says.

Our words have a lot of power. They can bring healing or destruction. Listen, for example, to James as he warns us of the power of the tongue:

> *The tongue is a small part of the body, but it makes great boasts. Consider what a great forest is set on fire by a small spark. The tongue also is a fire, a world of evil among the parts of the body. It corrupts the whole person, sets the whole course of his life on fire, and is itself set on fire by hell. . . . No man can tame the tongue. It is a restless evil, full of deadly poison (James 3:5–7, 8).*

Those are pretty strong words about the power of words. But it's not all bad, for as Solomon says, good things come from words as well: "The tongue has the power of life and death" (Proverbs 18:21). There can be tasty fruit from lovers talking together and growing closer, if they use the power of the tongue to give life.

The overall message is clear: when couples open their mouths, *something* happens, for better or worse. For that reason, it is important when thinking about talking to your spouse to—as business management expert Stephen Covey puts it—begin with the end in mind. Weigh each word carefully for its ultimate effect on the outcome. What are you trying to accomplish when you say that?

If you want to be understood, then you have to choose words and tones that will bring you that result. If words creep in that cause your spouse to resist or become defensive or hostile, some deeper agenda may have affected your communication. A little self-examination is helpful here. You might have to admit that you really have a different goal, like punishing your spouse for past failures. That is not going to help.

With that in mind, here are a few tips that will increase the likelihood of your being understood by your mate.

## Seek Connection, Not Alienation

Simply put, whatever you must talk about, seek maintaining the connection as the highest goal. So think before you speak. Will what you are going to say accomplish that goal? Will it make your mate see that she is loved and cared about? Or will it somehow drive her away? Stop before you talk and ask yourself what the end result is likely to be if you say what you're thinking. One good test is to remember what happened the last time you said it. Did you like that outcome? Remember, "He who guards his mouth and his tongue keeps himself from calamity" (Proverbs 21:23).

## Seek to Be Known

At the heart of relationship is the concept of being known. God uses that language often. He wants us to know him. In fact, the word *know* communicates such intimacy that the Bible's word for "having sex" comes from the word meaning "to know." That is probably why the word *intercourse* is used both for communicating with words and communicating with sex.

KNOW WHAT YOU FEEL AND WANT. To make yourself known means you must first know yourself—what you feel, think, want, desire, fear, or want to communicate. And that's not always easy.

It is incredible how much we talk without saying what we really feel. I (Henry) remember counseling Sharon and Tony. Sharon was angry with Tony for his irresponsibility. She was upset about how he handled the finances, and she was letting him have it.

"I can't depend on you for anything!" she said. "Every time I think things are OK, I find out that you haven't paid something, and we are in trouble again. And I don't even know it. I feel like I'm standing on quicksand." Her anger and contempt were strong, and you could see him moving away, becoming more alienated.

"That's ridiculous," Tony shot back. "I take care of everything, and then when one little thing goes wrong, you get mad. See what I mean, Dr. Cloud? This is what it's like to live with her. She is just mad all the time. I am sick of being judged and condemned for every little thing. Nothing makes her happy."

"Oh, give me a break," Sharon said. "I would be happy if I knew that the lights were not going to get turned off because you forgot to pay the bill. Is that too much to ask, Mr. Responsible?" You could see Tony's face getting redder by the moment.

"Stop it!" I interrupted. "Sharon, what are you feeling about this?"

"What do you mean, 'What do I feel?' Obviously I hate it. I hate living like this."

"But, past that, under that, besides anger, what do you feel?" I pushed.

At first she resisted and tried to give me more anger. But as I kept pushing her, finally it came out. She broke down and began sobbing, and then shaking. Tony was shocked, and his anger went away. He leaned toward her filled with concern, his whole body language changing.

"What is it?" I asked. At first she didn't respond, but slowly the words came out.

"I'm so scared," she said. "I'm so scared."

"Why? What are you afraid of?" I asked.

"I don't know . . . I just don't know . . ."

"Is it like when you were little and your mother would get sick?" I asked.

That was the key, and Sharon cried even harder. When she was growing up, her mother was a very undependable manic-depressive. Sometimes her mother was OK, but then at other times she turned the house into a chaotic nightmare. The entire structure of the family would fall apart, as her father was an alcoholic who was sometimes available and sometimes not. There was nowhere Sharon could turn for security and dependability.

The reason she got so upset with Tony was that when he was not dependable, all the old fears that she felt as a child would rise up and close in on her. She would react with rage at him, but the rage was not what she really felt. It was a cover, a defense against being known at her most vulnerable level, her fear. She was afraid of being alone with no one to care for her, and that was what her reactions were about.

Tony didn't know that at all. When he understood Sharon's feelings, everything changed. He was tender toward her, not at all angry. "I never knew my missing a bill made you feel that way," he said. And his behavior changed, as he became able to *know* her and truly understand how his behavior affected her. He did not want to hurt her, but he had never really understood that he did. He just had seen anger, not hurt or fear or vulnerability. She had never shown him those things deep inside that allowed herself to be known.

If you are going to be understood, you have to ask yourself, or get your mate to help by asking you, "What are you really feeling? What do you really want? Is it really more money to spend? Or more time at the basketball court? Or is it really something deeper, like more respect, or freedom, or feeling like you are not controlled? What do you really want your mate to know about you?"

If Sharon had known her own vulnerability and communicated that to Tony instead of blame, disgust, and contempt, he would have had something to connect with. It would have avoided a thousand screaming matches over the years and enabled them to heal each other at a deeper level. If she had said that she felt afraid that no one cared about her and she needed him to be there for her like her mother wasn't, chances are very good that he would have responded well. But when she just got angry, he never knew. He never understood. Learn from Sharon's negative example. Know what you really feel, and communicate it in ways that are not critical of your mate. Say those things. Your vulnerability is key.

It is good to bring up those things your spouse is doing that aggravate your vulnerability. But communicate them from the point of view of your vulnerability—how what he does makes you feel—not as judgment against him. The first way engenders empathy, but the second just drives your mate away.

OBSERVE YOURSELF. Another thing that keeps mates from being known is that they speak, yell, fight, or react without first knowing what's really punching their buttons. They don't monitor what they think or say; they just let their words fly without asking themselves what is really going on.

It's basic human nature to carry feelings inside from other times and places. Your mate may say something a little harsh or insensitive, but it feels like she said, "You idiot. You never do anything right." Regardless of what she really said, you know what she meant. So you have a reaction appropriate to your feelings. You are ready to defend yourself—either by fight, flight, or joining her in her opinion that you are worthless.

But while your reaction might be appropriate to what you felt, it is misplaced. It is not appropriate to what was said or meant. Your reaction is appropriate for some injury that happened to you in another time and place, perhaps caused by your family of origin or some past relationships, but not for now. Couples who do well together recognize those misplaced feelings, suspend their reactions, and monitor themselves. They don't react with rage or move away, but they do acknowledge that what prompts their feelings is coming from somewhere else, and they communicate that to each other.

Whatever has occurred in the past to spur that surge of feelings is in fact real, even if the reaction was more than what was called for. So talk with each other about it. "I feel like you don't think I do anything right, like I'm stupid. I know that's not what you said, but it's how I feel. Help me." More often than not, what comes back is "Oh, no! I wasn't saying that at all. I just wanted you to know that I wish you had remembered to pick up my shirt. I needed it for that meeting tomorrow. I'm sorry you felt that." These shared vulnerabilities help the couple move closer to each other.

The sad thing is that many couples, like Sharon and Tony, genuinely care for each another, but they just can't get to the care because *what needs to be cared about is never expressed.* The hurt is not owned by the person feeling it; instead, it is expressed in hidden overreactions.

When you feel strong negative reactions to your lover, stop. Count to twenty. Listen to your internal dialogues. Take a time-out. Research has shown that taking a moment to calm down, talk to yourself, and listen to yourself before you react is a huge key in improving communication. Doing so hooks different parts of the brain than those that are having those strong feelings. A moment of reflection helps you see your mate for who he really is and understand what he really meant to say.

GET RID OF THE THINGS THAT GET IN THE WAY OF BEING KNOWN. Do you want to be known? You want your mate to really understand? Then you have to take responsibility for the things you are doing that contribute to that not happening. You are human, so you have a tendency to hide what you are really thinking and feeling.

Don't get defensive or feel bad about this tendency. Yes, it's a dumb thing to do, but we come by it honestly, as everyone since Adam and Eve has done it. We cover our vulnerable selves, so we will be loved and approved of, desired and wanted. The paradox is that the very act of covering up keeps that from happening. Our defenses that are supposed to protect us from alienation and rejection ensure those very things.

What is the answer? The Bible puts it this way: "Each of you must put off falsehood and speak truthfully to his neighbor" (Ephesians 4:25). *Falsehood* means deception, and we humans create deceptions so well. We cover our feelings with smiles or independence or withdrawal. We cover our vulnerability with anger, our fear with pride and control. We cover our shame with performance and seeking admiration. We cover our inferiority with looking for approval from others. And we cover our pain by acting like we are OK when we are not.

If you want to be understood, then "put off falsehood." Stop acting in ways that cover up what you are really feeling. If you have any doubts about what those are, common ones include silence, withdrawal, overactivity, anger, argumentativeness, indirectness, sarcasm, nitpicking, blaming, meanness, bitterness, and jealousy.

You will have your own ways of hiding feelings that we did not mention here. Ask your mate to tell you the ways you hide your true feelings and the ways your defenses get in the way of being known. My bet is that he can tell you, for none of us hides as well as we think we do.

## The Guiding Principle

When you want to be understood, let this question be your guide: "Is what I am doing getting me closer to being known or farther away?" If you learn to ask this each time you feel a negative reaction, then you will bite your tongue before you unleash that angry statement on your mate. This question will force you to face your true goal of the moment, which is, as your anger shows, to make him feel bad. But when you get honest, you will realize that this is self-defeating behavior.

The good purpose for communicating is to make yourself known. That builds love. But there are some bad purposes of communicating that you must forsake. Assess what you say and do, and see if your deeper purpose is to:

· Make your mate feel bad, stupid, or guilty
· Off-load anger, tension, or stress
· Let him know how bad you hurt by hurting him
· Make yourself be seen as right
· Alienate her and make her feel alone
· Dominate or control your mate in order to feel in control
· Throw off responsibility to him in order to feel free from control
· Blame her so you won't feel bad or wrong
· Hide your real feelings, hurt, pain, or fear
· Hide your failures

If your response to your mate is intended to achieve any of these purposes, it may cause you to feel good for the moment, but in the long run it will work against the connection. Always consider that the "long run" may come sooner than you think. It doesn't usually take very long for responses like these to alienate a mate further. We have never seen anyone drawn into greater intimacy by any of these methods.

**A Lifeline:** AS YOU COMMUNICATE WITH YOUR SPOUSE, BEGIN WITH THE END IN MIND. WHEN YOU SPEAK OR ACT IN RESPONSE TO YOUR MATE, DO YOU WANT TO BE KNOWN AND UNDERSTOOD? BEING KNOWN AND UNDERSTOOD IS THE FOUNDATION OF CREATING LOVE, INTIMACY, AND CONNECTION.

## There's More to Listening than Hearing

"I feel like we aren't connecting," Sheila said to Wade. "I feel kind of alone."

"What do you mean 'alone'?" Wade answered. "We've been together all weekend! I haven't even left the house. You're not alone!"

"I don't mean that we haven't been spending time together. I mean I just don't feel like we have been close. It's more like we've just been hanging out, even doing things, but not really talking. I know we've been together and talking about a lot of stuff, but that's not what I mean. I mean really feeling connected," she explained.

"That's not true. We have spent every moment together since I got off on Friday. Of course we're connected. I've been right here with you the whole time," he retorted.

"Yeah, OK," she said. "You're right. We have been together. It's been great to have the time."

But inside, it wasn't so great for Sheila. She was shutting down, and her heart was sinking. She did not feel what she wanted to feel with Wade, which was a sense togetherness that time together should produce. Hope was fading into detachment and disconnection. She was slowly unplugging.

I (Henry) asked Wade why he didn't listen to her.

"I did listen," he responded. "I heard what she said. She said that she felt like we weren't connected and like she was alone. But she wasn't alone. I was *with* her for two whole days. I was trying to get her to see that she wasn't alone like she felt. What's her problem? It makes me feel like nothing I do is good enough. Like it won't make her happy. I mean, I could have been fishing all weekend, but I chose to spend the time with her and she doesn't even appreciate it."

Now *my* heart was sinking. As I listened to Wade, I felt exactly the same way Sheila did. *Even though he could tell me what she had said, he did not listen.* Thinking that you are listening just by hearing the words is another dumb attitude that can sink your love life. It is one of the biggest causes of disconnection, and if it's your problem, you've got to master it in order to reestablish your connection. In this section, we'll show you how to listen and not just hear.

## The Truth About Listening

Wade did not get the real meaning of what Sheila was saying. It was not a question of whether he intellectually understood the content of her words. That is only the beginning of listening. That is just receiving the information. Listening takes more than getting information, and that is what I told Wade. When I did, he made the second classic error.

"I know that listening is more than just getting information," he said. "It is also really understanding what the person is saying. I really understood what she was saying. She felt alone. I got it. I totally got it." He beamed a little as if he thought he was Mr. Empathetic Husband.

"No," I said. "Understanding is not listening either. Understanding is something you can do totally in your own head. It does not require any more connection on your part. But listening is more than just getting the information and understanding it. You can understand, and the other person may still say, 'He didn't hear me.' Listening has occurred only when the other person *understands that you understand.*

"And that is not happening with you and Sheila. She does not feel like you understand. In fact, you prove to her that you do not understand when you tell her that what she is saying is wrong and that there is no reason for her to feel that way. So, obviously, you do not understand."

"Well, what do you want me to do? Agree with her? I can't agree that she is alone. She's not. That's nuts."

"I did not say that you had to agree with her. We aren't talking about *you,* remember? We are not talking about how you feel or even what you think about what she feels. We are talking about what *she feels.* You just proved that you have difficulty understanding what she feels and thinks apart from what you feel and think. That's the problem. You have to let her know that you understand to the point that *she understands that you understand;* to the point that she really feels that you understand—not agree necessarily, but understand and care."

Sheila was now looking up with a hopeful expression. For the first time, she felt that someone knew what she was trying to say to Wade.

"How do I make her understand that I understand?" Wade asked.

"Like this: 'Gosh, Sheila, that's awful. We've been hanging out all this time, and you still feel alone . . . that's terrible. Even worse than if you had actually been alone."

Sheila nodded. "That's right," she said. "That is how I feel."

"Wade, who cares about anything else right now except that?" I asked. "Who cares about how she *should* feel, or whether or not you could have gone fishing? The only thing important is that she feels all alone. How does that make you feel?"

"Well, horrible," he said. "I don't want her to feel alone. I love her."

"OK, tell her that."

He turned to her a little sheepish about having to give what seemed to him a contrived performance, but I was serious. I could see that he cared, and I wanted him to be able to convey that to her. They needed this, badly.

"I hate that thought, Sheila. I never want you to feel all alone. That is an awful feeling. What can I do?" he said.

Sheila began to cry a little, and then she said, "You just did it."

He looked at me, a little puzzled, and I nodded. "She's right. You just did it. You made it clear that you understand, and now she understands that you understand. Worry about fixing the situation later. For now, this is what she has been needing from you," I said. "How do you feel, Sheila?"

"Better. Much less hopeless," she replied.

## Empathy Is the Key

The key to connecting with each other is empathy, *the ability to identify with someone else's experience, feelings, and thoughts.* The focus is on the other person and on communicating to the other person that you feel what she feels.

When Wade communicated that Sheila's feeling of loneliness was horrible, that he never wanted her to feel that way, and that he wanted to do something about it, he showed empathy. He showed that he was sensitive to her pain and was able to experience what it was like to be her for a moment. At that point, she felt understood and connected.

To empathize with your partner is to validate her experience. That doesn't meant that you agree with it or that it is right. It just means that you see that her experience is real. You recognize the truth that she feels that way. You say, "I see. What I did made you feel really hurt." You are not admitting to being a bad person or even admitting guilt for whatever caused the pain. You are just validating that the hurt is real and that you experience it with her and care for her.

## When Empathy Is Absent

The opposite of validation is *invalidation*, which means to discount, or treat as not real or not true, what the other person is thinking, feeling, or experiencing. Wade had invalidated Sheila's feelings. "That's not true," he had said. "You aren't alone." Even if he was trying to make her feel better, he just made her more distant by failing to understand.

It seems men do this a lot. In their attempt to make their wives feel better, they make them feel worse. They often want to solve the problem instead of just listen and understand. Research has shown that people, especially men, begin to feel overwhelmed, criticized, and sometimes fearful when their mate expresses her feelings. As a result, they will do anything to make her feelings go away so their own fear is dispelled.

Often when a woman speaks of a negative feeling or experience, the man takes it as a criticism or failure on his part. He may feel that she is about to abandon him, that she thinks he is inadequate, does not approve of him, and has come to like someone else better. As a result, he mobilizes his defenses, which causes him to quit listening. He wants to make all his fears go away, so he refutes her claim, and in the process says the most unhelpful things possible—like Wade did:

· "That's not true."
· "No, you don't feel that way."
· "You totally misunderstood."
· "That's crazy."
· "It's not that bad, really."
· "There's nothing to be afraid of."

Or worse, he might get defensive and go beyond trying to change what she is feeling—he might start attacking her. "Oh, really? Well you aren't always so easy to be around yourself, Miss Moody. You think this is a picnic for me?" His hurtful words certainly aren't going to help the situation, but in the moment, he is only thinking about getting the heat off of himself.

In reality, there is no heat on him. There is an opportunity for him to shine and get closer to the one he loves. If he will just listen without defending himself or devaluing her experience, she will feel heard. And most of the time, she will say something like what Sheila said: "I feel better."

And lest you men are thinking I am on your case, women do this as well, and they have their own ways of being defensive. It just seems that men (and there is research to back this up) do get mobilized to be defensive more quickly than women when hearing her express negative feelings. Who knows why? But if this is true of you, then by all means, learn to "get it." And women, if you do the same thing, then you need to get it also. Failure to listen will keep you from getting the connection you want in your love life, and all the defensiveness in the world will only defend something not worth holding on to, whether it's pride, ego, independence, old patterns, or whatever.

## Learn to Listen

Give up your defensiveness and pride, and learn to listen to your mate. Here are a few tips.

FOCUS. Look your partner in the eyes and give all of your attention. Observe your tendency to get out of the connection.

MONITOR YOUR THOUGHTS. As your partner speaks, are you listening or thinking of your response? Are you evaluating what he is saying? Stop that and just allow what your mate is feeling to sink in—to become your experience. Try to get inside his experience and feel what it is like to be him at that moment. Ask yourself how you would feel if you were in his shoes.

RESPOND NONVERBALLY. Are you nodding or saying "hmm," or something to let her know you are tracking? Let her know you are with her and truly listening.

WATCH YOUR DEFENSIVENESS. If you are feeling defensive, by all means, do not say anything. Count to twenty. If you need a time-out, take one and go away until you cool off. Do not defend yourself or counterattack.

EMPATHIZE. Communicate back what you have heard: "So, Sheila, you really feel by yourself, even when I am here. Wow." Use the formula: *content plus feelings equals being understood.* In other words, repeat back to your mate her content and what you understand her feeling to be:

· "With all the work you have to do, it's really feeling overwhelming."
· "So the way the kids act when I'm not here is just too much sometimes."
· "Yeah, I see. When I have to work a lot, you begin to feel that you don't matter to me as much as my job."
· "So when I am too tired for sex, you feel that I don't really desire you."
· "So when I want sex and we haven't really talked, you feel kind of used."
· "It's like so much is being asked of you that you just want to hide, or run."
· "That's awful. I don't want you to be in a place like that."

CHECK IT OUT. Ask your mate what you do that keeps her from feeling listened to. Check it out in the moment and ask, "Do you feel that I am hearing you?"

DON'T TRY TO FIX IT. Avoid advice, explaining, or trying immediately to make the feelings go away. There will be time for that. Connect first just through hearing.

DON'T MAKE IT ABOUT YOU. Don't answer with something about yourself. Listening is about the other person. "Oh, I know how you feel. The other day when my boss did that . . ." At this moment, who cares what your boss did? This is about the other person, not you.

## Connection Equals Being Known

As we have said, reconnecting with each other involves your hearts being known. And there is no way to be known if you are not listening to each other. Remember, "He who answers before listening, that is his folly and his shame" (Proverbs 18:13). And "The purposes of a man's heart are deep waters, but a man of understanding draws them out" (Proverbs 20:5).

**A Lifeline:** THE MORE YOU LISTEN AND DRAW OUT THOSE DEEP WATERS FROM YOUR LOVER, THE MORE YOU WILL KNOW EACH OTHER AND REESTABLISH THE CONNECTION AND LOVE LIFE YOU DESIRE.

## Common Communication Stoppers

When Wade (in the previous section) described his response to Sheila, my heart sank. I (Henry) had now experienced firsthand his failure to listen to her, and I felt the same kind of despair that she felt when trying to communicate to him. In an instant, he said something that made connecting absolutely impossible. It's as if we were building a bridge, and right in the middle of the process he dynamited everything.

As a marriage counselor, I only experience that kind of shutdown a fraction of the amount of times that it actually happens. Sadly, the couple lives with this kind of experience every day, and over time the experience drives them both to experience increasing loneliness. It is as if two people are caught in their own prison cells, both trying to send messages through the bars for the other to come and let them out. But the message never makes it through. They remain in their respective cells, even when there is great love and desire to be with the other.

While no one ever communicates perfectly, some do it much worse than others. They perpetually say things that not only do not help but make things even worse. It's a dumb thing to do, of course, but many do it without realizing what they're doing, and certainly without realizing there is a better way. But there is.

## Find and Fix Your Communication Stoppers

You've seen some of the following items elsewhere in this book, but the list below is a guide for what *not* to do when trying to connect with your mate. Learn them well—and learn to catch yourself *before* you do them. If you can avoid these communication stoppers, you will be way ahead in the journey toward reconnecting with each other. And you will go far in rescuing your love life.

When you find your behaviors in this list, make a covenant with yourself that you will do everything possible to avoid doing these things ever again. It's really that simple. To the extent that you have these issues running rampant in your relationship, you are doing harm to the very thing you want most: connecting with your mate. So do all you can to keep these dumb attitudes from sinking your love life.

DON'T DEVALUE WHAT YOUR MATE SAYS, NO MATTER WHAT YOU THINK OF IT. When your mate says something, take it seriously. Remember, it seems true to him, no matter how true it is in reality. That does not mean that you can't disagree or clarify. But to immediately say, "That's not true," or, "That's ridiculous," communicates nothing to help you connect. Treat your partner with respect. Really listen; don't just hear the words. Show that you are not there to criticize what he says but to understand it.

DON'T MINIMIZE IT. When your spouse feels something strongly or thinks something is significant, do not minimize it. Hearing you say, "Oh, it's not that bad" or, "It doesn't hurt that bad" shuts down her hope that you care about how things feel to her and that she has a chance of getting you to understand. Even if you do not see the problem as being as big as she does, that is not the issue at that moment. The issue is that it is big to her, and that is where her heart is. If you expect to find her heart, you have to connect with that feeling, not try to shut it down.

DON'T GET DEFENSIVE. Defensiveness is when you try to fight off anything that makes you feel bad. Anger, pouting, reactions to avoid what feels like an attack—all serve to shut the other person down. When you try to defend yourself, you communicate to the other person that you are closed and not willing to hear anything about your behavior. Excuses, explanations, justifications, and similar moves are intended to do away with the message—and when you do away with the message, you do away with the person as well. So listen to your partner, take in what he says, and embrace it. Doing so means that because you love your mate, you are more willing to hear than to defend yourself.

DON'T CRITICIZE OR PUT DOWN YOUR MATE. Complaints voiced in a critical spirit do not solve problems like constructive feedback does. Such criticism puts the other person down and makes him feel bad about himself. It finds wrong in everything, and it tends to become more of a pattern rather than something that is done when necessary to address a particular issue. Avoid faultfinding when it's done for no good reason. When you do have good reason, say what must be said in a way that is not a put-down or character assassination.

DON'T OVERREACT OR ESCALATE. The more emotional certain topics are, the more reactive and defensive we tend to get. The reaction takes different forms. Some people shut down, move away, or fight, while others tend to lose connection, rationality, and judgment. When you feel yourself overreacting, chances are that nothing good is going to come from what you are about to say. So tell yourself to take a time-out and calm down.

Learn your reaction patterns so you will know when the pressure gets to a place where you are not responding but reacting and overreacting. What do you see in yourself that tells you that you have crossed the line? Is it a feeling? Is it a certain behavior? Whatever it is, learn to recognize your reaction; and when it happens, stop and say, "I don't think I am being helpful right now. I need to take a time-out until I can talk about this in a better way." If you don't stop overreacting, you will have two problems. First, the problem that you started with and did not resolve; and second, your overreaction has caused new damage.

AVOID "SHUTDOWN" STATEMENTS AND BEHAVIORS. Shutdown statements are things that you say when you are mad, hurt, or overwhelmed that totally stop the communication. They are the interpersonal equivalent of slamming the door in someone's face. People say them when they want to stop talking, and they leave the other person feeling that something is really wrong and unresolved. Here are some examples of statements and behaviors that shut down communication:

- "Fine" (when it's not fine).
- "Nothing" (when it's something).
- "It doesn't matter" (when it does).
- "I can't do anything right."
- Silent treatment
- Walking away

DON'T SHIFT THE BLAME. When God confronted Adam with his behavior, Adam quickly shifted the blame to his wife: "It was the woman you gave me" (Genesis 3:12 NLT). Every couple has been doing that ever since. Shifting the blame means explaining away responsibility for your own behavior as being caused by your mate's behavior.

For example, the husband says, "It seems like you are a little harsh tonight. It doesn't feel good." His wife responds, "Well, that's because you aren't doing anything to help. You just come home and expect everything to be done for you. Maybe if you would lift a finger once in a while, I wouldn't be that way."

What has happened here? He has tried to tell her that she has hurt his feelings, and she blames him for it. So the one who is hurt becomes the perpetrator, and the one doing the hurting has become the innocent victim. She would not have been harsh, according to her, if he had done his share of the work. She is not denying her behavior, but she justifies it as being "because of him." Not true.

She could have chosen lots of other ways to respond besides being harsh. She could have talked to her husband about the problem, asked for his help, communicated her frustration kindly and directly, or any number of other options. His behavior might have bugged her, but how she handled it is not his fault. Responding to feedback with a counteraccusation always stops the connection.

AVOID SARCASM. Sarcasm communicates only disdain and lack of respect. Besides killing whatever message was intended, sarcasm hurts, closes down hearts, and turns things in the wrong direction.

AVOID EXTREMES AND GLOBAL STATEMENTS. Extreme statements do not communicate reality. They may communicate a feeling, but they do not communicate the real problem. When a mate says, "You always do this," it is rarely true. The times that she was responsible, or on time, or didn't spend too much, or was sensitive are not included. Such statements are neither true nor helpful; they just leave the other person judged and feeling bad. "You never show me that you love me" usually means, "I want you to do a particular thing, and you are not doing it." But the person on the receiving end is certain that he or she shows love in many ways, so the statement does not address the real issue. In fact, extreme statements are dumb things to say because they cut the partners off from what really is happening.

Don't immediately jump to your perspective. "I feel like we don't have enough time together," she says. "I wish that we could spend more time like we used to, taking walks, and just hanging out."

"Well, you don't understand all the pressure that I am under at work," he says. "I mean, my new division chief is on my back every day with e-mails and new things to do. It seems like it just won't ever end. Each time the phone rings, it feels like I have a new project coming. I am really under the gun."

Where is she to go with that? Have they connected? Think of how she feels at that moment. Do you think she feels closer or more connected or understood? Not likely. As soon as she expressed what she felt and wanted, he jumped to his perspective and what life was like for him. He left behind what she was feeling and moved ahead to himself.

Certainly conversation is give and take, back and forth. But some people do not connect with the other person's experience. They take a comment as the signal to talk about their side of things only. The other person is just left hanging.

Compare the conversation above with this one. "I feel like we don't have enough time together," she says. "I wish that we could spend more time like we used to, taking walks, and just hanging out."

"I know. It's hard right now, isn't it?" he responds. "You need more from me than you are getting, huh?"

Can't you see her softening and opening up even more about what she is experiencing? No doubt this response makes her feel more connected and understood than the previous one. They have not solved the problem, and nothing is different in the situation, but they are connected because he has heard her. Certainly, if they continue to talk, they will get to his side of things—that his work is taking more time from them. The difference in the second response is that he joined her in her experience first and did not immediately begin talking about himself.

DON'T TRY TO FIX IT. Most of the time, a problem that involves feelings can't be fixed until the feelings are heard and understood. Other times, the problem doesn't need to be fixed, just heard and understood. What if, in the above example, the husband said, "OK, how about we go for a walk tomorrow?" He might feel like he has solved the concern, but she does not feel connected. He's just putting a patch on her complaint. With the better response above, she feels like he has heard her and is with her. More often than not, once someone feels heard and understood, there is not much left to solve— or if there is, it is pretty easy to figure out. She needs him to listen to her and how she feels much more than she needs him to offer a solution. Solving this problem is pretty simple. Just shut up and listen.

DON'T GO "ALL BAD." One of the most infuriating things that people do in communication is to play the "all-bad victim." This happens when they take feedback as criticism and defend themselves by playing the victim.

"I feel like we don't have enough time together," she says. "I wish that we could spend more time like we used to, taking walks, and just hanging out."

"See, nothing I do is good enough for you," he retorts. "I can't please you no matter what I do. I can't help it if I have to work. I give you all the time I can, and nothing is good enough. I can't do anything right. I'm just the 'bad husband.'"

Where can she go with that? She was reaching out to invite him to find her heart, and he goes "all bad" and acts like he's the victim of her insatiable requests. That leaves her alone with her feelings and disconnected with nowhere to go. Now she probably feels that she should rescue him from his victim stance, so she says, "No, you're not the bad husband. I know you try. You try really hard, and I appreciate that." But when she does that, she and her feelings have been totally negated and forgotten. It has shifted back to taking care of him, and her needs are disregarded.

## Look at Your Communication Stoppers

We all have things that get in the way of communication. You can go a long way toward rescuing your love life if you find out what your personal communication stoppers are. Ask each other and talk about the way it feels when you do those things. Do not defend why you do them. Just listen to how it makes your mate feel.

Enlist each other's help to watch for these twelve communication stoppers. Make it a project. Make up a signal, if necessary, by which one can tell the other when it is happening.

**A Lifeline:** THE MORE YOU CAN STOP THE THINGS THAT STOP YOUR COMMUNICATING, THE MORE YOU WILL BE ABLE TO FIND EACH OTHER'S HEART, PRESERVING OR REESTABLISHING THE CONNECTION.

# DUMB ATTITUDE #6

## "My Lover and I Should Never Fight"

Conflict is normal in love. It is not a relationship-ender; it is part of love. You need to know this, because it is true. In fact, *good conflict enhances a good love life.* Are we kidding? No. This may not make sense, at least on the surface. But be open, and press on.

Sometimes couples have the impression that conflict is the main problem in their relationship. "If we could just stop fighting, we can get back the closeness we both want," they will say. It is true that some fighting can be quite destructive and love-destroying. Yet most of the time, conflict is not the problem. *The issue is the way that couples disagree and argue.* We are going to show you how to avoid the dumb ways to have conflicts, and how to do it in a way that helps. Because you *will* argue. You *will* disagree. You *will* have differences of opinion. If you don't, one of you is not necessary.

More than that, however, this section will provide you with tips and help on how to use conflict to enhance love, intimacy, and passion. Couples who know how to disagree in ways that redeem, heal, and connect find that they are closer and more loving.

So don't be dumb and continue to avoid conflict. Learn instead how to rescue your love life through the right types of conflict.

## Fighting for a Win-Win Solution

Bruce and Kris looked at each other in amazement. "We did it!" Kris exclaimed, and they high-fived each other. I (John) said, "Way to go, guys."

The couple wasn't celebrating making a great financial investment or running a marathon together. They were happy about something even more important: they had their first successful fight. By "successful," I mean that they argued over an issue, resolved it, and still felt connected to each other. This time it was over dinnertime. Bruce was often late from work, and Kris wanted dinner to be earlier. It sounds like a minor issue, but I had been through many of these issues with them, small and large, and they had always gone nuclear—until today.

That's why Bruce and Kris had come to see me. She felt alienated from Bruce because she couldn't bring up any problems to him without him becoming defensive and blasting her. On her end, Kris would disconnect from Bruce, leaving him feeling lost. The problems never got resolved; and on a deeper level, the alienation was starting to jeopardize their love.

When I told them that my goal was for them to be being able to argue and still stay attached, they thought I was crazy. They couldn't imagine that after the anger and the coldness. But they worked hard, using the tips we'll share in this chapter, and they were finally successful. Learning to fight successfully takes a little effort, but it yields a very high return on your investment.

## Why Fight Anyway?

Couples who know how to fight right will love right. Healthy arguments are an important part of connection, reconnection, and passion. After all, at its healthy core, fighting is about love. It is an attempt to resolve differences so that love can return or grow. When people fight, they are defining themselves so that two distinct people can be close and yet keep their distinctness. A fight is a vigorous way to solve the problem of two people disagreeing while wanting to remain connected.

Ironically, a benefit of good fighting is that it can lead to passion and romance. Fighting clarifies the definitions of the two people. He becomes aware that she is not an extension of himself and has her own thoughts and feelings, and vice versa. This awareness creates a healthy space between the two lovers. That space is necessary to create passion, longing, and desire. Like chemicals need their space in a test tube to interact and become volatile, two people can't become excited about each other if they are not sure who is who.

There are many kinds of fights. Some are about preferences (movies and restaurants). Some are about values (honesty and faithfulness). Some are about communication ("I never said I thought you looked fat in that dress"). Some are about our own issues (baggage from the past). No matter what sparks the fight, you need a way to address these and any other disagreements you might have.

## Keep the Goal in Mind

Couples who fight well keep the goal in mind: connection. It's all about your love life and about the relationship. It's not about fixing, being right, or proving wrong. Certainly you must focus on the problems themselves, but that is not the ultimate goal. *What is important is not the problem; it is how the problem affects the relationship.* It distances the two of you. It works against the connection.

This is easy to miss in the heat of the argument. Fighting can bring out the three-year-old in us, and it can easily escalate to power plays and revenge. But you must begin and end with the goal in mind: *This is about our relationship. This is about having a better connection.*

In the heat of a fight, beware of the need to get things off your chest. We all need a little catharsis now and then, but realize that this may work better in a subsequent conversation with your lover in order to keep the present fight from needing too much damage control. Some relationships can do well with this kind of unloading, and others can't. Sometimes people need somewhere else to blow off steam so that they can keep the relational goal in mind.

## Be Direct and Specific

Good fighters are direct and specific. When you are direct, you give your partner someone to talk to. Being indirect causes distance and anxiety. The other partner knows something is wrong but has nowhere to go with it, because his indirect partner is being evasive. So he either gets really mad or shuts down.

When you are specific, your partner knows exactly what you are seeing as the problem and, hopefully, what steps are required to change things. Many fights center on vague charges, such as, "You do the wrong things and don't do the right things." Where can you go with that?

If your husband isn't doing his share with the kids after work, tell him that: "I don't think you are doing your share with the kids after work." That gives him somewhere to go. Tying criticism to the relationship is key. "When you disappear on the Internet, I feel really alone and disconnected from you. It's not good for me or for us." Then follow up with, "Go ahead and take a few minutes to unwind. But I really need you with me and with the kids as soon as you're done." Now you are being direct and specific.

## Keep It Two-Way

Good fighting is much more than conveying your feelings and requests. It is a dialogue between two people. Don't get caught in thinking that if you say your piece, it's all done. Most likely, your lover has his own realities and emotions about the situation, and he needs equal time. Only after he has his say can you solve the problem. If you fail to make it a conversation, things will only end up with alienation or escalation.

As a couple, learn to keep the conversation two-way. Each of you should become as concerned about hearing the other's viewpoint as you are about being heard. For starters, get used to saying, "When I am done I want to know what you think, because I want this to be about the two of us. And then we need to come up with a solution together."

## Have a Structure

Ever notice how some of your fights are often the same fight over and over again? Each of you knows what the other will say. That is a signal that the issue has not been resolved. It needs to be resolved for good if possible, and that will require some structure. Here are four examples.

TRAFFIC COP. When discussion involves a lot of diverting, missing the point, blaming, defensiveness, and moving into separate issues, one of you needs to be the traffic cop. Stop the flow for a moment and say, "We're losing focus here. This is about our relationship and getting in a better place. I brought up your temper because it cuts me off, and I get scared of you. I need to get back to that so we can get it resolved."

TIME LIMITS. The fight shouldn't get in the way of life, activities, and schedules, unless it is some sort of a crisis. Sometimes the disagreement seems to be the only reality for one of the partners, and she feels she must go into every nuance and detail of the situation—which is seldom necessary. If the discussion is not moving forward, set a time limit. Having a time parameter will often help you stay focused and more mindful that you have a goal to reach.

AGREE BEFOREHAND ON ESCALATION. If one of you doesn't tend to stay in control but gets extremely loud, raging, or even violent, agree beforehand that escalation isn't all right and will not be tolerated. Determine what you will do when that happens so that both of you are aware. You might say, "If you go beyond normal anger to yelling and cursing at me, I will end this and walk out. We'll address this at some other time." If your partner has a real problem with escalation, you may have to follow through with this several times, sometimes with the help of others, to ensure that you require a certain level of self-control on your mate's part.

DON'T AVOID ALL ANGER. Relationships have passion, and anger is part of passion. But pay attention to the degree and tone of anger. The degree should not be so great that it distances or scares your partner. (If one of you is afraid of anger in general, however, that's an individual problem that needs its own work.) The anger should also be "clean" in tone. That is, it should not be sarcastic, vengeful, or "guiltifying." It should be appropriate to the matter at hand. When the issue is dealt with, the anger it sparked should go away. If it does not, something else is going on inside the person that needs to be dealt with.

## Normalize Fighting

Normalize your arguments by taking the fear and power out of them. Couples who become anxious and avoidant about fighting either will not solve their problems or will have enormous blowups when they do argue. It is not uncommon for couples in love to have some sort of disagreement every day, ranging from what time dinner was to how much someone spent. These disagreements don't have to be a big deal, but they will be if you try to avoid them.

When you and your partner are not fighting, refer to your fights as a part of your life together: "Remember that trip we took to the river? It was the day after that fight we had about your mother's visit." And when you are fighting, talk about it in the "now": "Look, I know we're both mad right now, but I want you to know that I love you and I want us to be safe with each other." These sorts of things help integrate love, truth, reality, and passion into the connection.

**A Lifeline:** ABOVE ALL, REMEMBER THAT FIGHTING IS NOT DONE FOR ITS OWN SAKE. FIGHTING IS FOR THE SAKE OF LOVE, RELATIONSHIP, AND CONNECTION. ANY ARGUMENT SHOULD BEND ITS KNEE TO LOVE.

## The Fatal Flaw in Fairness

Life is not fair. Neither are relationships. Deal with it.

I don't mean for this to sound cold. But it is true, and it is important, especially if you want to forge passion and connection out of conflict in your love life. The reality is basically this: *if you demand fairness, you stand to ruin your love life.*

At first blush, this seems logically upside down. Shouldn't we be fair with each other? Isn't that what give and take is about? If I don't require fair treatment, won't I receive bad treatment? To answer these concerns, let's look at what a demand for fair treatment really means and go from there.

What is fairness? In relationships, it means that each partner should receive to the degree that he gives to the connection. In a marriage relationship, the thinking would go something like this: *I have been kind and loving to my lover. He has not reciprocated. Therefore, I am justified in withdrawing my kindness and love from him, for I am not receiving fair treatment.*

## Fairness and Connections

The truth is, this principle works in business and tasks, but not in connections. Connections are not meant to be based on fairness, and here is why.

THE FOUNDATION OF INTIMACY IS ATTACHMENT, NOT PERFORMANCE. Relationships are established on closeness, vulnerability, and love. But when someone takes the stance that he will give no more than he receives, the entire foundation has been shifted to performance. Now he is in the relationship for what he can get, and he won't give until he gets that. Love has to take second place.

For example, suppose that your lover has been neglectful of you. She's been immersed in her friends and her activities. You're feeling somewhat unappreciated. With the fairness doctrine of relationship, you have every right in turn to drop the ball: disconnect from her, hang out with your friends, and engage in your own activities. That is technically a fair thing to do.

Then play out the scenario. Your lover feels the disconnect. That hurts her feelings, so she disconnects more. So do you. As this continues, there is very little relationship left between you and your partner, and the connection is in trouble.

Relationships based on performance and fairness can't work. There is not enough love and grace to hold things together. Watch how a five-year-old gets angry with her friends, then takes her ball and goes home. She has her ball, and she doesn't have her friends. But she feels that fairness has been accomplished.

It is far better to base the relationship on love and attachment rather than fairness. Forget fairness; opt for humility. Say to your partner, "I am really feeling left out of your life, and I'm lonely. What's going on? Am I doing something to bug you? Can we get back on track with each other?" Humility and fairness don't get along, but humility and love do just fine together.

FAIRNESS IS ANTI-LOVE. Fairness is *giving to get*, a concept that has no place in love. Scorekeeping is just a way to make sure you'll get yours back, which reveals the intent that you were in it for yourself in the first place. Giving to get will never result in the love you need. Ask yourself how you would feel if your partner said, "I'll spend time being close to you and connecting to you, if you'll pay me." You don't even want to think that your connection has any similarity to that sort of scenario, so get out of the fairness game.

Couples who give more than they get tend to receive more too. The practices of grace, patience, and sacrifice are planted in each other's hearts and minds, and each knows that he or she is special and valuable to the other. And that, in turn, generates more love in a way that fairness never could.

FAIRNESS DISTORTS REALITY. Living by the fairness ledger doesn't work because we have a tendency to distort the ledger the way a funhouse mirror distorts our reflection. Fairness distorts reality. We tend to minimize the ways we fail our lover and maximize how she fails us. So even when we are on the fairness system, we inadvertently cheat and skew the results. Better by far to forget the whole fairness thing and move on to love.

GOD IS NOT "FAIR." Look at how God models His relationship with us. When we see how we have treated ourselves, each other, our world, and God, do we really want fairness? It would be our worst nightmare! Fairness from God would mean reaping everything we have sown in life, and nobody in his or her right mind would want to experience that scenario. (Of course God is ultimately fair and just, but He does not insist that we be perfect in order to receive His love.)

One of the most profound and comforting realities of life is that God "does not treat us as our sins deserve or repay us according to our iniquities" (Psalm 103:10). Theologically, God accomplished ultimate fairness by Christ's death for us; the innocent was substituted for the guilty for mercy's sake. Our response is to love Him back. In the same way, when you let go of insisting that your lover play fair, you are extending that sort of mercy to her. And that will increase her capacity to love you.

## How to Transcend Fairness

It's easy to be trapped in a five-year-old's "But that's not fair!" mentality. Here are some ways to grow beyond it and into true love and connection:

TALK ABOUT NEED INSTEAD. When you have a conflict or a problem in the relationship, agree together that instead of keeping score of who's being the better partner, you discuss need. Here are a few examples:

- Instead of saying, "I am nicer to you than you are to me," say, "I need more kindness from you."
- Instead of saying, "I am the one who always solves the problems and keeps things going; you never do," say, "I need more help in running things, I am feeling overwhelmed and alone without your help."
- Instead of saying, "I asked you about how your day was every night last week, and you only asked me once," say, "I really need more initiative from you in asking me about my life and how I'm feeling."

AGREE THAT YOU WILL GIVE TO GIVE, NOT GIVE TO GET. Get the issue out on the table, and admit that sometimes you are kind or attentive in hopes that the scorecard will qualify you for treatment in kind. That kind of behavior is very common, and there is no shame in it; just deal with it. Tell each other, "I am going to love you because I love you, not so that you will love me. If you catch me keeping score, you have the right to bust me for it."

SOLVE PROBLEMS IN TERMS OF DISTANCE, HURT, AND RESPONSIBILITY, NOT FAIRNESS. Having said all this, you will most likely still have to solve problems where one partner is not shouldering her load in the relationship. She may not be connecting, taking ownership of problems, or caring enough. These issues need to be addressed, but stay away from crying, "Not fair!" Instead, discuss the issues in terms of distance, hurt, and responsibility:

- "When you got so mad at me and yelled, it cut me off from you inside, and I went far away from you."
- "What you did really hurt my feelings, and I need for you to own what happened."
- "You are not taking responsibility for the finances, and it's getting really hard for me. I need some changes."

These are direct, accurate statements, and they lend themselves to solutions for conflicts. They also keep you out of the scorecard.

WHEN YOU RECEIVE MERCY, GIVE LOVE AND GRATITUDE. Couples who get out of the demand for fair play enter the world of grace, mercy, and true love. Realizing that your lover no longer has you on the ledger and is treating you with kindness simply because he loves you will help open your heart to him.

Follow that openness and give your vulnerability, your heart, and your passion to him. Being loved for ourselves—experiencing authentic love, with no strings attached, the way it was designed and intended by God—frees us, heals us, and brings us closer together in a way that most of us can hardly imagine.

**A Lifeline:** STORE THE FAIRNESS LEDGER SOMEWHERE ON THE SHELF SO YOU CAN TAKE IT DOWN SOMEDAY AND REMINISCE ABOUT IT JUST FOR GRINS.

## Love Is Eternal When Forgiveness Never Ends

Most new couples, whether newly dating or newlyweds, seem to have a certain blind spot in their relationship. They are, for the most part, keenly aware of their love and feelings for each other, and they are actively pursuing their goals and dreams for the relationship.

When I (John) ask them, "How did you meet?" they get a little giddy and tell me their story. When I ask, "What do you like about the other person?" they fall all over themselves with praise for their partner. But the blind spot pops up when I ask another question: "How do you guys forgive when one of you hurts the other?" They look at me and cock their heads like my dogs do when they don't know what I am talking about (which is often).

Couples come by this blind spot honestly. Most of us learned about forgiveness as part of religion, not as part of relationships. So we don't really have a place for it in our connection. But we must make a place for it, because forgiveness establishes a principle that's key to keeping our love life afloat: *your ability to connect and reconnect will depend largely on your ability to forgive each other.* In other words, good lovers are good forgivers, and vice versa.

### The Debt

Simply put, forgiveness is when you *cancel a debt.* It is a legal word. It first assumes that one person has hurt another, and there is a debt to be paid. That is what the law is all about. A crime is punished in order to achieve justice and vindicate innocent people. But forgiveness takes justice in another direction. Though there is a justifiable debt to be paid, with forgiveness *the penalty is cancelled.* There is no punishment. The guilty go free.

Strictly speaking, forgiveness flies in the face of justice. Innocent people should go free, and guilty people should pay a fine, go to jail, or be punished in some way. But forgiveness transcends all that. It says, "Let him go." It gives a person another chance at life and growth. And nowhere is that more clearly illustrated than at the Cross.

Forgiveness is the foundation of the Christian faith. We all have missed the mark, the Bible says. We all owe a debt—one that we cannot pay in full. That predicament is what moved a just and fair God to send His Son to die for our sins, the just for the unjust: "This is love: not that we loved God, but that he loved us and sent his Son as an atoning sacrifice for our sins" (1 John 4:10).

Why go through all this law and theology in a book on rescuing relationships? Because *forgiveness is the only hope any connection has to grow and flourish in intimacy.*

There are only two ways to relate to each other: through the law and through forgiveness. No third alternative exists. When one of you is selfish, irresponsible, or hurtful, you can choose one of these two paths. The first path is to extract an eye for an eye, insisting that a debt must be paid. In relationships, this means partners keep a scorecard of hurts and transgressions. They withdraw love and empathy until the other person has paid the price. They stay disconnected until they have gotten justice, revenge, or both. And no relationship can sustain that amount of law. The connection goes away, and the relationship often just dies.

Forgiveness, the other path, is the only hope. When one partner incurs the debt, the other feels the pain and knows she has been wronged. *But she lets go of her right to demand justice.* She lets the prisoner go free, so to speak.

## The Benefits

If we stopped here, we would not have made a strong case for a couple to learn forgiveness. It just doesn't seem right, fair, or healthy. But there are strong benefits in building this capacity into your love life. Let's take a look at them.

BOTH PARTNERS GET ANOTHER CHANCE. Think about the times you have not been the lover you should have been. Perhaps you snapped at your partner, or maybe you were controlling. Think about how you would like to be handled. Do you want to receive the law, or do you want a chance to be reconnected, loved, and reconciled?

It's natural for us to want our partner to receive law and for us to receive forgiveness. But what is natural is not always what is good. You can't have it both ways. Healthy couples realize that they both will fail each other and that they both need to be forgiven—often.

GRACE WINS. Your relationship must be fueled by love and grace. When you live in forgiveness with each other, you both experience grace. When you and your mate learn to forgive, you are off the performance track, you are not being judged or condemned, and you are *for* each other and the relationship. Forgiveness unlocks the grace you both need to keep the connection alive.

Couples who forgive well know how deeply they both need the grace that comes from forgiveness, and because they receive it from each other, they are secure in the relationship.

THE FORGIVER IS FREE. Many people have a hard time forgiving, because it seems like the hurtful partner gets off scot-free, and the hurt one is left with the pain. But that is not the way it is at all. *When you do not forgive, the hurt still owns you.* You are not free. The hurt controls you.

I (John) can think of times in my life in which I was slow to forgive. I brooded. I withdrew. Thoughts, emotions, and memories of the hurt filled my mind. The incidents controlled my conversations with others. This is not a picture of freedom; it is a prison.

When you cancel your partner's debt, you are free to move ahead and live your life. Forgiveness is a benefit to the wounded party.

FORGIVENESS BRINGS GRATITUDE. When you tell your partner, "I forgive you for what you did," you are bringing him a tremendous gift. You are lifting a burden of condemnation from him. In healthy people, this results in a deep and profound sense of gratitude.

I (John) was working with a couple once, and the husband had been very controlling with his wife. It hurt her deeply, and they began drifting apart. He didn't really think he had done anything to cause it. But over time, and with a lot of confrontation from me and from others, he finally saw what he had done to her.

When he saw the problem though his wife's eyes and understood the hurt he had caused her, he broke. He felt horrible and remorseful. He cried and asked her if she could ever forgive him. The wife said, "Of course I do. All I ever wanted was to get this solved and for us to be in love again." I cannot tell you how grateful he was for the second chance she gave him.

YOU CAN BE REAL. Couples who forgive don't have to hide their faults from each other, fearing rejection. They are secure enough in the forgiveness to know that they will make it through. So they are real, authentic, and honest with each other. Why hide when you don't have to?

## Blast Through the Obstacles

Forgiveness is always the right thing to do, but it's not often easy. It does get easier over time as the couple experiences the benefits, but you will need to blast through a couple of obstacles to get to the good stuff. Here they are.

EQUATING FORGIVENESS WITH RECONCILIATION. Sometimes, people think that once they have forgiven their partner, they are now reconciled and close again, almost as if nothing had happened. But often the hurtful behavior is still ongoing or has not been dealt with.

This is a common error. Forgiveness and reconciliation are not the same. Forgiveness is your obligation to cancel the debt, as your own debt has been cancelled by God: "Be kind and compassionate to one another, forgiving each other, just as in Christ God forgave you" (Ephesians 4:32). It takes only one person to forgive, but it takes two people to reconcile. If your partner is still being hurtful or is not showing necessary attitude changes, you aren't reconciled. Keep confronting and dealing with the problem today, but let go of the past debt.

HOLDING ON TO UNFORGIVENESS TO MAINTAIN DISTANCE. Sometimes a partner will not forgive because he is afraid he will get too close to his mate too soon and be hurt again. So anger and distance prevails. This is a normal reaction, and it has to do with how our need for contact and love can put us in vulnerable positions.

Fortunately, there are solutions to this problem. There are ways to stay safe other than withholding forgiveness. Setting healthy boundaries and limits is one. Learn how to guard your heart and your vulnerability with good boundaries while engaging in forgiveness.

For example, you might say, "Ron, I don't hold your temper against you anymore. I know I have resented and judged you for it, and I am sorry about that. I forgive you, and I hope you will forgive me. At the same time, it's not OK for me to receive it from you anymore either. So the next time you start yelling or cursing, I will either leave the room or the house. I hope you will work on this, and I would like to help." This keeps you in control of your life, while not having to live in the misery of withheld forgiveness.

INCREASING DEFICITS IN GRACE. Sometimes a partner will try to forgive, but the debt keeps reemerging in the form of angry feelings, protesting the injustice, recurring thoughts, memories, or dreams.

Sometimes this is due to a lack of sufficient grace resource inside the hurt partner. It takes a lot of love, comfort, and grace to let go of our resentment and anger over wrongs. And if we are alone, isolated, or disconnected from good relationships, the time needed to let go is extended. Get good and safe people around you, and let them in. Allow yourself to receive the grace you need to let go of the debt. Grace comes from the outside and transforms us so that we can forgive.

## Become a Forgiving Couple

Here are some ways to add the awesome power of forgiveness to your love life.

AGREE ON THE REALITY. At some point you need, as a couple, to agree that you are both going to fail each other all through your relationship. (For some of you, this will not be a hard thing to admit!) Agreeing on the reality of failure sets the stage for the need of forgiveness.

TALK ABOUT WHAT YOU WANT AND NEED. People need different things from their partners regarding forgiveness. One may say, "I just want you to admit it and not excuse it." Another may say, "I just want to know you aren't holding it over my head." This dialogue helps you see what needs to happen in your relationship so that both of you can experience the benefits of forgiveness.

PRACTICE RECEIVING AND GIVING FORGIVENESS. Swallow your pride. "Would you please forgive me for . . ." and "I forgive you for . . ." need to be part of your normal vocabulary. It just doesn't work to assume, *Well, she knows what I mean.* She doesn't, and we all know what assuming makes out of us! Using the words, facing each other eyeball to eyeball, brings home the reality of our transgressions and the depth of forgiveness.

HAVE A "NO-WAITING" POLICY. When you have a problem, go to the other person as soon as it is realistic and get the forgiveness ball rolling. *Do not* wait for your partner to come to you with an apology. Always take the initiative, whether you are the hurter or the hurtee. It doesn't matter who goes first; it only matters that you start the process. (However, if there is a pattern of passivity in one person, that should be confronted as its own issue.)

GO ALL THE WAY. When you forgive, *really forgive*. Cancel the debt and let it go. Don't hold on to the offense and bring it up later as ammunition in another argument. Grieve it, feel your sadness, and say good-bye to the right to punish.

We're not saying that you should never bring up or talk about the issue requiring forgiveness. You may have to talk about someone's behavior, selfishness, or irresponsibility if it is an ongoing problem. That is how problems are resolved. But talk about it as a problem to be addressed, not as a blame from the past.

**A Lifeline:** MAKE FORGIVENESS A PART OF YOUR WORLD IN THE SAME WAY FISH EXPERIENCE WATER: IT'S SO MUCH AROUND THEM THAT THEY DON'T EVEN KNOW THEY ARE WET. MAKE FORGIVENESS A LIFESTYLE FOR YOUR LOVE LIFE. FORGIVENESS WILL KEEP YOUR LOVE LIFE FROM SINKING.

## Humility Is a Door, Not a Doormat

I (John) love how television sitcoms teach us about love and relationship, especially about handling conflict. My favorite is a theme that I have seen a thousand times. It goes like this: One person does something that upsets his partner. Then the other does something to get him back. They blow up at each other and go to their friends, saying, "I don't know what I ever saw in him." Then, before thirty minutes are up, somehow they manage to reconnect and become close again—until the next episode.

These shows can be entertaining, but they often display a problem that many couples face: *a failure to understand the value of humility.* You can usually see pretty toxic levels of self-righteousness and pride infecting sitcom connections. In real life, however, when couples learn how much they receive when they exercise humility, things can transform quickly from alienation to intimacy.

### The Misunderstood Trait

Humility doesn't get a good spin in our culture. But, properly understood, it really opens up things in a connection. Basically, humility is *the capacity to experience the reality of who you are.* A humble person is one who has no grandiose illusions of herself in either direction—good or bad, strong or weak. Humility affects several main areas of love relationships.

HUMILITY RECOGNIZES YOUR NEED FOR YOUR LOVER. When we toss aside our natural pride and self-sufficiency, underneath it is need for your lover. That is, rather than saying, "I don't know what I ever saw in him," a humble partner says, "We aren't doing well right now. I don't feel close to you with this problem. But I know that I still need you and I need our relationship. So I want to work on this."

Of course that is difficult to say and think. It makes you vulnerable. It makes you accessible. And it doesn't allow you to hide behind a wall of strength and disconnection. But *humility is the key to the resolution of not only conflicts in love, but also the love relationship itself,* because love is about allowing the other person to get inside you. It doesn't work any other way.

We are not saying that if the other person is going to hurt you or wound you, you should allow it. You should not. You are the guardian of your own heart, and protecting it is the right thing to do. Some relationships need to be very structure- and protection-based in order to keep things safe. As the Bible teaches, "Above all else, guard your heart, for it is the wellspring of life" (Proverbs 4:23).

Ideally, you won't have to worry too much, if at all, about self-protection. In that case you can embrace the value of humility: it keeps you in touch with your need as a pathway back to love.

HUMILITY ACCEPTS YOUR INABILITY TO CHANGE OR CONTROL YOUR LOVER. Remember that humility is about admitting reality. And one of the toughest realities is that you really have no ability to change or control your lover. You cannot:

· Make her love you
· Force him to see your point of view
· Cause her to stop a troublesome attitude or behavior
· Make him see you the way you think you really are
· Force her to want to be close to you

Relationships are rescued only when both lovers are free and have choices. Love cannot exist without freedom. The relationship becomes just a fear-based compliance with no real connection. When you are humble, you understand that you simply can't remove your partner's choice, no matter how much you would like her to see things your way. Couples who have this sort of humility know that they are only bound to each other by love, not by fear.

This does not mean that you cannot or should not influence your partner. That is part of being in love. You were designed to be a force for God, for love and for growth with your partner. So absolutely be an influence with him. Say what you want and need. Be an example. Be strong and direct. But *do not attempt to control*. Be as protective of your lover's freedom as you are of your own.

HUMILITY RECOGNIZES YOUR OWN IMPERFECTIONS.

Humble people don't pretend to be someone they are not. They admit and confess their weaknesses and failures to their partner.

A relationship is like a plant in a garden. The soil has to be healthy, or the plant can't be healthy. The soil of your connection is that both of you have the humility to own the things you don't like about yourself *but that are nonetheless real*, with each other. That is the only way love and growth can occur. If you hide your bad parts or pretend they are not there, *you are not present in the relationship*. Your body is there, but you are not in the room. Humility ensures that you both "show up."

HUMILITY ALLOWS YOU TO SHOW HURT WITHOUT RETAL- IATING. Remember the conflict resolution played out in the sitcom? "When your lover bugs you, bug him back." The problem is, this approach doesn't bring resolution, love, or connection.

When we act in humility, we don't give back what we receive; we give back better than we receive. As the apostle Paul once wrote, "Do not be overcome by evil, but overcome evil with good" (Romans 12:21). It is certainly natural to withdraw love when you are with- drawn from, to blame when you are blamed, to blow up when you are being controlled. *But that natural response is its own reward.* If all you want is to know that you paid someone back in kind, then when you've done it, you should be satisfied. Most people want something much stronger and deeper than revenge and payback however. They want love. And humility paves the way to love.

Being hurt by your lover is never a good thing. The person you love can hurt you the deepest; we all know that. The best response, however, is not to lash back or retaliate, but to show your hurt to your partner. Tell him, "When you dismissed my feelings about our sex life, it really hurt me." Or, "When you made fun of me at the party in front of our friends, it really hurt my feelings."

The humble approach cuts out the pride and payback issues, and it gets right into the real issue: one partner has hurt the other. Instead of having to defend himself and deflect your anger, he sees what he has done to someone he loves. He looks into your eyes and is face to face with the hurt he alone has caused. His empathy, compassion, and remorse are activated, because it is safe to do so.

Humility brings about the best result because it doesn't play the fairness card. It plays the love and reality cards, which trump everything else in making a connection and rescuing love.

## How to Create Humility in Your Love Connection

Here are some ways to build good and healthy humility into your relationship so that you can keep your conflicts constructive.

AFFIRM THAT YOU DO NEED EACH OTHER, EVEN IN CONFLICT. Practice saying these words out loud: "I need you, and I love you. Even when we are fighting, the need doesn't go away. And I want to resolve our conflicts so that it's easier to be safe with my need for you." Yes, you are taking a risk by showing your partner that he can hurt you because of your need.

In a way, this display of your need is a test of character. If your partner uses your humility against you and deliberately hurts you with it, you must stop everything immediately and insist that the problem be addressed, possibly by a competent therapist. Do not go further until this has been dealt with directly. Empathy should rule.

REVEAL YOUR FEARS TO EACH OTHER. Why have you not been as humble as you needed to be? Why have you been proud or self-sufficient? Have you been afraid of rejection, being put down, controlled, or disrespected?

Tell each other about these fears, and reassure each other that you don't want to be the cause of them. Give each other grace and safety so that humility can emerge, along with the real person.

ADMIT YOUR FLAWS BEFORE YOUR PARTNER BRINGS THEM UP. One of the greatest signs of a healthy couple is that neither partner waits to be caught or confronted on an issue. He brings it up himself, because he doesn't want it to get in the way of the love, because he wants the issue resolved, and because the relationship is safe enough to do so.

Commit yourself to taking the first step: "Honey, I overspent; here's the credit-card statement. I screwed up, and let's deal with that." "Honey, I got too mad at you over your staying at work too late again. That was my fault, not yours. I want to not do that again."

Remember that humility is about embracing what is true and real about you. If you have been together for any significant amount of time, it is not likely that the admissions are any surprise to your lover. Rather, you are bringing into the relationship what you both know to be true, so that you can deal with it.

CELEBRATE HUMILITY AND CONFRONT PRIDE. Couples with humility have no toleration for the false, arrogant, grandiose self. They confront it in each other and work on growing past it. At the same time, when one of you admits need, limitation, or faults, throw a party. Humility should draw you closer together and into the deeper aspects of each other's hearts and souls.

In relationships, as in the law of economics, there is no such thing as a free lunch. You can't have it both ways. It's either pride or humility. Pride feels good for a short while, but eventually it isolates you.

**A Lifeline:** MAKE HUMILITY THE EXPECTATION AND PRIDE THE ABERRATION IN YOUR LOVE RELATIONSHIP. HUMILITY MELTS THINGS DOWN INSIDE SO THAT LOVE CAN FLOW FREELY. YES, HUMILITY IS A HARD PILL TO SWALLOW IN THE SHORT TERM, BUT IT BRINGS UNBELIEVABLE RESULTS IN THE LONG TERM. LIVE IN REALITY, ADMIT REALITY, AND GET ON WITH THE BUSINESS OF TWO REAL PEOPLE LOVING EACH OTHER.

# How to Underreact to Overreactions

One of you gets a little peeved about some ordinary matter and says something like, "It really bugs me that you don't listen to me." The other partner reacts by exploding in rage, hurt, or both, in a manner far more intense than the initial statement justifies. The first person tries to calm things down, but nothing works. The explosion goes on for a while. In time the dust settles, but neither of you knows where to go from there, so you just hope it doesn't happen again.

Unfortunately, most of the time it does happen again. Whatever caused the explosion didn't go away, and all the avoidance, positive thoughts, and good intentions in the world won't make it do that. These explosions—called *overreactions*—must be understood and resolved for you to achieve the lasting intimacy you want in your love life. Read on, and we'll help you understand overreaction and resolve it.

## What an Overreaction Is and Isn't

When a person overreacts, she is experiencing an emotional response (hurt, fear, rage, and guilt, among others) that is greater than normal, given the circumstances. If you scream and cry when you are falling off a cliff, that would not be an overreaction. However, if you scream and cry when you trip on a step, that would probably qualify.

Couples are alarmed by the intensity of overreactions. They often don't have experience in dealing with them. The overreactor may be labeled crazy, sensitive, manipulative, or attention-seeking. The partner of an overreactor may be labeled insensitive, judgmental, or unloving. Obviously, overreactions can get in the way of the love connection.

Understand that, in one sense, overreactions are not overreactions. In objective reality, the emotions exhibited are greater than the situation, but *for that person's inner world, the emotions are entirely consistent with that situation.* He is living or reliving something that is still present within his experience. This has to do with hurt or pain that has not been dealt with, processed, or healed.

When a person is hurt—emotionally, physically, traumatically, or in other ways—it causes a deep reaction inside. Withdrawal, fear, anxiety, and anger are typical reactions to being hurt. It can be about something far back in the person's past. It can be a pattern in the couple's connection. It can be a symbolic representation of something that has occurred before.

The normal process of resolving this sort of pain is through love, support, grief, forgiveness, and healing. Support and acceptance from a caring environment renders the person capable of expressing the pain, working through it, and letting go in the grief process. Over time, and with the right steps, most hurtful events can be transformed into normal memories that instruct, teach, and warn us about life. But when this healing process does not occur, those *unprocessed memories are still experienced as occurring in the here and now.* Whatever the specific cause, the overreactions you or your lover are experiencing could be mild or severe hurts that have not yet been healed.

## What Triggers Overreactions

There are many triggers that can set off an overreaction. Returning to the example of the person who explodes when her partner gets peeved, her overreaction could be caused by several reasons:

- She came from a family background filled with rage and was traumatized by it.
- She came from a background where no one ever admitted anger, and therefore she has no skills to deal with it.
- She feels unloved when he is angry and gives up hope on the relationship.

- He may have contributed to her deep fears by being habitually and excessively angry about a lot of things.
- She is a people-pleaser and falls apart when she is obviously not pleasing him.

Whatever the cause, the triggering event somehow is similar to or represents a bad or dangerous event or relationship, and she reacts to it as a little child would. In her experience, she is back there when the bad thing happened to her. This can be very confusing, and it is often misunderstood. For example, the exploding person may look hostile and enraged. But inside, she may be terrified and simply trying to protect herself. She feels weak and feels forced to act strong to get out of danger.

I (John) was counseling with Randy and Melissa, a married couple who were having communication, intimacy, and conflict-resolution problems. I began to notice a pattern in which Randy would do anything to ward off Melissa's disappointment and anger at him. Melissa tended to be somewhat distant and critical, but Randy was afraid to say anything. So they stayed in a superficial connection that made neither of them happy.

During one session, Randy took a risk and confronted Melissa on her emotional unavailability. She did not respond positively but lashed out at him, saying, "You're never real with me anyway, and you don't appreciate all I do for you."

To my surprise, Randy abruptly burst into tears and curled up in his chair. Between sobs, he said, "I'm sorry, I'm sorry, I'll change, I'm sorry, I'm sorry." Instead of a thirty-year-old man, I was looking at a small boy who was terrified of his mother's rage. I felt compassion for him. Fortunately, Melissa did too. Seeing his fear and terror melted her own coldness, and she reached out to help him.

We found that Randy's mother had been many times worse than

Melissa. She was very unloving, harsh, and even cruel. Randy had never been able to move past the age when he was paralyzed by his need for a loving mother and his desperate fear to cross the cruel mother he had.

In time, Randy was able to move past his dependency and fear. He became stronger and more autonomous inside. He was then able to connect in healthier ways to Melissa. The process also helped her to warm up to him and become more emotionally available. In a way, his overreactivity, caused by his childhood wounds, finally helped bring them together and enabled them to connect in deeper and more satisfying ways.

### How to Help the Person Who Is Overreacting

Here are some solutions to this issue of overreactivity.

DON'T ATTACK THE IRRATIONALITY. You can't talk a person out of her feelings. Instead, stop the argument and become safe. Exercise a little warmth and tenderness. Speak softly and empathize with her hurt, anger, and fear. This will help increase the internal safety she needs to resolve the problem.

DON'T TAKE THE NEGATIVE EMOTIONS AS A PERSONAL ATTACK. When your partner overreacts, remember that you merely served as a trigger or symbol for the sins of someone else against her. The more you make it about you, the less available you are to help her, and it is she who really needs the help. Treat her as caringly as you would a small child who is having an emotional storm, and stay present, real, and containing with her.

PUT YOURSELF IN HER POSITION. Think of times you have been totally panicked or hurt, and how out of control and frightened you have felt. Remember what it was like, and how much you needed space, care, and time to calm down. This will help you have empathy, patience, and compassion for your lover's discomfort.

PROVIDE STRUCTURE AND REALITY IF NEEDED. Let your partner know that you aren't mad, that he is not in trouble with you, and that you will get through it. Tell him, "I will be here, and I will help you." Let him know that if the overreactions get too bad, you will get help. In most cases, the storms will subside with enough empathy, space, and time. Again, think of how a small child's reactivity gradually resolves as you hold him and keep him safe.

TALK ABOUT WHAT IT WAS LIKE FOR HIM. Don't avoid the problem of overreactivity and hope it goes away. Your partner needs to discuss his overreactions during normal times, so that he feels connected to you. Ask him what might help the next time it happens. Develop an approach consisting of things you can do to help create an environment of comfort and safety. This routine will help him stabilize that hurt part inside by increasing his internal sense of security and control.

ROLE-PLAY AND PRACTICE SAFE CONFRONTATIONS. Practice how to have disagreements that avoid the triggers. Write your own script—or at least the opening scene—and then be willing to ad lib. Help your partner become aware of what triggers the overreactions so that you both can know what might be coming. Develop the ability for both of you to give and receive feedback in loving and constructive ways.

GET HELP IF NEEDED. If your partner's condition does not resolve itself in a reasonable amount of time, seek help. Many therapists are well-trained in helping people work through their overreactions, and the results can be quite positive.

**A Lifeline:** ULTIMATELY, THE HURT THAT CAUSES YOU OR YOUR LOVER TO HAVE THESE INTENSE EMOTIONS CAN BE TRANSFORMED AND MATURED. OVERREACTIVITY CAN GIVE WAY TO RESPONDING APPROPRIATELY, IN BOTH EMOTIONAL AND INTELLECTUAL WAYS, AND YOU CAN MOVE ON AS A COUPLE WITHOUT THE WILD EXPLOSIONS SINKING YOUR LOVE LIFE. BE A PART OF YOUR LOVER'S GROWTH, AND IN SO DOING, HELP THE RELATIONSHIP GROW IN LOVE.

# "My Lover Should Trust Me Without Question"

T hink about your spouse for a minute, and ask yourself the question, "Do I love him?" Unless you are in severe trouble, the answer is probably yes; you do love him. Now ask yourself, "Do I trust him?" You may have to ponder that one for a while.

The reality is that you can love someone and not trust him *at the same moment in time.* Though love and trust are often confused, they are very different parts of a relationship. Love is a gift that you give your lover, even when he doesn't deserve it. He must be proven worthy of your trust before you will provide it. Love is free. Trust is earned.

Trust is something that every good relationship has in the fabric of its being. Often, it is the thing that must be built—or rebuilt—for intimacy and rescue to happen. In this section, you will learn what trust is, how powerful it is, and how you can create a relationship based on both love *and* trust.

# Trust Is a Risk You Have to Take

Karen looked at me (John) and took a deep breath. "OK, I'm ready," she said.

In the couple's work I was doing with Karen and Jim, her fiancé, I had noticed her shutting down in the sessions. She would withdraw, not talk, and seemed distracted. I had asked Jim if it would be OK if I talked to her privately. Jim had agreed.

In the private meeting, Karen told me that not too long before she and Jim had started dating, she had an abortion. She felt horrible guilt and remorse over it, and she had never told Jim about it. Karen was deeply in love with Jim, and it troubled her that he didn't know, for she wanted their connection to have no secrets.

I told her to tell him. "But what if he hates me or leaves?"

"There is always that possibility," I said. "I don't tell every couple to tell everything, as long as deception isn't involved. But I think Jim has the character to handle it. And I think he loves you a lot."

So, in the next session, Karen told Jim. She cried as she did, not even looking at him, because she was so afraid of what he would say.

When she finished, Jim also had tears in his eyes. He reached out to her and comforted her. He said, "I am so sorry that this happened. And I am so glad you told me. I want to know everything about you, and this just brings me closer."

Karen was deeply moved by Jim's grace and acceptance. She knew, at a level she had never known before, that she could truly trust him with all of herself. They are now happily married, and that trust has taken them through several years of growing in love and life together.

Trust is *the ability to be totally real, authentic, and unguarded with your lover.* It means being able to bring all parts of yourself to him, good and bad, strong and weak, without fear of condemnation or judgment. It has to do with not needing to edit or color what you say or who you are for fear of his reaction.

In the Hebrew Scriptures, there is a word for trust (*batach*) that actually conveys the idea of "carelessness" (Psalm 22:9). When you trust someone, you aren't paranoid about what you say or do. You let things slip sometimes, and even if that causes a problem, it's a little problem, not a catastrophe. Who wouldn't want to have a connection with her partner that was characterized by the ability to be "careless" in this way?

Think about the last time you opened up with your partner about a failure or a fear. When you were vulnerable with him, did he move toward you, make it safe for you, and draw you out? Or did he move away, become critical, or even dismiss the issue? This exercise is not meant to be an indictment of partners. It is simply a way for you, as a couple, to begin to evaluate the level of trust the two of you have in each other.

Couples who have learned how to trust receive many benefits in return. They are able to connect at deeper levels. They desire to be with each other and want to give to each other in gratitude. They are able to have more passion, as passion can emerge only in a safe and trusting context. Trust forms the foundation of the love life you want to have.

## The Three Elements of Trust

Couples can work on trust and improve it. Let's look at three primary elements that, when present in the relationship, create an atmosphere of trust and safety.

RISK. No risk, no trust. To develop trust, you will need to extend yourselves out of your comfort zone and take a risk. Risk in a relationship involves exposing vulnerable parts of yourself to your partner. You will need to let him know about your thoughts, feelings, and experiences that are negative, painful, or fragile. This might include fears, hurts, mistakes, sins, and parts of yourself that you are ashamed of or wish you didn't have.

Before taking this kind of risk, you must first deal with some internal conflict. How do you think your lover will respond? Whatever your partner's response might be, you need to take the risk anyway because *you are designed to bring every part of your being into the relationship.* God made you to connect at all levels. Couples who can navigate risk well are on their way to the benefits of trust.

Here are some things lovers sometimes need to say that involve risk:

· "I need you more than I would like to sometimes."
· "I get afraid that you will see all my flaws and disconnect from me."
· "I pretend that I'm OK sometimes when I am not."
· "I get mad at you and don't like you sometimes, and I pull away from you."
· "I don't know how to be who you need me to be."
· "I can be really selfish and demanding with you."
· "I secretly judged you for things I didn't like, and I never let you know."
· "I have a bad habit that I've been keeping from you."
· "I spent the money in a way that I had agreed not to."
· "When I said I was late because of traffic, it was really because I was hanging out with my friends at work."

Some risks are small; some are large. You will need to determine how much risk to take to begin this journey in your connection. But at some level, it is time to jump into the water and start swimming. Couples who refuse to risk because they are afraid of the consequences may think they are protecting the relationship, but they are actually doing a dumb thing that can sink it.

WELCOME. Appreciate the effort and humility of your partner for doing something uncomfortable for the sake of the relationship. Extend grace and love with no hint of condemnation. You do not have to agree with what your partner says or does to be welcoming. The best way to understand it is that *you are welcoming your partner's vulnerability,* not necessarily the right or wrong of what he is saying. Think how hard it is for you to take a risk with him and give him the same grace you would need.

Effective welcome may require a little work, because often the person taking the risk is not expecting it. Rather, he may anticipate the judgment or distancing from you. You may need to reassure him by your words, emotional presence, and body language that you want to know this part of him. And you will most likely need to do this more than once, over time. As the two of you welcome each other's risks, you will grow able to believe, on a heart level as well as a head level, that your willingness to reveal your darker parts is truly welcome in the relationship.

TRUSTWORTHINESS. Trustworthiness has to do with the character of the two of you as individuals. Not only are you to risk and welcome, but you also need to earn each other's trust by how you handle these more fragile things.

Trustworthiness means that you take your partner's investment in you very seriously and that you will not do anything to break the trust between you. This aspect requires time. Trustworthiness can only be proven over a series of experiences, all of which add up to show that you are truly that kind of person. A couple who is trustworthy puts a high value on faithfulness, loyalty, and reliability.

Here are a few examples of being trustworthy:

· Maintaining your welcome for your lover as a constant thing
· Restraining yourself from ever using against your lover anything she shares with you
· Keeping your promises and commitments

· Saying no to any form of deception or lying, large or small
· Being an authentic person—that is, being who you say you are
· Owning up when you make mistakes, and changing what needs to be changed

Without risk, you will never know if you can trust your lover. Without welcome, you will simply detach or pretend. Without trustworthiness, you will not believe the welcome is real. Make all three a covenant in your connection with each other.

Trust has a dynamic nature. It is not static. It moves and changes as the couple exercises it. As you find success in trust, it will open you up to each other at deeper and deeper levels.

## How Much Trust Is Too Much?

Ideally, you cannot trust too much. A love relationship was meant to give light and grace to all parts of you, so that you can safely know and be known and grow from that. In reality, however, you will need to find out what is possible at this point in your relationship and move on from there.

While figuring out where you two are on the spectrum of trustworthiness, the best rule of thumb is to risk at a level somewhere beyond comfort but not to the point of injury. If your relationship is fragile or has a history of untrustworthiness, you don't want to open up at a level that will cause real damage. See how your partner handles your little risks before you take the big ones.

Couples working on trust are often concerned about confessions of indiscretion. They wonder, *Should I tell her about the lust or the affair?* This question is not easy to answer, and it must be determined on an individual basis. Here are some guidelines: if the indiscretion is going on in the present, and you are not ending it, you probably need to tell your partner. It is not fair to her for you to be actively involved in something that hurts and deceives her. Think how you would feel if she were living a lie with you, and you didn't know.

If the indiscretion is in the past, and you have dealt with and ended it, it is ideally best to tell her, because that is the nature of intimacy. At the same time, however, evaluate the relationship: is it strong and adaptive enough at this point to handle the information, or would this revelation damage it? Also determine your own motives. If your motive is to get something off your chest, that is more about your own relief and less about the relationship. If it's because you think she would want and need to know, and if it somehow is blocking closeness, you may want to share it. Obviously, these are matters that require safe and mature counsel from others, and much prayer for wisdom and sensitivity.

### Building a Legacy of Trust

At a party several years ago, I found myself talking with a small group of guys. One of the men, Frank, was an older gentleman who had been married to his wife, Ruthie, for many years. The conversation turned to marriage. And since Frank had a lot of seniority, we began asking him questions about his success in that arena.

At one point, one of the guys made a somewhat inappropriate remark to Frank: "What about when you were overseas on military duty? I bet you've got a few stories Ruthie's never heard!"

The remark was out of line, but Frank didn't take the bait and do the expected wink-wink, shrug-shrug that guys do. His matter-of-fact response was, "I don't have any secrets from Ruthie." And that was it. The conversation moved to something else.

I remember thinking about Ruthie. How safe she must have felt with Frank. At a moment when she was not around him, she was still being protected and loved by a trustworthy husband. Small wonder their marriage had lasted so long.

**A Lifeline:** TRUST IS NOT A MYSTERY. IT'S NOT AN "EITHER YOU HAVE IT OR YOU DON'T" KIND OF THING. TRUST CAN BE DEVELOPED AND MATURED, AND IT'S WELL WITHIN YOUR POWER TO DO IT.

## Broken Trust Can Be Repaired

My friend Carl is one of the most welcoming, warm, and caring people I (John) have ever met. I don't think there is a critical bone in his body. He has what another friend of mine, my agent Sealy Yates, refers to as "a large grace window." For a long time, however, Carl was not the trustworthiest of people. Though he cared deeply for others, he had difficulty being honest and reliable.

It comes as no surprise that Susan, Carl's wife, went through some pretty dark waters in not being able to trust Carl. He let her down often, and the breaches in trust were serious ones. She knew he loved her, but she had been disappointed enough that she shut down and withdrew from the relationship.

As often happens in these situations, Carl finally hit bottom, and he hit it hard. His deceptive lifestyle cost him his career, and his marriage was not far behind. Fortunately, Carl valued Susan and their connection enough to get help, and things began to gradually change. He began to be more truthful, more responsible, and more dependable with Susan and her feelings. He worked on doing what he said he would do.

Regaining trust with Susan was not an overnight success; broken trust never is. Susan did not at first believe that Carl was trustworthy. She was hesitant to hope that he had changed, as she had seen many false restarts with lots of promises, none of which had lasted. But Carl hung in there, and Susan did her part, which we will show in this chapter. In time, they began to rebuild the trust between them. Susan began to see a new man emerging who was far different from what he had been. They not only weathered this storm, but they grew closer in ways they had given up hope of ever experiencing.

Carl and Susan's journey illustrates the point that, while trust is often broken, *there are ways to repair and rebuild it.* These ways involve work, humility, courage, and patience; but this process works as long as both parties engage in it.

## Trust Problems Are a Serious Matter

Trust issues are in a relational category all their own because trust underlies and supports the entire fabric of the connection itself. When trust is broken, it's as if the foundation of one's home is cracked, and the home is no longer a suitable place to live. When trust decreases, love decreases, and vice versa.

Trust can be broken in many ways, such as deceit, manipulation, white lies, financial indiscretions, sexual unfaithfulness at any level, minimizing the hurt you have caused your partner, saying one thing and doing another, broken promises and commitments, and inconsistency as a person.

When you cannot trust someone, *you no longer know who he is.* If he is deceptive or untrustworthy, you have lost the capacity to be safe and depend on his character and nature to be there for you. Furthermore, if you have trusted your lover, you have exposed some vulnerable parts of yourself to him—weak, shameful, fearful, or bad aspects that can be fragile and easily wounded.

Breaches in trust penetrate and hurt those deeper and more fragile parts of ourselves. When one partner is deceptive, untruthful, or unfaithful, the other doesn't just get annoyed; she is wounded and sometimes devastated. Trust problems are matters of injuring the very same fragile parts of the heart that she entrusted and exposed to you. Her weakest aspect is the part that gets torn up the most.

Some of the most difficult relational issues are those involving breaches of trust. Trust issues must be taken seriously. Rebuilding trust is hard work, but it's dumb not to tackle it. The work is definitely worth it. As Carl and Susan demonstrated, people do make great and lasting changes that rescue their love lives. Let's go into what you can do to correct problems in trust.

## Six Steps to Repair the Breach

If you have a trust problem, think of it as a crack in the foundation of your connection. How do you, as a couple who wants to rescue your love life, repair the breach? Here are the basic steps.

AGREE WITH REALITY. State and discuss what really did happen, and bring it into the light of your relationship. That is, talk about it frankly, while at the same time reaffirming the love and safety you have for each other. If you do not agree, work on that. But do not negotiate or compromise with facts, reality, or right and wrong.

If one of you insists on denying or rationalizing a breach of trust, stop the process and talk about the meaning of this. The injured person may have to say, "I can't continue giving you the benefits of being with me until we get this resolved. I need for you either to come clean or I will have to make some changes." You may need to bring in a third party. The point is, you just cannot proceed unless both people agree on the basic realities of what happened.

TREAT IT AS SERIOUS. Trust problems can rip a couple apart like no other issue can. It is paramount for both of you to be truthful and honest about not only what happened, but also its effects. The likelihood for healing is much greater when the couple recognizes the seriousness of the problem. You may have to face some painful realities between the two of you in order to know what can be done, such as:

- Your heart is broken.
- Your partner has hurt you deeply.
- You are unable to feel close to your partner.
- You don't know if you will ever be able to feel close again.
- You don't know if you are still in love with him.

YOU CANNOT HEAL THAT WHICH IS NOT BROUGHT INTO THE RELATIONSHIP. It simply will not happen. It's not pleasant when your contractor tells you how badly the house's foundation is cracked. But if you simply patch it over with mortar, the house will crumble. Cosmetic solutions will not heal the real situation.

It is very, very important for the partner who broke trust to learn to listen and to contain his lover's negative feelings about the problem and especially about him. She has a lot to process and to confess about what she is going through. And she needs the experiences of you listening, containing her hurt, being there, and being emotionally present.

It is extremely important—even critically important—for the partner who broke trust to listen closely to his mate's hurt. He must accept her negative feelings about the problem and about him without retaliation or self-defense. He must put himself in her shoes. She has a lot to process, and she needs to express to you frankly and honestly what she's going through. And she needs to know that you are listening—really listening, understanding and empathizing with her hurt, and being emotionally present.

Never dismiss or minimize how your partner is feeling about your betrayal's effect on her. Never say things like, "It wasn't that bad" or, "You're overreacting." Statements like these will compound the problem and build walls that will be extremely difficult to bring down. There may even be some truth to your observation, but this is definitely not the time to press the point. Your job is to shut up, listen, and just swallow it—no excuses, no clarifications, no justifications, and especially no blaming the victim for provoking you. Have zero tolerance here, for these things can permanently sink your love life.

DEMONSTRATE REMORSE AND REPENTANCE. The partner who violates his lover's trust needs to express and demonstrate authentic remorse and contrition. If you love someone, you aren't merely sorry you got caught. You feel bad for the hurt you caused. Let the one you love know how deeply you regret what you did.

Don't make this into a guilt trip or center it on yourself by saying, "I feel so bad; I'm the worst person in the world." Statements like these convey self-interest, rather than other-concern. You want him to know that your remorse is based on how much he has been through. It's not about you; it's about your partner.

Make real and true changes. Whatever the indiscretion, you will need to show that your remorse involves more than just words. Then do what you say. That is the nature of what the Bible calls *repentance*. To repent is to turn from our erroneous ways. For example, Luke 17:3 says, "If your brother sins, rebuke him, and if he repents, forgive him." The Greek word translated "repents" here means action.

The offending partner may need to make herself accountable to the wounded one and submit to him in the area of concern. That means you might need to give up certain freedoms to rebuilt trust, but it must be done. For example:

· He can reach you at any time on the cell phone, and you will tell him where you are and what you are doing.
· You will give him control and access to all financial information.
· You will bring any decisions you need to make to him, before you make them.
· You will get help for an addiction.
· You will get into an accountability group or therapy to help you stop lying.

If these examples seem restrictive, it's because they are. You are submitting to a process of growth and repair for the sake of helping the person you hurt and the relationship you damaged. Accept these restrictions, and follow through. You want to do whatever it takes to keep your love life intact.

The injured person also has a task. You must hold to requirements and standards about these matters of change. Insist on them, talk about them, and don't waver. All too often, the hurt person gives in to his love and loneliness and accepts "I won't do it again" as enough. That may be OK for a single, minor incident. But for repeated and severe hurtful patterns, you must stand firm. This is a burden you must carry, but you don't have to carry it alone. Get people to stand with you to keep the requirements intact.

GIVE THE PROCESS TIME. Time alone never healed a trust issue; just as putting the ingredients into a bowl won't produce a cake. Time is necessary as you both work together on renewing trust.

If you have broken trust with your lover, get into the process of growth, rather than trying harder or starting over afresh as if nothing has happened. Put your shoulder to the long haul of personal growth and change. Give your partner and other trusted people some sort of monitor power over you, so that they, not just you, will decide when you have truly changed from the inside out.

If you have been betrayed, you will need to take responsibility for learning to forgive, to cancel the debt. This is not easy, and it may take time, but it is the only way. You will need to let go of the demand to punish and vent wrath on your partner. That process will involve growth, grieving, and loving support from God and others.

You will also need to observe the changes your partner is making over time—for at some point, you will need to take another risk with him. When you are ready, and the healing is happening inside you, and he has been proving himself a changed person, it will be time to dip your toe into the water and let him back into your heart. It is probably best to do this under the counsel of some wise people who are *for* both of you as well as the relationship.

DEAL WITH BAGGAGE. Sometimes when trust has been broken, the problem is compounded because the hurt person has had to deal with trust issues from previous relationships. That kind of baggage makes the woundedness even greater. Sometimes it causes the wounded person to take on a victim mentality, meaning she feels totally without fault and that all problems are his fault. Most of the time it is an exaggeration. Yet in such cases the past and present can fuse in the victim's mind, which significantly slows down healing and reconciliation.

If you are the wounded person and realize you have brought your own trust issues into the relationship, get help to resolve them. You need to free your relationship from the past so that you can deal with the present problem. I have seen too many cases in which the injured person refused to work with a genuinely remorseful and repentant partner because of past baggage, and it sank the relationship.

**A Lifeline:** IT IS NEVER EASY TO CONFRONT TRUST PROBLEMS. BUT THE GOOD NEWS IS THAT LOVE RELATIONSHIPS THAT DEAL WITH TRUST ISSUES WITH HONESTY, OPENNESS, AND PATIENCE CAN HEAL AND GROW INTO A REWARDING CONNECTION OF TRUST AND CARING.

## Trust Thrives on Independence

When I was in college, my friend Mike explained to me (John) how my breakup with Cindy, my girlfriend, was my fault and not hers. I didn't ask him for his perspective, but he thought it his duty to give it. I'll tell you what he said, because sometimes autopsies of old relationships help to point out patterns and problems we can use to improve our present connections.

Cindy and I had a lot of the same interests and friends. The early days of our relationship were fun and enjoyable. I soon felt I was falling for her in a big way, and I hoped she was also becoming really interested in me.

We started spending more alone time together. The more time I spent with her, the more I wanted. I wanted to be with her as much as I could. When I was away from Cindy, life didn't seem as bright as it was with her around. In my mind, that was a sign that she was the right girl for me.

So far, so good. However, when I really became interested in Cindy, she seemed to move the other way. She became somewhat distant and seemed preoccupied or even irritable at times. We began to have tiffs over meaningless things. Finally she started becoming less available to me. Other activities and people were always getting in the way.

Ultimately, we broke up, and I felt terribly disappointed. I wasn't really sure what the breakup was about. So I talked to my friends about it, wondering if she had just lost interest, if someone else had come along, or if she had been faking her interest in me.

Finally, Mike gave me some straight talk. He said, "Well, it seemed to me that you wanted too much from her."

I didn't get it. "What are you talking about?" I said. "I did everything for her." I listed all the times I helped her with homework, walked her home, and did odd jobs on her apartment.

Mike agreed with all that, but he took it further. "Yes, you did all those things. And that's not all. You pouted when she had other things to do, gave her a hard time when she wanted to be with other people, and didn't like going out in groups with her. I think you suffocated her."

As I thought about Mike's analysis, I realized that I had pretty much smothered Cindy. At the time, I had thought my actions and attitudes were what people do and feel when they are in love. But in reality, it was more about me than about her.

The autopsy of my relationship with Cindy points out a key element in rescuing a love life: *you both need to encourage and develop independence and freedom within a context of love and connection.*

This relates to the issues of dependency we covered previously, but here we enter a new arena. In this chapter, we deal less with your personal dependency issues, and more with establishing a strong relationship based on two people supporting each other's freedom and choices.

## I and We

It takes two "I"s to form a "we." The "I"s don't disappear or melt into the "we"; they still exist. But something new has been added, which is the connection itself.

Your love connection is intended to focus on the needs of the individuals and the needs of the relationship. This focus must shift and change at times as seasons and needs change. Whenever the focus shifts, both of you must continually approve and support these two elements: the needs and interests of the individuals as well as those of the relationship.

THE "WE." There is built-in tension and sacrifice in being part of a "we." While you want to love and connect, you will probably resist giving up personal things in order to get that connection. After all, it's easy to think in terms of your own perspectives and interests, but it takes effort to think of what is best for your lover and the relationship.

However, deeply attached couples who practice this do not find the sacrifice excessively burdensome. The benefits are simply so much greater. What you receive, in terms of love, closeness, intimacy, and passion, transcend what you had to give up.

In a marriage, this might mean a wife puts off her career for a while for the sake of raising children. Or a husband may give up a promotion in another city to keep the family where they are doing well. Choices for the "we" aren't easy, but they need to be faced from the perspective of what is best for the entire team.

THE "I." In the other direction, paying exclusive attention to the "we" is not good for the relationship either. Each individual's choices, preferences, needs, dreams, and desires are important.

Supporting the "I" brings many benefits. A couple who supports the growth and interests of the individuals brings good things to the connection. The relationship itself is better and more whole, because the individuals are better and more whole.

This is why corporations send their executives to professional growth conferences. They gain skills in leadership, vision, management, and motivation. Then, armed with their new abilities, they make the corporation a better and more productive place. When you and your lover encourage each other to pursue your own interests, hobbies, and friendships, you enrich the connection and make it a better place to live and love.

Supporting your efforts to fulfill a goal can give your mate much happiness, knowing that your desire is being fulfilled. Then your own gratitude for her support can urge you to help her fulfill her own dreams as well.

### Yes and No

Another important aspect of keeping your love life in balance is making the relationship a safe place to say no. Love grows when both partners are free to make choices. And it can't exist when that sort of freedom is resisted.

It is important to pay attention to the balance in the relationship, because it's so easy for relationships to become unbalanced. For example, when one partner is more assertive and the other more compliant, one person's interests will tend to take over the relationship. The assertive one may tend to get her way more because she takes more initiative. In more serious instances, one partner will actually resist and restrict the individuality, choices, and freedom of the other. He may try to control her or react negatively when she does not agree. This dumb attitude must be confronted and addressed before it sinks your marriage.

Your relationship needs to place a high value on personal freedom. Otherwise, neither of you ends up getting what you want. If you want closeness and passion, let your lover have choices. If you want distance and coldness, try to control your mate. Which is the dumb attitude?

As a couple, you need to take a negative word and turn it into a positive: the word *no*. Having the freedom to say no, to disagree, to have your own opinion and decisions, is the paradox of love. Couples who have the freedom to move apart in their own choices and minds have more of a chance to connect and engage. Couples who don't have that freedom may look like they're close, but in time, that closeness generally shows its true colors as an external compliance that often results in a cold heart and a dead connection.

It's not easy to make the word *no* an accepted and encouraged part of your relationship. Couples often feel threatened, unloved, or unable to have any control over the relationship. So, as I did with Cindy, they resist and punish, in crazy ways, their lover's attempts to have independence.

If one or both of you has trouble hearing the word *no,* it may be helpful to look at the situation in three ways. First, don't you want your own choices also? What you want for yourself, you must also provide for the other. Freedom must be mutual, or it doesn't work. Second, if your lover stays around only because she's afraid to say no, you don't have her anyway. And surely you want to change that! And third, your resistance to independence is probably a problem in other areas of your life, like work, friends, and family. Learning to accept *no* will help you not just in your love connection, but also in your success and happiness as a person.

## Declare Your Independence

Pay attention to the choices and independence each of you has in the connection. The less control you have, the more connection, desire, and love will develop. Here are some tips and suggestions for declaring your independence in the relationship.

HAVE A "FREEDOM OF CHOICE" TALK. Talk about the fact that freedom and love go together. Express your desire, love, and need for each other. Reassure one another that you are committed to the relationship. Lack of this reassurance is a big reason that some partners become controlling. They fear losing their mate, so they use control to hold on more tightly. When reassurance is firmly established, you can talk about how you want more choices and independence within the parameters of your connection.

ESTABLISH A VISION FOR INDEPENDENCE. Discuss the advantages of independence. For example, you both can make free choices that increase your value as an individual. This will make each of you stronger, giving the other more strength to rely on. When you are there for each other, you are there wholeheartedly and by choice, not out of guilt.

This in no way implies that independence means selfishness or irresponsibility. Independent adults are more responsible to be loving, dedicated, faithful, and caring, because they do it freely instead of under compulsion. That is the purpose of independence—to produce a mature person.

Immature people want more freedom simply because they don't like the normal constraints of relationship. This is one of those dumb attitudes that must be confronted, for commitment brings with it certain constraints. You cannot, nor should you, have all the same freedoms in a committed relationship that you had in your single life.

In healthy connections, both mates give up certain freedoms because the advantages transcend what they had to surrender.

ESTABLISH AN ONGOING SYSTEM TO MONITOR FREEDOM. Agree that if one of you feels controlled, smothered, or guiltified by the other, it's OK to say, "Hey, it felt like you just guiltified me when I said I wanted to go out with the girls this weekend. That pushed me away from you. I need to talk about this." Often the freedom resister is unaware that he is doing this, and he may need a little feedback, reminding, and coaching.

PAY ATTENTION TO THE BENEFITS. As you take the risk of being independent within your connection, become aware of what you should be getting in return. Couples who learn to exercise freedom often find that they miss their mates all the more. They look forward to being with their spouse and sharing what they are experiencing and learning in life. They feel an expanding space in their hearts that creates more room for love.

> **A Lifeline:** ALLOW AND EXERCISE RESPONSIBLE FREEDOM IN YOUR RELATIONSHIP, AND YOU SHOULD BEGIN TO NOTICE AN INCREASE IN THE THINGS BOTH OF YOU REALLY WANT IN YOUR LOVE LIFE: PASSION, CLOSENESS, HAPPINESS, AND INTIMACY. DECLARING INDEPENDENCE TO GAIN INTIMACY MAY SEEM LIKE A DUMB THING TO DO, BUT IT CAN WORK VERY WELL.

## A Little Structure Won't Kill Romance

Randy was a good-natured but controlling guy. He constantly ran over Sandra's opinions, interrupted her in conversations, and tended to take over the decision-making process. His dad had been that way, and Randy took after him. When they came to me (John), Sandra was pretty much ready to throw in the towel.

I told Randy, "The only way you'll get her to connect with you again is to humble yourself and give her room, space, and respect."

Randy didn't understand what I meant. "I already do that," he said.

"No, you don't. Nor do you me. So far in our time together, you have interrupted not only Sandra, but me several times, and changed the course of the conversation. I don't think you do this on purpose, but I assure you that she is right about this complaint."

Randy sighed. "OK, what do I do?"

I said, "Look at this like a little game, though it isn't. I'm going to have Sandra tell you about a problem she feels about you, and I want you to follow three rules, First, you cannot say a word until she says she is through. Second, before you can say your opinion, you must let her know you understand her experience, to her satisfaction. Third, you must agree to change anything she is right about. Then you can talk about your side."

Randy said, "That sounds really hard."

It was. When Sandra would start talking, he would begin to clarify what she "should" be thinking and try to "guide" her to the right perceptions. But I kept stopping things, over and over, until Randy began to be aware of how controlling he was. In fact, he became sad when he saw how much of a jail he had kept Sandra in, thinking that he was being caring and protective.

We kept on with our "game" for several sessions. Randy's dominance was deeply ingrained, so I imposed these rules for a while, until I felt that Randy and Sandra could handle differences without them. In time, I let them talk without the structure, and things got better. But I don't think Randy would ever have been able to acknowledge or resolve his dominance without that little game.

## The Need for Relational Rules

Reflect for a minute on your first date with your partner. Remember where you were, what you did, how you felt, and how you experienced the other person. At any point during that evening, did you discuss what kind of rules and structures you should put in place in order to get to know each other?

No way! That just doesn't happen, nor does it make any sense. People don't become interested in each other and fall in love because they are into rules. The relationship starts with love, commonality, excitement, meaning, safety, and passion. Rules are the farthest thing from their minds.

However, as time moves on, many couples have found that they can be forgetful, hurtful, and selfish with each other. Love can break down and become wounded. Trust and understanding can be somewhat fragile and easily bruised. It takes time to develop these two qualities in a love connection in the first place. So when one partner hurts the heart of the other, that sets the entire relationship back many steps.

Couples often don't know what to do when this happens. They don't have the tools to deal with this hurt. Sometimes the wounded one will try to ignore it, but the heart doesn't forget. Sometimes she will try to have more love and patience, but that doesn't help the partner grow or change. So a little wall grows between them that can, over time, become a giant block. And all the understanding, patience, and grace in the world won't fix it.

It's like having a broken arm and hoping it will go away. All the good intentions in the world won't heal it until you get a cast to provide safety and structure, so the healing can happen. This is where relational rules and structure come into your love life. There are times when they are necessary to treat the wound. Like a cast on a broken limb, relational rules can preserve, protect, and even repair the love you want.

This applies to a host of problems, ranging in their effects from mild to severe, such as emotional unavailability, control, irresponsibility, defensiveness, chronic tardiness, overspending, unfaithfulness, and rage. These behaviors—and others as well—can bruise love and trust. They must be dealt with.

## Not the Ideal, but the Real

Just as broken limbs aren't ideal, neither is having lots of rules for your relationship. Problems in connection are real, though, and we need to accept the rules to deal with the problems.

One of the long-term goals of any love relationship is to have as few rules as possible. If you and your partner have made responsibility, care, sacrifice, and freedom parts of your normal behavior with each other, you don't need a lot of rules. You can trust your partner to act in your best interest, and you can rest in that. Love is sure to follow, as the environment is safe for it to grow and develop.

For example, if your partner is romantically faithful, how often do you say, "I want you to make sure you're behaving appropriately with other women you meet at work"? Probably never. You don't need the rule because he lives the rules. Rules that are lived don't need to be stated.

But suppose he flirts or has a history of unfaithfulness. This is a real problem for you, and it should be addressed. Romantic love is a one-to-one proposition. To ignore a pattern of unfaithfulness is to run the risk of continually being hurt, or even destroying the relationship you have so carefully constructed. You may have to establish some sort of accountability with him until he proves trustworthy, from bringing in a counselor to being able to reach him at any time and require that he tell you who he is with.

Think of rules as elements that protect and preserve. Use them when needed, and use as few as possible, so that freedom and love can flourish as much as possible.

## When Do We Need Rules?

There are two criteria for the structure of rules. First, one of you is hurting the other and causing alienation and distance. Second, appeals to the offender on the basis of relationship aren't working.

Ideally, when one person is harsh or hurtful, his partner says something to let him know how it affected her: "That really hurt my feelings. I was trying to tell you that when you come home late, it's hard for the kids and me. And you cut me off and didn't even try to listen. I need you to understand what I am saying here, because I go a million miles away from you when you respond like that."

That kind of statement is direct but not unloving. It is always the place to begin. The mate who offends the other should get a chance to hear an appeal to the relationship: *what you are doing affects how I am feeling about you.* Ideally, the kind of statement just modeled will help your lover see himself through your eyes, feel sad that he has hurt you, and make the change. The two of you will reconnect, and love will go on.

But sometimes the appeal is not enough. Your lover can't hear you, won't hear you, is defensive, or is in an egocentric frame of mind. That is when you may need rules and structure. For example, "I've brought up the problem of your coming home late several times, but nothing is changing. And now your dismissing my feelings is becoming a big problem for me, bigger even than the lateness. I think if you'd really understand how I am feeling, you would probably try to change the lateness. But since you're not hearing me, I am going to do this. For a while, if you dismiss my feelings and stop listening, I will just stop talking about it and solve the problem myself. But for a couple of days, I will just not be open at all to you. I won't be mean. But I won't be available or accessible. I don't like doing this, but my words aren't working. When you start trying to hear me again, I'll drop all this, but not until then."

If you have not had a lot of experience setting limits, this may sound harsh or mean. But notice that this action was taken only when nothing else worked—and notice that it is about reconnecting, not punishment. And notice that it all goes away if the lover gets it and changes. She reconnects, gives him the love he needs, and he is more of a loving person with her. This is all reasonable and appropriate.

Say one of you is a spendaholic. As a couple, you have goals and dreams that you are saving for: a home, kids' college, or retirement. But the spendaholic keeps running up credit cards and going into the account to spend frivolously.

When reminders and appeals don't work toward solving a problem, you must impose structure. Tear up credit cards. Take over the finances. Keep separate accounts if you have to. Bring in a third party to control things. If the spender dreams of a new home, tell her clearly that she will have to be financially responsible for some meaningful period of time before you will sign for a home loan. You will probably find lots of ways to address the details, but the point is, you need to call in external structures until the problem is solved.

Imposing rules is not meant as some sort of character diagnosis of your lover. It doesn't mean that he is narcissistic or has a controlling disorder. Some people simply need experiences to make them aware of their effects on others when words don't work.

### Next Steps

If your connection is being hurt by your lover's behavior or attitudes, and if words aren't working, call in the rules. Protect yourself and preserve the love you want to have.

BRING IN A THIRD PARTY. Most people need to talk to someone, like a safe and responsible friend, to process what is going on. Seeing what the problem is, what exactly needs to change, what rules will help accomplish the change, and how to deal with your own anxiety about the process—it is very difficult to do all this in your head. You need to borrow the head of a wise and trusted friend. Talk to someone who is balanced and *for* the relationship.

BASE THE RULES ON RELATIONSHIP. When you decide what you are going to do, appeal to the connection. Make it clear that this is not about wanting to change or fix her. It is because you want to trust and love her, and you can't because of what she is doing. Always come back to the goal: *I am doing this because I want you, and I want us.* If you need a lot of support from sources other than your partner, don't hesitate to get it. You are getting that support so that you can solve this issue and reconnect with your lover.

FOLLOW THROUGH. If rules are needed, set them and live them. If you are afraid you won't follow through, stop and get more resources and help, or you will make things worse for the two of you. Giving in to your feelings or his pleas destroys the effectiveness of the treatment by showing that bad behavior has no consequences.

**A Lifeline:** COMMIT AT THE OUTSET OF THE PROCESS TO HOLD ON TO YOUR STRUCTURE FOR THE ENTIRE TIME NEEDED. OFTEN, THE TIME WILL HELP YOUR LOVER EXPERIENCE YOUR FIRMNESS AND REALIZE THAT YOU ARE SERIOUS. AS HE COMES TO RECOGNIZE HIS NEED FOR YOU AND FOR YOUR GRACE, HE WILL BE MORE ABLE TO CHANGE HIS BEHAVIOR. KEEP THE RULES, GIVE GRACE, AND GIVE IT TIME. YOU'LL BE GLAD YOU DID.

## DUMB ATTITUDE #8

## "My Lover Should Be Perfect at Sex"

How can anything so wonderful, so sensational, so desirable, and so *fun* often go so wrong, as sex does? Whatever the reason, this playground often becomes a battleground. What is meant to be a union of the sexes becomes another battle of the sexes. What is meant to lift couples to the heights of joy plunges them into the depths of misery. Sometimes this comes from things that one or both partners bring into the relationship. At other times it comes from things that are produced within the relationship. Either way, it can be very discouraging and often undermines the connection.

If you are among the couples who have encountered the downside of sex, we have good news for you. You can get the ecstasy back. You can restore the joy, the satisfaction, the love, and the sheer fun of sex. You can learn to get the desire back, as well as the ability to take it to fulfillment.

What we offer here is not a sex manual; it's more of a hope manual. You will realize that, if you have sexual problems, you are not alone. We will help you identify the most common sexual problems so you will know how to address them. We will also tell you what kinds of help are available, giving you a point and a shove in the direction of healing.

If sex is the thing that needs rescue in your love life, here is the lifeboat that can bring you back to solid ground.

## Good Sex Doesn't Just Happen

What is healthy sex? It depends on whom you ask. From Hugh Hefner to *Cosmopolitan* to Dr. Ruth and beyond, there is no shortage of opinions regarding what good sex is. The common assumption is that the man's answer is "more" and the woman's is "more connecting." A poll would probably reveal about as many answers as there are couples.

Sex is a very individual topic—and for good reason. It draws upon the most personal and vulnerable aspects of the man and the woman, as well as their relationship. Sex therapists long ago figured out that sex therapy was not the same as fixing plumbing. They found that to be successful, they could not just fix the equipment malfunction. Instead, they had to focus on the relationship itself. They discovered that sex was an easel upon which the relationship painted a picture of itself. If the relationship is loving, the sex will be loving too. If the relationship is self-centered, the sex will reflect that. If the relationship is connected, the physical experience will further the connection. But if the partners are detached from each other, the sex is in danger of being just a routine physical act.

One thing is for sure: *sex is important and powerful.* It is the place that God has reserved for the unity of a marriage to be expressed in a unique and tangible way, by two bodies becoming "one flesh." Sex is both symbol and reality—surely one of God's most incredible designs. And since love and oneness are the highest values in the universe, He endowed the sexual experience with an ecstasy like no other. With that endowment comes incredible power as well. The sexual experience in marriage has the power to do many good things for the partners, as well as for the relationship. And when it is not going well in some way, sex has its own set of threats.

In light of the high and honorable place that God has reserved for sex, and in light of the pleasure and pain that it can bring, it is good to look past Heffner and *Cosmopolitan* to determine what good, healthy sex really is. You need to know, for it is an important part of preserving and reestablishing your connection.

## Healthy Sex Knows Best

From the Creator's view, sex is the ultimate expression of *knowing* someone. As we mentioned earlier, the Bible's word for "having sex" comes from the Hebrew word that means "to know." In other words, to have sex with someone is to truly *know* him or her in the deepest way. That is why it is not something casual or unimportant. On the contrary, sex is the deepest expression of intimacy and of knowing another person.

It is no coincidence that when Adam and Eve fell, the part of their bodies that they covered with fig leaves was their genitals, for that symbolized their deepest vulnerability. They had gone from "naked and unashamed" to being afraid of being known (Genesis 2:25). Shame, inadequacy, fear, guilt, and disconnection had all gotten in the way of their ability to be known at the deepest levels of who they were.

First and foremost, healthy sex is sex that expresses *knowing one another in the deepest sort of intimacy with the absence of fear, shame, hurt, or guilt.* Sex is where total vulnerability is expressed; it is a knowing of the other person's heart, mind, soul, and strength. Let's look at some of the things that help couples truly know each other in the deepest biblical, or sexual, ways.

## Healthy Sex Is Connected Sex

"He doesn't put the mental and the physical together sometimes," Amanda told me (Henry), referring to her experience having sex with Jason. He would rush her to the physical act, but she would feel like he was leaving her heart and soul behind. As a result, she felt disconnected from her husband while making love to him. Why? Because he was only making love to her body and not the rest of her. He was "making sex," not love.

So they began to work on it. We made a rule that Jason could not move forward physically without talking first and "finding" her. He had to express to Amanda what he was feeling toward her, the things he loved about her, and his desire to be close to her. He had to listen to what she was feeling toward him and what she wanted as well.

As Jason and Amanda started talking more, they began to share other things that were on their minds as well, and the verbal intercourse turned into a deep knowing that led to sexual intercourse that now was not only mental, but also much more physical than they had ever known. In the end, Jason got more of what he was looking for in the beginning, but not by getting physical first. He found that the physical followed the connection.

Strangely, the best sex manual may be *Merriam-Webster's Dictionary*. Look up *intercourse* at www.webster.com, and here is what you find: "(1) connection or dealings between persons or groups, (2) exchange especially of thoughts or feelings, (3) physical sexual contact between individuals that involves the genitalia of at least one person."

If couples would just work through the order the dictionary prescribes, things would work out better in the end: (1) deal with each other in a way that connects, (2) exchange thoughts and feelings, and (3) go for it!

In the end, good sex is connected sex—sex between a connected couple.

## Healthy Sex Is Freely Given

As we have said, where there is love, you will also find freedom. Where there is control, love breaks down. Love is something that is freely given. If a person feels controlled into giving sex, it is no longer love, but slavery.

Healthy sex is sex where both parties feel like they are there, in the act, by their own choosing. They have said yes with their bodies and their hearts. The problem comes when they say yes with their bodies and no with their hearts.

When people are free to engage in sex voluntarily, they can be truly "there." So an important aspect of connecting with each other sexually is talking about the degree of freedom that each of you feels in saying no either to having sex at any particular time or participating in any particular aspect of sex. The good and satisfying sexual relationship is one where neither person is coerced or forced either to have sex when they don't want to or to do sexual acts that they don't want to do.

Just as other areas of your relationship will display different preferences, desires, and leanings, so will sex. Just as one of you might prefer dining out more than the other, one of you might want sex more than the other, or on one particular day when the other doesn't. Or just as one might prefer Italian and the other a French menu, you will have different tastes in what you desire and enjoy sexually as well. Here is the key: *in good relationships, lovers do not view these preferences as a problem, but as natural.* And in good relationships, as in the rest of life, the two lovers listen, understand, and compromise to give to each other in ways that are the most satisfying for each. Neither one gets left behind.

Compromise means giving sometimes when it would not be your preference, as an act of love. Compromise also means doing without sometimes when it would not be your preference, also as an act of love. Lovers both give freedom and act out of freedom. That is what it means to truly *know* each other.

## Healthy Sex Is Accepting Sex

One of the biggest dumb attitudes couples have about sex is that everyone should be an expert, and if they are not, something is wrong with their sex life. It's as if the rest of life requires practice and working out problems, but this one area should come complete, preassembled, with batteries included. That is never the case.

Good sex is not expert sex, but rather sex where both people feel accepted, right where they are—and where the relationship feels OK, right where it is, at whatever level of sexual health or competency it has. *Good sex is "failure-free" sex.*

Give each other the freedom not to get it right. Give your relationship the freedom to fail sometimes. Some of the most sexually satisfied couples report that they moved from the fear of things not going well to the ability to laugh together at those times when it just wasn't working.

If you want a great sex life, then work on accepting each other in all areas of life. When a person feels totally accepted by her lover, barriers go down in the entire person. It is the beginning of being naked and unashamed, and it translates into passion and sexual freedom. Get judgment, performance anxiety, guilt, lack of forgiveness, and other unrealistic expectations out of your relationship—and out of your sex life.

## Healthy Sex Is Fun

OK, enough of all this heavy stuff. Healthy sex is not only for deep communion, but for fun and recreation as well. (You probably already knew that.) Healthy sex involves knowing *all* of each other—body, heart, mind, soul, and strength. And part of that is the physical act itself. There is physical sex that is simply passion, desire, and the coming together of two people as "one flesh."

Then there is "soulish" sex that comes from your personality, feelings, interests, and expressions of who you are in various ways that are unique to you and your mate. There is also sex that comes from connecting intellectually, with your minds and your beliefs coming together. But sometimes sex is just the physical hunger that you have for one another. It may not be the deepest meeting of the hearts at all, but simply a moment of pure fun.

Some couples need to have permission for that kind of sex, as well as to get out from the seriousness of it all. Have fun, and get physical. But remember this: couples who enjoy times where sex is just fun and physical have that because all the other more connecting aspects are in place. If your heart's connection is secure, and you and your spouse are really "knowing" each other in all the ways we have talked about, you can have fun, physical sex and no one gets hurt. Safety and connection are already there, so you are free to be physical.

## Healthy Sex Requires Communicating

Couples with the greatest satisfaction are those who talk to each other about sex—about their wants, desires, likes, dislikes, fears, pains, insecurities, and whatever else comes into the picture. These couples have a safe space just to get to know each other sexually, apart from having sex.

Strangely, some couples often seem to think that they will just automatically know what to do in all sexual situations. After all, isn't sex supposed to be a natural instinct? Nothing could be further from the truth. Talking is imperative to healthy sex. But opening up to each other requires safety. Create a space where you can connect about sex apart from connecting through sex. Do not criticize or judge your partner about the things listed above. Make it OK to communicate openly without either of you taking it personally. Remember, the goal is to know each other better, and to do that you need the safety to talk.

## "Knowing" Each Other Is a Process

Putting into practice the things we have talked about here all take time. Sex means "to know" someone, and you must remember that it takes time to know a person. Healthy sex is just like any other aspect of your relationship: it takes time to build.

Couples with healthy sex lives give each other time to get to know each other. They never assume they know everything about themselves or each other and are always learning. They allow the necessary time to be sure the right things happen.

**A Lifeline:** WE ALL DEAL WITH WORK, KIDS, PERSONAL PRESSURES, AND LIFE ISSUES. DESPITE ALL THAT FILLS OUR SCHEDULE AND DRAINS OUR ENERGY, WE HAVE TO GIVE SEX TIME AND SPACE SO THAT IT GETS THE ATTENTION IT DESERVES IN OUR MARRIAGE. IF YOU INVEST TIME IN GROWING TOGETHER AND KEEP WORKING ON YOUR SEX LIFE, THE RETURNS WILL BE WORTH IT ALL.

## Untangling the "Nots" in Unhealthy Sex

In the last chapter, we talked about some of the ingredients that create healthy sex. Before we go further, let's review them quickly:

- Knowing each other
- Being connected
- Being free
- Being accepting
- Having fun
- Communicating
- Seeing sex as a process

If those are the ingredients for healthy sex, then what are the ingredients of unhealthy sex? Answer: the absence of those same things. Let's take a look at the other side of healthy sex for a moment, so you can rid your relationship of the dynamics that destroy your connection in the sexual arena and beyond.

## Not Knowing or Connecting

If "being known" is what sex is about, then the *absence* of being known is unhealthy sex. Unhealthy or disconnected sex occurs when one of the partners is not relating to his mate as a whole person, but he still wants sex. He takes no time to find out where his mate's heart, mind, soul, or strength is; he wants to have sex that is disconnected from the rest of the person.

That kind of sex feels awful to the other partner, and the overall connection breaks down sexually and relationally. It is not uncommon for women to say that sex feels like a totally lonely experience, leaving them empty. I have worked with some women who said that at times they would cry silently during sex and their husband would not even know it. That is very disconnected indeed. Others just report rolling over afterward and crying to themselves. Obviously when this happens, the woman's heart is not in the act at all.

When men engage in disconnected sex, they often take aspects of their own heart outside the relationship. This disconnectedness is one of the chief reasons for pornography addiction and infidelity. When one relates to his mate with his body only, and not the rest of himself, he is in an unhealthy state. If the only way that he ever connects with his mate is through sex, then the connection is loveless and something is wrong.

If you feel that you are being treated like a sex object or that your physical relationship is without heart and soul, then it is time to talk about it—about your fears, hurts, needs, desires, and the like. Make a strategy to have your physical connection be equal to your relational connection. Agree to have sex only when you are both feeling like you are heard, understood, and connected with each other. Then, working together, come up with a strategy for having your physical connection be equal to your relational connection. That will be good for both of you.

## Not Being Free

Remember, you must have freedom to have love. So if one of you is putting pressure on the other, controlling the other into having more sex than he or she wants, or having some kind of sex that he or she doesn't want, that is not healthy. Couples must talk through such differences and negotiate, compromising and sacrificing. That is normal.

What is unhealthy is when those sacrifices are made against a partner's will. It is not good when pressure of personality, manipulation, guilt, or other subtle but coercive means causes one partner to go past where he or she feels comfortable going.

Talk about this issue. Talk about the freedom that exists in your relationship to say no, easily and simply, as in, "Not tonight, please. I'm tired." You do not have to have a headache to say no. Part of a loving relationship and a healthy connection is the freedom to say no to sex just as you would say no to anything else you didn't want at the moment.

If you don't feel that kind of freedom in your relationship, the problem may be coming from your own head, or it may be a dynamic between the two of you. Sometimes you cannot know which until you talk it out. Likewise, it is important that you talk about what you agree to do or not do sexually. Make sure that the agreements are not due to pressure or coercion of any kind.

You must have freedom to have love. At the same time, if freedom is exercised without concern for the other person's needs, then love loses as well. To just say no to everything and not consider your mate's sexual needs or desires is not loving either. That is taking advantage of freedom. So balance the two: freedom and love.

Freedom extends past the bedroom but comes back to haunt couples *in* the bedroom. If there are control dynamics in your relationship, then chances are your sex life is going to be affected. This is often the cause for a man's lack of desire for his wife and his attraction to pornography or other women—to the extent that he feels controlled by her, he moves away from her sexually, as sexuality and power are intertwined for men. There is a reason that the word *potency* is used to describe male sexual ability; it has to do with power. If he feels relationally powerless with her, then it will show up often in their sexual relationship. Lack of desire, impotence, premature ejaculation, and sexual addiction can all come from control dynamics. Make freedom one of your highest goals in your relationship (Galatians 5:1).

## Not Being Accepting

Few dynamics cause more sexual dysfunction than the lack of acceptance. If a man feels like he is under performance dynamics, for example, he can suffer impotence. If a woman feels like she is under performance dynamics, she can suffer from everything from lack of lubrication to being nonorgasmic. Good sexual response requires the lack of tension, and performance anxiety causes tension. Obviously, the two are incompatible. One of the most helpful things a sex therapist does is cure impotence by just getting rid of performance anxiety. It can be that simple, but it seems like such a miracle.

There are other areas of nonacceptance that enter into sexual performance as well. Not accepting your lover's body, the way he makes love, or other aspects of him can all put him under a shame dynamic, creating feelings of inadequacy. Those feelings inevitably lead to some sort of sexual response issue. In short, *no one should ever have to worry about not being "good enough." That is a sex killer.*

There is nothing wrong with talking about ways that each of you wants the other to do things differently. But there is everything wrong if that is done in a critical, shaming, or judgmental way. Take an inventory to see how you are making requests with each other. Is there a hint of disapproval, anger, guilt, shame, or comparison in your voice or body language? Are you implying a loss of love or connection because of something about your partner's performance? It is great to be talking with your partner about this, but you have to watch the way that you talk. Ask each other how accepted you feel by the other. Ask how you can give requests or feedback in a way that does not hurt, apply pressure, or become deflating.

In a healthy love life, there *must* be acceptance of the bad stuff— each other's fears, feelings, fantasies, desires, hurts, inadequacies, weaknesses, past, or whatever else is lurking between one's heart and the connection—as well as the good. Accepting everything about each other is part of a formula for healthy and good sex. Make it so neither of you has to be ashamed of anything, and both of you will feel comfortable having all of your feelings known.

Self-acceptance also affects sexual health. Lack of self-acceptance can really get in the way of sexual expression. If you tend to reject your own body, desires, sexuality, or whatever other aspects of yourself you do not like, your negative perspective will affect your sexual responsiveness. Working toward self-acceptance will improve your sex life. Listen to the way that you talk to yourself, especially during lovemaking. Are you critical of yourself? Are you evaluating yourself in some way? You must shut down that voice and move toward acceptance.

## Not Having Fun

Sex should be fun. For most couples, that's a given, especially at first. But for some couples, sex becomes routine, a duty, or an obligation; and that is unhealthy.

If your sex life is lacking in spontaneity, freedom, and enjoyment, then something is wrong. Sometimes it can be caused by personal hurt or injury, such as past abuse, which needs to be understood and healed. Other times it comes from rigid religious teaching or parental messages that need to be reworked in one's head. Remember, even missionaries had one position that was OK! That old joke probably originated from some of the religious taboos on sex, viewing it as only for making babies and not for pleasure or enjoyment. Wherever those religious taboos came from, they did not come from God. Read the Song of Solomon in the Bible and you will find one of the most explicit descriptions of marital sex ever recorded. If that book were read in church, it would make the choir director blush.

Obligations and inhibitions are unhealthy to good sex. Both partners need more freedom so the joy can return to the bedroom (or wherever you happen to be).

## Not Communicating

Sadly, many couples are afraid to really talk about what they want or don't want in their sex life. As a result, they are doomed to stay stuck, as each partner has no way of knowing what the other really wants.

If you are not having verbal intercourse, then your sexual intercourse is sure to be lacking as well. But if you are not talking, then there are probably other dynamics contributing to the problem. Take a look at why you aren't communicating about sex.

Is one of you reactive? Defensive? Judgmental? Takes things personally and can't accept feedback? Moralistic? If those dynamics are at play, talk about them as they relate to sex. Whatever is in the way of your communication, get it out of the way.

Maybe your communication failures are not about the relationship at all, but about your own fears of being open. Why are you afraid to talk? Look at those fears and face them. Your sex life will benefit from that kind of risk-taking.

## Not Seeing Sex as a Process

You can't hurry sex. If there is pressure in your sexual relationship to have your sex life all together right now, then that is not healthy. It's a dumb attitude, and you need an attitude adjustment that makes sex more like a journey together, with total safety and lack of time pressure to get there.

Your sexual journey with your partner is a trip of discovery, pleasure, self-knowledge, other-knowledge, and adventure. Realize that you are never going to "arrive," but you will learn more and more about each other and how to make better love til death do you part. We know now from research on aging that sex continues much longer and much better into old age that many people realize. You have well into your twilight years to be together sexually, so see your sexuality as a lifelong adventure.

And there is the microcosm version of that same truth. Just as you have to give yourselves time over the course of your relationship to get it right, you also have to also give yourselves time in any one sexual encounter. Do not hurry! That is what foreplay, patience, lack of pressure, and all of those things are about. Give yourselves the time it takes to get relaxed, pleasured, loved, connected, and the like. Sex is not a race.

## False Sexual Expectations

Another way that sex can become unhealthy is when it faces false expectations. This problem is rampant today, especially with the way our society has sold sex as the cure-all for humanity's ills. Sex is being asked to do more than it was designed to do, and it has been elevated to the most important thing in life.

Sex cannot *be* the entire relationship, as many magazines and movies ask it to be. This is sex glamorized beyond all possibility of reality. Trying to make your sex life follow the patterns presented in the media is similar to women trying to look like pictures of a model who has been airbrushed to perfection. She does not exist in realty.

False sexual expectations can come from anywhere—comparing your partner or yourself to a fictional movie character, reading a magazine article about the frequency or kinds of orgasms one is supposed to experience, or determining the longevity or intensity of the experience from what your friends report. You should ignore all this dumb stuff. These kinds of sexual fantasies are meant to sell movies and magazines, and there's not an ounce of truth in them. The truth is that sex is very individual, and every person and every relationship is different.

Your sexual performance, aside from real dysfunctions, is your sexual performance. Your relationship is your relationship. The only standard that is important is your own satisfaction and fulfillment with each other. Don't let false expectations rob you of what is good and fulfilling for you. Let reality be good enough, and let loving each other be the real expectation you try to meet.

## The Good News About Unhealthy Sex

The good news about unhealthy sex is that it can be helped. Resolving sexual problems is an area of counseling that has great success. If you struggle with sexual issues, then we encourage you to get help from a qualified sex therapist. Chances are good that he or she can help you greatly.

The really good news is that sexual problems are resolved in tandem with relationship problems. The things we have talked about here all have to do with improving your relationship as well as your sex life.

**A Lifeline:** WORKING ON YOUR SEX LIFE IS A GREAT PLACE TO FOCUS ON REBUILDING YOUR CONNECTION, AS IT GETS INTO SO MANY AREAS OF FINDING EACH OTHER AGAIN. GET STARTED!

## Keep the Home Fires Burning

The music plays in the background; the moon glistens above. The lovers look at each other from the balcony, as the reflection of the city lights shine pathways to heaven. They caress, and then he leads her through the open glass door, the draperies gently blowing in the wind. The lights fade, and the lovers disappear into the depths of romantic and sexual bliss, leaving the audience to fill in the blanks.

Sound familiar? Hollywood depictions of sex are engaging to watch, but they lead many couples to expect that all they need for a fulfilling sexual relationship is moonlight, a little breeze, and the right music in the background. The movies never show the couple five years later, three kids later, fifty-hour workweeks later, forty pounds later, or any of the other "laters" that make for real life. In reality, sustaining a sexual connection in your marriage takes focus, attention, and work. The good news, though, is that anything worth having takes effort, and the effort is worth it in the end. In this chapter, we will give you a few tips on how to keep your sex life alive and healthy.

### Talk, Talk, Talk

We simply cannot overemphasize how important talking is to your sexual connection. You've got to talk to each other about things like:

- How do you feel about your sex life? How would you like your sex life to be different?
- What are your areas of insecurity?

- What areas would you like to explore?
- How do you feel about your foreplay, and how do you want it to be different?
- What does your mate do that you really like and wish he would do more of?
- What does your mate do that you don't like and wish he would not do?
- How do you feel inhibited, and what could your mate do to make you feel less so?
- What positions do you like, don't like, or would like to try?
- What makes it hard for you to communicate about sex?
- What fantasies do you have that you want your mate to fulfill?
- What fears do you have about sex?
- What makes you tense?
- What makes you relaxed?
- What turns you on before sex and makes you begin to desire your mate?
- What do you want your mate to know that you feel like he doesn't know?
- What attitudes, actions, and words would help you feel safer and more fulfilled?

Be nonjudgmental so that you are safe to talk freely without hearing each other's comments as criticism. If you can't get to that safe place with each other, that indicates another problem, and you need to talk to a counselor.

### Become Self-Aware

Sometimes your own feelings about sex or about yourself stand in the way of your responsiveness. Become aware of your own beliefs, self-talk, guilt, and thought life about sex and during sex. Work on those patterns and beliefs that are interfering and need to change. Talk about them to your mate or to a good friend or counselor. Both men and women who experience sexual arousal or performance problems have thoughts that lead to those symptoms.

Also, become more aware of your own body and sensations. Take time to get in touch with your body, and learn what turns you on and makes you feel safe, as well as the things that make you feel tense or nervous. There is nothing wrong with learning about your own body—what makes it tick, how your body relaxes, and how it is aroused. So take a warm bath, and learn to feel your body. Touch yourself, and find out what feels good and where your most sensual feelings are. Share those with your mate, and instruct him or her about your body and your feelings.

## Have Nonsexual Sensual Exercises

One of the most important things that sex therapists have couples do is nonintercourse, or nongenital, pleasuring exercises—sometimes referred to as sensate focus. This involves making a rule of either not having genital-to-genital contact, or no genital contact at all. There are proven reasons that sensate focus is helpful for couples who want to improve their sex life.

SENSATE FOCUS TAKES THE PERFORMANCE PRESSURE OFF. Nothing hampers sexuality more than performance anxiety. The pressure is off because there is no goal—to become aroused, to be orgasmic, to "do it right," to please your mate, to get there quickly, or whatever you feel pressured to do. The idea is to pleasure your mate through full body touch, massage, stroking, caressing, and so on. There is no way to fail, so there is nothing but pleasure, relaxation, care, and tenderness.

SENSATE FOCUS ALLOWS YOU TO GET IN TOUCH WITH YOUR BODY. It helps you find out what feels good, emotional, erotic, relaxing, intimate, connecting, and the like. It helps people rediscover—or discover for the first time—their sexuality. It does much to cure arousal problems that are caused by anxiety.

SENSATE FOCUS IS A CONNECTING EXPERIENCE IN AND OF ITSELF. It is connection without sex, which is the opposite of most sexual problems, which are sex without connection. It gets the horse in front of the cart, sometimes for the first time. This is very healing and very powerful.

SENSATE FOCUS EDUCATES EACH PARTNER ABOUT THE OTHER. You will learn things that you did not know that your mate feels, likes, and dislikes. At times you can talk about what you are feeling during sensate focus, and at other times you can just enjoy the experience and then talk about it later when you can focus.

SENSATE FOCUS TRAINS MEN TO SLOW DOWN THEIR TENDENCY TO PUSH TOWARD THE GOAL. When they do, they often find that she really is sensual, responsive, and even erotic after all. The problem has been that he has never taken the time to know that.

## Kill Evaluation

There are few bigger desire- and performance-killers, as we have said, than evaluation and performance anxiety. Watch what is going through your head while you are making love. Do any of your thoughts sound like the following?

· "He thinks I am taking too long."
· "She doesn't think I am a good lover."
· "She is not getting aroused. It must be me."
· "He thinks I'm not sexy or too fat."
· "I hope he is enjoying this. I want him to love me."
· "I don't want her to think I'm a pervert. I'd better tone it down."
· "I want to express more, but he would think I am weird."

These are actual sentences that people have reported going through their minds that are followed by inhibition, delayed arousal, inability to perform, dissatisfaction, and other problems. Remember, your most powerful sex organ is your mind. That is where sex begins and ends. So don't allow sex-killing evaluation to be in your mind. Stop evaluating and begin experiencing. Get into the moment and feel it. Focus on it. Talk about it, but don't judge. That only leads to fear and shame.

## Sex Begins in the Kitchen

As the old saying claims, "Sex begins in the kitchen." In other words, if a husband avoids helping his wife or connecting with her earlier in the evening away from the bedroom, he can't expect just to turn her on instantly in the bedroom. She will go to bed feeling disconnected, perhaps even ignored and unloved. And if men are nagged, controlled, or judged, their libido plummets.

Sex does not begin when you begin "sex." It is an outgrowth of the connection, love, and tenderness that you have shown up to that moment. That moment is only a culmination of what's already going on. If the atmosphere is negative or unloving before that moment, it will not magically change in an instant. So, both of you, begin sex sooner. Men, pursue her in nonsexual ways throughout the day. And pursue all parts of her, not just her body. In short, be loving, kind, tender, initiating, and helpful in the kitchen, over the phone, throughout the day—and chances are, she'll make you glad you did.

## Eliminate Pressure

Pressure of any kind works against everything that sex is designed to do. Get performance pressure out of your bedroom—and out of your relationship. If he is not erect, or it takes time to get there, make that OK. Enjoy being close and just caressing each other. Many erection problems are cured when it's OK not to have an erection. Similarly, she must not feel pressured to have to have an orgasm or get aroused in a certain amount of time. If she is, the effect will probably be the opposite.

Men, above all else, *slow down*. Women need much longer to become aroused than men do. Research shows that most women need to be caressed, touched (nongenitally), stroked, talked to, relaxed, and the like for twenty to thirty minutes before they are ready for genital contact. Some take longer.

The problem is that some men see this as some sort of dues they have to pay, to "get there" instead of part of the experience itself. The word *foreplay* implies that it's merely a preliminary to the really important thing coming later. But foreplay is a very important part of good sex. She is not ready as fast as you may be. Go along the connecting journey with her, and slow down.

*Women need to be close and aroused slowly to get to desire. Men get desire first and then move to being close.* This is good in that it makes the man the pursuer, leading the woman to feel wanted and loved. It is God's design.

And women, have no standard for yourself to be aroused or even to climax in some particular way. You may not be like the women in the movies (not many are, by the way). You may have some experiences that are very subtle, if climactic at all. They may at times just be moments of feeling relaxed and connected. Fewer than half of all women experience orgasm through intercourse; the majority of women need direct stimulation instead. Don't feel bad about that. And husbands, don't judge yourself as a crummy lover if this is the case for your wife. If she needs direct stimulation, let her tell you how to do it.

Also, ladies, go easy with your husband's fragile male ego. For some reason, men are often prone to take sexual feedback as criticism of their virility or manhood. Give feedback in a way that does not put him under pressure or imply that he is not performing well enough.

Stroke his ego as well as his body. Just as you need to feel loved to respond, he needs to feel strong and like he is good enough. Offer compliments and build him up. Basically, show him that you approve of him and are positive toward him. For starters, smile! In short, be *with* him in the time together.

The bottom line here is that sex is about a relaxed, emotional, loving, relational, and physical response. You are a team to pleasure each other, not to perform for each other or judge each other or even judge yourselves. By all means, if you can't solve these issues, see a good sex counselor for help.

## Get Physical

Research shows that people in better physical condition have better sex. You have heard this before, from many sources, so why aren't you doing it? Get in shape, and eat healthy. Get more rest, and cut down on stress. All of these disciplines have been shown to improve sex.

For example, research shows that men who exercise have fewer erectile problems. That should motivate you. Exercise leads to higher libido, hormonal and chemical changes in the brain, greater blood flow, and many other sexual benefits. People in good shape feel better about their bodies, so they are less inhibited. Women feel better about being in control of themselves. Both sexes function better into old age. There are a zillion reasons for this, so get over that dumb couch-potato attitude, and get healthy.

Do whatever it takes. Get a buddy system, hire a trainer, or join a class. You have been waiting long enough, and if you are just depending on yourself to change, you won't. Get some kind of help.

## Make Time

Loving takes time and space. If you are doing it as an afterthought— with whatever few minutes and little energy happen to be left at the end of the day—then that will be the quality of your love life. Working late at night, pressure of an early morning meeting on the mind, weary from the day, worried, exhausted—these elements do not add up to great lovemaking. Yet many couples put their love life at the tail end of such a schedule.

Be more proactive. Make time. Schedule time for sex. Protect it. Vary it. Have a date night in your schedule that does not get tinkered with short of emergencies. Go on overnighters. Have sex appointments. However you do it, make protected time for making love.

## Support Each Other

When either of you has a struggle or needs to grow in some way, support each other. You are a team. Supporting and accepting each other in all situations is a move toward better sex. You need each other, and you both are on the same team.

Remember, you and your partner are one flesh; when one of you struggles, both of you struggle. So get with each other and bring each other along. Loyally supporting and accepting each other in all situations is a move toward better lovemaking. Supporting each other in any struggle you may have will strengthen your connection with each other.

As we said earlier, this is not a sexual manual or instruction book. It is broader than that. What we have tried to do here is give you some time- and research-tested information that should prove helpful in your relationship. But don't end here. There is so much good information out there to help you continue to learn and grow sexually as a couple.

**A Lifeline:** Becoming a student of good sex in marriage, as well as a student of each other and yourself, is one of the healthiest things you can do to rescue your love life.

# Unfaithfulness Is More than Just Adultery

As we have seen, sexual fulfillment in marriage has little to do with sexual technique or attractiveness or any of the other things that Hollywood urges us to think. Satisfying sexuality goes much deeper than looks or mechanics, and research attributes it to the quality of the connection between the couple. How well do they listen to each other, tend to each other's needs, see sex as another way to know each other, and feel safe and free to be all of who they are with each other?

In this section on rekindling your sex life, we will address one of the biggest things that destroy it: *taking your sexuality outside the marriage.* If sexual fulfillment is about total connection, then taking parts of yourself outside your marriage for sexual gratification is certainly an enemy of that fulfillment.

There are many ways of taking sex outside marriage, the most obvious one being an affair. Most people in their right minds see infidelity as a problem for a marriage, and if they are the one in the affair, they know that they are doing something wrong and destructive. We've already discussed resisting the temptation to have an affair, so we will not dwell on that issue in this section.

## The Cycle of Sexual Addiction

There are other ways besides affairs in which people take their sexuality outside of the marriage. We all remember the media frenzy over President Bill Clinton's escapade with a White House intern. In defending himself, he insisted that since the intimate acts they engaged in did not involve actual intercourse, they did not fall under the definition of *sex* and therefore were not to be considered adulterous. So did the nation buy the president's explanation? Did it get him off the hook? Not for a moment. Virtually everyone in America saw his dalliance as an affront to his wife, an affront to sexual morality, and an affront to the people who had elected him. Everyone understands that when a person indulges in any kind of sexual expression or intimacy outside the marriage, a breach of faith has occurred that inflicts damage to the relationship.

The biggest examples of this breach are pornography, romantic novels or videos, and fantasy crushes on other people. While people who engage in these practices are not having an actual affair, they are taking sexual parts of themselves in directions other than their mates. These activities may not have all of the same repercussions as physical adultery, but they still defile the person and the relationship, as Jesus and any good marriage therapist will tell you (Matthew 5:28).

It all began innocently enough for Jason, or so he thought. He was tired. He had worked late at the office every night for three weeks on a project crucially important to his company and his career. Every night as he wearily drove the twenty miles to his suburban home, he passed the Triple X Video Arcade, always lit up with alluring neon lights. His wife, Jenny, was always in bed when he arrived at home, so she would never know if he stopped for a few minutes. After all, because of his late nights, they had not had sex since the project started, and he thought he deserved a little sexual diversion to compensate. So he stopped and went in.

The girls in the videos were luscious—always willing, always loving, always compliant. Before long, Jason was stopping almost every night. At first his conscience bothered him a little, but soon he convinced himself that he wasn't actually doing anything wrong. He was not having sex with these girls. In fact, they were not even real girls, but merely photographic images on a screen. What he was doing would have no effect on Jenny. So what was the big problem?

Here is the problem. When a partner turns to pornography, for instance, the parts of him that engage in the activity run from the marriage and are not available to the relationship. People turn to pornography or fantasy relationship for a lot of reasons, such as fears, conflicts, or feeling overpowered, inadequate, criticized, or afraid of intimacy. Those feelings and dynamics are common and understandable. Most marriages have issues like these to work out at some level or at some time.

But the one who goes to pornography or fantasy relationships does not have to work out those issues at all. The fantasy relationship never rejects, disappoints, has conflict, overpowers, or criticizes. The fantasy is always there and, like any other idol, always under the control of the user. So there is no risk and lots of reward. That is why pornography is the preferred "drug of choice" for so many people. They get all the feelings (at least they think) that they want in real sexual relationships, but without any of the hurt, pain, fear, or risk. The gratification is powerful. The person in the pornography or fantasy always approves, always serves, and always loves. It is a tough relationship for a real person to compete with. With pornography, there is no nagging and no cellulite.

So the person gets hooked in deeper and deeper. What he does not realize is that he is getting further and further away from his wife and from reality. His real sexuality is splitting further and further from love and real relationship. As a result, he begins to withdraw, relationally and sexually, from his wife. And his libido goes away. He feels guilty, but he can't stop. Sexual and relational interest wane. The addiction has taken its toll. There is no driving force to work out the relationship because the pain continues to get medicated by the addiction. It is a cycle, with nothing pushing the person back to the mate.

But it gets worse. When we are cut off from real life, God's life of real sex and real relationship, we are never satisfied. There is a continual lust for more and more, and there is never enough. That is why people get addicted to pornography or romance novels or masturbatory fantasies. When the thrill of those substitutes begins to wane, they need more and more to stimulate and satisfy, and then the cycle is set. There is never enough, so more and more is continually sought.

When a partner is involved in pornography, romantic novels or videos, or fantasy relationships, the marriage is the victim. So are both partners. Intimacy suffers, walls are built, sexual desire goes away, interest vanishes, and isolation ensues.

### What to Do

If this cycle of addiction describes you, get help. Do not think that you are just going to stop your addiction through will power. You need God's help and the help of others who understand sexual addiction to help you get out. Call a counselor with experience in sexual addiction or go to a group such as Sexaholics Anonymous or other recovery groups designed for this kind of problem. Sexual addiction can certainly be overcome, but you need help to make it happen.

If this describes your spouse, put your foot down. Set some boundaries. Tell her that you are not going to share her with someone else, even a fantasized person. Tell her that you want all of her, and you want your marriage to work. Tell her that you will deal with anything about yourself that has made it difficult for her to come to you, and you will help her deal with anything that might be causing fear or pain. Make it clear that what you will not do is continue to pretend that there is not a problem and enable it to go on. Make the appointment. If she will not go, go yourself to figure out with a professional the correct stance to take. Do not just allow it to go on. Pray for her and get others praying as well. This can be overcome.

If neither you nor your spouse has this problem, don't think it could not happen to you. No one is above temptation to fantasy, even people who think they would never be cheaters. In the literal sense, people who think this way may be right; they would never cheat on their mate by committing adultery. But those who would never act out an affair can become victims to fantasy to make themselves feel better when they hit some sort of hard time or dry season.

**A Lifeline:** "BE CAREFUL THAT YOU DON'T FALL!" WE ARE WARNED (1 CORINTHIANS 10:12). A STRONG SUPPORT GROUP IS KEY TO NOT FALLING. A SUPPORT SYSTEM WILL HELP YOU REMAIN FAITHFUL TO YOUR MATE IN EVERY SENSE AND TAKE ALL OF YOUR SEXUALITY TO HER, FINDING IN A COMMITTED RELATIONSHIP ALL THE FULFILLMENT GOD INTENDS YOU TO ENJOY.

## Facing Sexual Dysfunction

This section has two purposes. First, we will educate you about sexual dysfunctions that are very common with normal people. Many times, those who struggle with their sexual functioning may think they are the only person who has their particular problem. They may not even know that their problem has a name and is well understood and highly correctable. If you have such physical challenges, we want you to be able to put a name to whatever you are struggling with and know that it is common and treatable.

Second, we want to give you hope and motivation to face your problem and get help. The reality is that most sexual problems are treatable, some in relatively short order. The key is to stop minimizing the problem and its effect on your marriage, and get help from a seasoned professional. The results can be amazing, and your marriage will benefit. But for that to happen, you have to be honest about your problem and deal with it directly. Get over the shame, fear, guilt, or whatever is holding you back.

It is beyond the scope of this book's length to give you self-help for these conditions. There are good books available that can do just that. We encourage you to locate these books and read more about what you can do at home. Much can be accomplished in that way. Most of the time, a trained sex therapist is the key. We encourage that approach whenever self-help fails.

Since sex is a very personal issue, many couples simply hide and avoid dealing with sexual dysfunction. Don't choose that option. If you are solidly on each other's team and *for* each other, if you are willing to extend total love and acceptance of each other's hurts and weaknesses, you can get past the problem. We say, "Go for it!"

## Common Sexual Dysfunctions

Here are some of the most common sexual problems.

LACK OR LOSS OF SEX DRIVE. Many couples find themselves at some time or another in a situation when one of them experiences a lack of sex drive. She may describe it as lack of interest or motivation toward sex. Often there is no reason to be found in the relationship, as she is feeling very positive and loving toward her mate; she simply finds herself without libido.

First, investigate biological or medical causes for your loss of libido. Sex drive is a complex physical and psychological function, and there can be causes in either direction for it to go away. Hormonal changes, depression, drug interactions or side effects, diabetes, stress, or other medical illnesses can cause sex drive to wane or disappear. You may have a perfectly logical biological cause that can be treated. It is not natural to have no libido, so its absence may mean that something needs correcting medically or biologically.

Lack of sex drive can also result from relational or psychological issues. It may be a problem in the dynamics of the relationship, or it may result from one partner's psychological dynamics. A good therapist can help with either of these causes. It is not uncommon to have a sexual shutdown because of self-image problems, past hurts that are not healed, or reminders of problems with parents that cause a person to become sexually repressed. A good therapist can identify and treat those problems quite effectively. We encourage you to get that help.

IMPOTENCE. Impotence is the inability to achieve or maintain an erection for intercourse. It is one of life's most painful emotional experiences for men, and it is often frustrating for their wives as well. It is not uncommon for the woman to blame herself for not being exciting enough or to feel responsible for making it better somehow. So it puts a lot of strain on both partners.

Again, the causes of impotence can be either physical or emotional. Our advice about impotence is the same as above: get the medical aspect of it checked first. Many causes of impotence are medically related, and medical treatments have great results. Contact your physician before you do anything else.

Psychological, emotional, and relational causes for impotence are not uncommon, and they can be successfully treated as well. Performance anxieties can often be at the root of impotence; as soon as those are dealt with, things advance readily. The problem may also be rooted in relational dynamics or the need for some reconditioning. But whatever the cause of impotence, proven treatments are available. So don't put it off another day: get help from a qualified doctor or counselor.

AVOIDANCE OF SEX. At times when the relationship is strained, one or both parties may avoid initiating or agreeing to sex. If that is the case, it's generally because someone is hurting in some way. Sexual avoidance can be due to personal issues as well, such as unhealed abuse issues, inhibitions or guilt, repressive spiritual or religious teachings, parental messages, addictions, fear, shame, or many other issues. Talk with your mate about these things to get a handle on whether this is an issue with your relationship that you need to work through together, or a personal issue that requires help. Even if it is a personal issue, it is also a relational issue because it affects your mate, and his help and support are going to be important.

PREMATURE EJACULATION. Premature ejaculation is also a great source of distress for both the man and woman. He often feels inadequate and considers himself a lousy lover because he cannot last long enough for her to get as much out of the experience as she would like. For men with this problem, the real killer is the powerlessness that they feel to correct the problem.

The good news is that premature ejaculation is very treatable, even with do-it-yourself treatment. A good sex therapy book can walk you through exercises proven to be effective, and you may find your problem cured in short order. At other times the problem can be a little more involved, but a good sex therapist can help you.

Like other sexual problems, premature ejaculation can be relational, psychological, or medical. You would do well to consult your doctor first to rule out medical conditions. Be sure to ask him at the outset if he is aware of the sex therapy treatments for the condition, just to be sure that you are getting the whole array of possible helps. You and your mate should work on this together with the same kind of sensitivity and support that you would give each other with any problem.

RETARDED EJACULATION. Retarded ejaculation is a problem that many men do not even know exists, and when it appears, they wonder what is wrong. Like other sexual problems, it can put a lot of strain on the relationship. The wife may feel that something is wrong with her or his attraction to her. She begins to feel responsible for his climax. Sometimes men even blame their wives, thus adding to the problem.

There are certain medical conditions and certain medications that can cause retarded ejaculation. Talk to your doctor first to get a good physical diagnosis. If he gives you a clean bill of health, seek sex therapy. Many men who have this problem are able to ejaculate when masturbating, but not during intercourse. There are sex therapy techniques that can overcome the problem, whether it is relational or psychological.

VAGINISMUS. Vaginismus is a disorder that makes penetration of the vagina impossible because of an involuntary contraction. It closes, and nothing is able to penetrate. Like other sexual problems, vaginismus can be caused by physical conditions or relational and psychological factors.

Vaginismus is very treatable, and many times it can be cured by exercises a good sex therapy book or counselor can prescribe. At other times, more extensive sex therapy may be needed. But in either case, if you suffer from vaginismus, don't wait; get help. It is available, and it works.

ORGASMIC DYSFUNCTION. As we said earlier, in more than half the cases, women need additional stimulation other than intercourse in order to reach orgasm. Some couples do not know this and see her inability to climax as something wrong. This is simply not the case. Move together to provide for her stimulation in addition to intercourse. The techniques may vary, and you can intermingle them in any sequence that works for her. There is no right way that works for every woman, and you can have a great time finding what works for you. But there is one wrong assumption, and that is that every woman is going to climax through intercourse.

Orgasmic dysfunction can also be caused by emotional, psychological, or relational pressures. The orgasm is a "letting-go" response, and a woman is wired to let go when she is in a relaxed and safe place. Anything, whether internal or external, that makes her anxious or causes her to feel under pressure, afraid, or uncomfortable can work against her. Examine the kind of dynamics in your relationship that may trigger these tensions.

Sex therapy for orgasmic dysfunction can be very helpful, and we recommend it. If you take advantage of the help that is widely available, not only will your love life improve, but your overall health will improve as well.

## Get Together

Where there is love, there is a way. Couples who are committed to being for each other and for the relationship can overcome huge obstacles or, in the case of sexual dysfunction, very curable obstacles that only feel huge. These problems feel huge because sexuality is a point of vulnerability for both men and women. Furthermore, a lot of feelings are wrapped up in one's view of oneself and one's performance.

The term *performance*, as we have seen, does not belong in your sexual vocabulary. Focusing on performance is a trap that can destroy sexuality, and it is often at the root of sexual dysfunction.

**A Lifeline:** ONLY LOVE AND SAFETY CAN HELP A COUPLE OUT OF THE PERFORMANCE TRAP AND INTO WHAT SEX IS MEANT TO BE: A DEEPER WAY OF *KNOWING* EACH OTHER. IF YOU NEED HELP TO GET THERE, BY ALL MEANS, GET IT. YOUR SEX LIFE—AND YOUR LOVE LIFE—WILL THANK YOU FOR IT.

# Conclusion
## On to the Rescue

So here you are. You have finished the book, which says something hopeful about your marriage. It means that your relationship is important to you and that you were willing to put in some time and effort. There will be more work ahead, but people who work on love are far more likely to find it than those who wait and hope for it to happen.

Hopefully, you found your relationship within these pages. Maybe you don't experience the loving feelings you want together. Perhaps intimacy has been an issue, or trust hasn't been what it should. Maybe the conflicts have been painful, or a character issue has gotten between you. At the same time, however, we hope that you have also found solutions, principles, and tips that apply to your situation. Because we believe that the answers are there for all of us. They have worked with many, many couples, and they continue to work. You just have to find the right ways to apply them to your relationship.

We would suggest that you do not try to rescue your love life all by yourself. Marriages that are grounded in healthy community are marriages that do better. Find a good church with small groups in which couples are welcome to open up safely about their struggles and can identify, pray for each other, and find support, feedback, and grace for each other. Fortunately, many good churches provide such groups for couples and families.

Often, couples will ask, "Where do we start? We need to work on more than one area." There is a way to approach this question. Start with this principle in mind: *the concern that most gets in the way of intimacy is the one to begin the rescue with.* That is, look to the connection as your guide. Whatever disrupts love, attachment, safety, trust, and passion is where you should start talking to each other, vulnerably and honestly. Let each other know that all you really want is to love each other, and begin the work.

Plans and structure are important here. Hopefully, you now have some ideas not only on the conversations to have, but also what applications to make. For more help with personal applications of these principles, we encourage you to use the *Rescue Your Love Life Personal Discovery Guide.* This helpful workbook is filled with insights and discussion questions designed to help individuals and small groups process the information in *Rescue Your Love Life.*

Make your love life a planned and active part of your real life, just as you do with working out, entertainment, and churchgoing. You will be surprised at the progress you will make on rescuing good things and avoiding dumb things, if you do a little work, a few times a week.

We hope also that you have caught the vision that *growing marriages are made up of growing individuals.* As you both become open, accepting, vulnerable, honest, and searching for spiritual and personal growth, you will experience a natural progression in your marriage. Because you are more whole inside, the marriage can become whole. You will find many benefits in growing personally in addition to what happens in your connection, such as the areas of other relationships, family, kids, friends, and work. You cannot lose when you become a growing person.

Finally, we want to leave you with some hope. Not only have many couples found the love and intimacy they have always wanted using these principles, but in a greater and deeper sense, remember also that the Designer of marriage has not left your relationship alone to fend for itself. God has provided the truths and principles you need to grow and love together. And He is also personally involved in helping your love grow. He wants love for your relationship, because He is involved in love. In fact, He is the very source of love. So when you look to Him and ask Him for help in rescuing your love life, you are reaching out to the One who cares the most about love and relationships. Your marriage is important to God, and He will help in substantial ways that you may have not even expected.

We pray that, as you work the steps in this book, the day will soon come when you and your mate look at each other and know that you are experiencing the love, intimacy, and romance that you have always wanted.

God bless you and your relationship.

# Works Cited

Henry Cloud and John Townsend. *Boundaries Face to Face: How to Have That Difficult Conversation You've Been Avoiding.* Grand Rapids: Zondervan, 2003.

———. *Boundaries in Dating.* Grand Rapids: Zondervan, 2000.

———. *Boundaries in Marriage.* Grand Rapids: Zondervan, 1999.

———. *How People Grow.* Grand Rapids: Zondervan, 2001.

———. *Rescue Your Love Life Personal Discovery Guide.* Nashville: Integrity, 2005.

John Townsend. *Hiding from Love: How to Change the Withdrawal Patterns That Isolate and Imprison You.* Grand Rapids: Zondervan, 1996.

———. *Who's Pushing Your Buttons? Handling the Difficult People in Your Life.* Nashville: Integrity, 2004.

# ALSO AVAILABLE FROM
# JOHN TOWNSEND

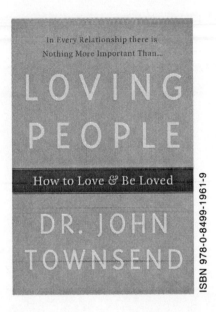

*In Every Relationship there is Nothing More Important Than...*

## LOVING PEOPLE

How to Love & Be Loved

## DR. JOHN TOWNSEND

ISBN 978-0-8499-1961-9

*Your personal guide to learning how to love.*

When you say or hear the words "I love you" it can change your life forever. Love is one of God's most important gifts to anyone, yet there are many misunderstandings about how to make love work in our families, friendships, marriages, and dating relationships. In *Loving People*, best-selling author Dr. John Townsend shows you that love can actually be learned, and gives you the steps and tools to become skilled in love.

**AVAILABLE WHEREVER BOOKS ARE SOLD**

### THOMAS NELSON
**Since 1798**

For other products and live events,
visit us at: **thomasnelson.com**

CPSIA information can be obtained at www.ICGtesting.com
Printed in the USA
LVOW040701220113

316697LV00003B/13/P